MITZVOT

MITZVOT

A SOURCEBOOK FOR THE 613 COMMANDMENTS

Ronald H. Isaacs

JASON ARONSON INC.
Northvale, New Jersey
London

List of commandments from the *Encyclopaedia Judaica* copyright ©1972 by Keter Publishing House Ltd. Used by permission.

Material in chapters 5 and 6 was developed from ideas in *Mitzvah Means Commandment* by Elliot N. Dorff. Copyright © 1989 United Synagogue Youth. Published by United Synagogue of America. Used by permission.

This book was set in 10 pt. Garamond by Aerotype, Inc.

Library of Congress Cataloging-in-Publication Data

Isaacs, Ronald H.
    Mitzvot : a sourcebook for the 613 commandments / Ronald H.
Isaacs.
        p.   cm.
    Includes bibliographical references and index.
    ISBN 1-56821-900-8 (alk. paper)
    1. Commandments, Six hundred and thirteen. I. Title.
BM520.8.I74 1996
296.1′8—dc20   96-13668
                                                                      CIP

Manufactured in the United States of America. Jason Aronson Inc. offers books and cassettes. For information and catalog write to Jason Aronson Inc., 230 Livingston Street, Northvale, New Jersey 07647.

CONTENTS

INTRODUCTION

The Jewish people are a varied lot. They live in almost every country in the world, speak many different languages, and have many different customs and ceremonies. It is not surprising that they also differ in how they understand and apply the tradition that they share. There are Jewish people that believe that God dictated His will at Mount Sinai, while others believe that the Torah was written by human beings who were inspired by God.

Judaism has always been more a religion of action and deed than belief and creed. Learning was intended to lead to doing. To that end, Jewish conduct has been governed by a series of commandments, known in Hebrew as *mitzvot* (singular, *mitzvah*). The scope of meaning of the word *mitzvah* is a wide one. It denotes commandment, law, obligation, and deed, while connoting goodness, value, piety, and even holiness.

Today, in modern times, Jewish people expect that if their understanding of a particular tradition is going to command their allegiance, it must make sense to them. Thus with a renewed interest in spirituality and ways of connecting oneself to God has come an increased interest in the understanding of the rationale behind the various *mitzvot*.

This volume attempts to present an overview of the commandments and the answers to the myriad of questions, related to their categorization and rationale, that both Jewish and non-Jewish people may have.

I dedicate this volume to my wife and partner, Leora, in gratitude for her love, devotion, understanding, and cheerful help during the course of my work on this and many other pursuits. May we all be blessed to see our children and our children's children occupied with Torah and the joyous desire to fulfill *mitzvot*.

1

ABOUT *MITZVOT*

What Is a *Mitzvah* and How Many Are There in Judaism?

The word *mitzvah* (plural, *mitzvot*) means a commandment, specifically a divine one. It has also come to mean a good or pious deed. Undoubtedly, the most common associations with the word *mitzvah* are Bar Mitzvah and Bat Mitzvah, the two religious ceremonies that mark the passage from Jewish childhood to religious maturity. According to Jewish Law, a Jewish boy becomes a Bar Mitzvah at age thirteen, according to his Hebrew birthday, while a girl becomes a Bat Mitzvah at age twelve, according to her Hebrew birthday. Historically, the Bar Mitzvah and, later, the Bat Mitzvah represented a Jewish rite of passage when a child reached the age when he or she was responsible for the performance of *mitzvot*.

The original source of the commandments is the Torah, also known as the Five Books of Moses. Although the commandments are present in the Torah, they are neither specified nor enumerated there. One must go to the Talmud, the rabbinic interpretation of the Torah, to find the tradition of the specific enumeration of the *mitzvot*. It was Rabbi Simlai, a third-century Jewish scholar, who first taught that the commandments of the Torah total 613. Specifically, he stated (Talmud *Makkot* 23b) that "six hundred and thirteen commandments were communicated to Moses; three hundred and sixty-five negative commandments, corresponding to the number of days in the solar year, and two hundred and forty-eight positive commandments, corresponding to the number of the parts of the human body." This long-standing tradition has generally been accepted as the legal frame for the codification of all of Jewish Law. These 613 commandments are also referred to in Hebrew as the *Taryag Mitzvot,* since the Hebrew letters of the word *Taryag* have the

1

number value of 613 (*tav* = 400; *resh* = 200; *yod* = 10; *gimel* = 3; total = 613). The observant Jew is said to keep the *taryag mitzvot.*

What Are the Various Kinds of *Mitzvot?*

Over the centuries, Jewish thinkers have classified and categorized the *mitzvot.* This was done in an attempt to make them easier to follow and understand. The following is a summary of some of the more important basic classifications:

1. Positive and negative *mitzvot:* the talmudic rabbis divided the *mitzvot* into the categories of positive and negative. The positive commandments (called *mitzvot aseh*) are the commands that require a person to do something, such as to give charity, to keep the festivals, or to love one's neighbor. There is general agreement that there are 248 positive commands in the Torah. The negative *mitzvot* (*mitzvot lo ta'aseh*) are the commandments to refrain from doing something, such as not to steal, not to bear false witness, and not to be jealous of a neighbor's possessions. There are 365 negative commands.

2. Time-bound and non-time-bound *mitzvot:* time-bound *mitzvot* are those that must be observed at a particular time each day. Examples of time-bound commandments include reciting the *Shema* (Hear O Israel . . .), putting on a prayer shawl, and eating *matzah* (unleavened bread) during Passover. Women traditionally were not required to observe positive time-bound commands because of their responsibilities for raising children and managing household affairs.

Non-time-bound *mitzvot* were those that were not related to specific times in the day and could be observed at any time. Non-time-bound commands might include caring for animals, helping the poor, keeping promises, and so forth.

3. "Light" and "serious" *mitzvot:* the talmudic rabbis some twenty centuries ago made a distinction between what they called a "light *mitzvah*" (*mitzvah kallah*) and a "heavy *mitzvah*" (*mitzvah chamurah*). For example, the famous medieval philosopher Maimonides considered the celebration of a Jewish festival as a "light *mitzvah,*" while he considered the *mitzvah* of learning Hebrew as a more serious or weighty commandment.

4. Rational and nonrational *mitzvot:* the ancient scholars distinguished between commands whose reason for doing them was easy to discern and those *mitzvot* that appeared less logical and sometimes even nonrational. Most of what are called today the ethical commands, such as "do not steal"

or "honor your parents," are called rational commandments (often referred to in Hebrew as *mishpatim*). An example of a nonrational *mitzvah,* which is called in Hebrew a *chok* (*chukim,* plural) would be the keeping of the Jewish dietary laws (*kashrut,* in Hebrew).

5. *Mitzvot* that guide our relationships with other people and our relationship with God: centuries ago, the rabbinic teachers also distinguished between those commands that help people better relate to one another (in Hebrew, *mitzvot bay adam lechayvayro*) and those that guide people in their relationship with God (in Hebrew, *mitzvot bayn adam laMakom*). Examples of people-to-people *mitzvot* might include prohibitions against jealousy of things your neighbor owns and against stealing those things. Eating in a *sukkah* on the festival of Sukkot or affixing a *mezuzah* on one's doorpost are all part of the group of *mitzvot* that help to connect people to God and their Jewish identities.

What Are the Commandments Given to Noah's Descendants?

Even before the revelation at Mount Sinai, there were certain laws, according to the ancient rabbis, that were binding on all humanity. This view held that while the Jewish people were subject to the extensive provisions of the Torah, non-Jews were required to observe at least a number of fundamental precepts deemed essential for the maintenance of a just and decent society. These laws came to be known as the "Noahide" laws as they were believed to have been incumbent on the sons of Noah, and therefore to have become obligatory for all people, since from Noah's sons "the whole world branched out" (Genesis 9:19).

The rabbis, in interpreting chapter 2, verse 16, of the Book of Genesis, established six such basic commands:

1. People may not worship idols.
2. People may not blaspheme God.
3. People must establish courts of justice.
4. People may not kill.
5. People may not commit adultery.
6. People may not rob.

A seventh law, that people may not eat flesh cut from a live animal, was added after the Flood (Genesis 9:4).

Interestingly, this rabbinic tradition is reflected in the apostle Paul's teaching about the Noahides. He required of all Gentiles that they abstain from idolatry, from eating blood and the meat of strange animals, and from fornication.

Are There Rewards Suggested in the Torah for the Performance of *Mitzvot?*

Of all of the commandments in the Torah, there are only two that are associated with receiving a reward for their performance. In both cases, the reward is an added length of days:

> Honor your mother and father, that your days may be long upon the land which God has given you. (Exodus 20:12)

> If a bird's nest chances to be before you in the way, in any tree or on the ground, with young ones or eggs, and the dam sitting upon the young, or upon the eggs, you shall not take the dam with the young. You shall let the dam go, but the young you may take for yourself, so that it may be well with you, and that you may prolong your days. (Deuteronomy 22:6–7)

Since rabbinic times, the rabbis have emphasized that one ought not to be a reward seeker when performing a commandment. Antigonos of Socho, one of the first noteworthy scholars to have assumed a Greek name, best sums up rabbinic opinion: "Do not be like a slave who ministers to God for the sake of receiving a reward, but be like a servant who ministers to the Master not for the sake of receiving a reward" (*Ethics of Our Fathers,* ch. 1, *Mishneh* 3)

Are There *Mitzvot* Not Based in the Torah?

There are seven commands that the rabbis determined to be observed but that were not based on any verses in the Torah. They have come to be known as rabbinic *mitzvot* (*mitzvot de'rabbanan*). The seven rabbinic commands are:

1. Washing one's hands before eating.
2. Lighting Sabbath candles.
3. Reciting the Hallel psalms of praise.
4. Lighting Hanukkah candles.

5. Reading the Scroll of Esther at Purim.
6. Making an *eruv* (a technical term for the rabbinical provision that permits the alleviation of certain Sabbath restrictions).
7. Saying a blessing before experiencing pleasure in worldly items, for example, before partaking of any food, before smelling a fragrant plant, and so forth.

2

CLASSIFICATION OF *MITZVOT*

As mentioned in Chapter 1, the tradition of the 613 commandments was first recorded in the Talmud (*Makkot* 23b) by Rabbi Simlai, who stated: "Six hundred and thirteen commandments were given to Moses; three hundred and sixty-five negative commandments, corresponding to the number of days in the solar year, and two hundred and forty eight positive commandments, corresponding to the numbers of parts of the human body." This tradition was generally accepted as the legal framework for the codification of Jewish Law.

The actual enumeration of the 613 commandments first appear in the Jewish legal compendium entitled *Halakhot Gedolot,* produced during the gaonic period. This work departs from the numerical division of Rabbi Simlai and includes several rabbinic laws in its total number. It also classifies the commandments according to the degree of punishment incurred in transgressing them and according to their common character. Maimonides, the eleventh-century philosopher, likewise structured his *Sefer HaMitzvot (Book of the Commandments)* on the system of the 613 commandments, though he differs with the *Halakhot Gedolot* in that he does not include rabbinic laws in his count. Maimonides' *Book of Commandments* treats exclusively their legal aspects since his work was intended to be an introduction to his great Jewish Law code, the *Mishneh Torah.*

Among the foremost of the codes of law that groups the commandments using the 613 *mitzvot* system is the *Sefer HaHinnuch,* the *Book of Education,* which is attributed to the thirteenth-century scholar Rabbi Aaron Ha-Levi of Barcelona. Unlike Maimonides' *Book of Commandments,* his book deals with the legal aspects of the commandments and also attempts to understand their religious and ethical roots.

In the nineteenth century, Rabbi Israel Meir haCohen, known as the Chafetz Chayyim, wrote a book called *Sefer Ha Mitzvot Hakatzar* (*The Short Book of the Commandments*). In it he includes a listing of both the positive and the negative commandments that are still applicable today.

The following are summaries of the classifications of the commandments by the Hinnuch, Maimonides, and the Chafetz Chayyim.

Classification of *Mitzvot* According to the Hinnuch

The Hinnuch grouped the commandments as follows:

a. Commandments that are obligatory upon all Israel, both men and women, everywhere and in all time.

b. Commandments that are obligatory everywhere and in all times, but only upon Israelites, and not upon priests or levites.

c. Commandments obligatory upon levites only.

d. Commandments obligatory upon priests only, everywhere and in all times.

e. Commandments obligatory only upon the king of Israel.

f. Commandments obligatory upon the whole community, and not just the individual.

g. Commandments that are obligatory only in a specified place and in a specified time, namely in the land of Israel and in the time that the majority of the people of Israel are there.

h. Commandments whose obligation differs between men and women, and between Israelites, priests, and levites.

i. Commandments that are constantly obligatory, such as the commandments to love God, fear God, and the like.

j. Commandments that must be observed at a specific time, such as the commandments of the Sabbath, *lulav* (palm branch), *shofar* (ram's horn), recitation of the *Shema* (Hear O Israel), and the like.

k. Commandments whose observance is contingent upon a given circumstance, and that are therefore not obligatory unless that circumstance should arise. For example, the commandment to give the hired man his wages in the appointed time is obligatory only upon one who has hired workers.

l. Commandments that apply only in the time of the Temple.

m. Commandments that are binding upon all humankind.

n. Commandments punishable by death or by stripes.

o. Commandments not legally punishable but nevertheless morally binding. (Note that commandments "l" through "o" are not included in his official list, although they are made apparent in his discussion of the *mitzvot*.)

Of the 613 commandments, 369 are applicable in our day. Of the 369, there are 78 positive commands and 21 prohibitive ones that are contingent upon certain conditions. Of those commandments that are binding upon every Israelite unconditionally, there are 270 in all: 48 are positive and 222 are prohibitive.

Six commandments are obligatory at all times:

1. To believe in God.
2. Not to believe in any other besides God.
3. To affirm God's unity.
4. To love God.
5. To fear God.
6. Not to stray after wayward thoughts.

The Hinnuch arranges the commandments according to the order in which they appear in the Torah. He does this in order that they may be studied along with the weekly Torah reading in the synagogue. His exposition of each commandment is divided into four parts:

1. The nature of the *mitzvah,* its Torah source and rabbinic explanation.
2. The root of the *mitzvah* (i.e., its rationale).
3. The specific laws of the *mitzvah,* as derived from the Talmud and other sources.
4. The conditions of each of the *mitzvot* (i.e., where a *mitzvah* applies, to whom it applies, and what punishment is meted out if it is transgressed).

Maimonides' Classification of the *Mitzvot*

Maimonides arranged the positive commandments in ten groups, dealing with the following:

1. Belief in one God and our duties toward God (1–19).
2. Sanctuary, priesthood, and sacrifices (20–95).

3. Sources of uncleanliness and modes of purification (96–113).
4. Gifts to the Temple, the poor, the priests and levites; the Sabbatical Year and the Jubilee; preparation of food (114–152).
5. Holy days and their observances (153–171).
6. Functioning of the Jewish State (172–193).
7. Duties toward our fellow men (194–209).
8. Duties attached to family life (210–223).
9. Enforcement of criminal law (224–231).
10. Laws relating to property, real and personal (232–248).

Maimonides' negative commands also fall into ten groups:

1. Idolatry and related subjects (1–59).
2. Duties to God and sanctuary (60–88).
3. Sacrifices, priestly gifts, priests, levites, and the like (89–171).
4. Prohibitions affecting food (172–209).
5. Cultivation of land (210–228).
6. Duties toward our fellow men, employees, and the poor (229–270).
7. Administration of justice, authority of courts, and the like (271–319).
8. Sabbath and festivals (320–329).
9. Forbidden degrees of marriage and related subjects (330–361).
10. Head of the Jewish state and its officers (362–365).

Maimonides also enumerates those commandments that a Jew in the ordinary course of life has always the opportunity to fulfill and are applicable to this day. These commandments, 60 in number, are as follows (numbers in parentheses correspond to the enumeration of the commandments in Maimonides' *Book of Commandments*):

1. (1) Believing in God.
2. (2) Unity of God.
3. (3) Love of God.
4. (4) Fear of God.
5. (5) Worshipping God.
6. (6) Cleaving to God.
7. (7) Taking an oath by God's name.
8. (8) Walking in God's ways.
9. (9) Sanctifying God's name.
10. (10) Reading the *Shema*.
11. (11) Studying the Torah.

12. (12) *Tefillin* of the head.
13. (13) *Tefillin* of the arm.
14. (14) The fringes.
15. (15) The *mezuzah*.
16. (18) Acquiring a scroll of Law.
17. (19) Grace after Meals.
18. (26) Priests blessing Israel.
19. (32) Honoring the Priests.
20. (54) Rejoicing on festivals.
21. (73) Making confession.
22. (94) All oral commitments to be fulfilled.
23. (143) The priest's due in the slaughter of every clean animal.
24. (146) *Shechitah*.
25. (147) Covering the blood of slain birds and animals.
26. (149) Searching for the prescribed tokens in cattle and other animals.
27. (150) Searching for the prescribed tokens in birds.
28. (152) Searching for the prescribed tokens in fish.
29. (154) Resting on the Sabbath.
30. (155) Proclaiming the sanctity of the Sabbath.
31. (156) Removal of leaven.
32. (157) Recounting the departure from Egypt.
33. (158) Eating unleavened bread on the fifteenth of Nisan.
34. (159) Resting on the first day of Passover.
35. (160) Resting on the seventh day of Passover.
36. (161) Counting the omer.
37. (162) Resting on Shavuot.
38. (163) Resting on Rosh Hashanah.
39. (164) Fasting on Yom Kippur.
40. (165) Resting on Yom Kippur.
41. (166) Resting on the first day of Sukkot.
42. (167) Resting on Shemini Atzeret.
43. (168) Dwelling in a booth during Sukkot.
44. (169) Taking a *lulav* on Sukkot.
45. (170) Hearing the *shofar* on Rosh Hashanah.
46. (172) Hearing the Prophets.
47. (175) Abiding by a majority decision.
48. (184) Removing sources of danger from our abodes.
49. (195) Charity.
50. (197) Lending money to the poor.
51. (206) Loving our neighbor.
52. (207) Loving the stranger.

53. (208) The law of weights and measures.
54. (209) Honoring the scholars and the elderly.
55. (210) Honoring parents.
56. (211) Respecting parents.
57. (212) Be fruitful and multiply.
58. (213) Law of marriage.
59. (214) Bridegroom devoting himself to his wife for one year.
60. (215) Law of circumcision.

The listing of the above commandments was guided by Maimonides' fourteen principles, which he created to enumerate the commandments:

1. We are not to include in this enumeration commandments having only rabbinic authority.
2. We are not to include laws derived from Scripture by any of the thirteen exegetical principles by which the Torah is expounded or by the principle of inclusion.
3. We are not to include commandments that are not binding for all time.
4. We are not to include charges that cover the whole body of the commandments of the Torah.
5. The reason given for a commandment is not to be counted as a separate commandment.
6. Where a commandment contains both a positive and a negative injunction, its two parts are to be counted separately, with the one among the positive commandments and the other among the negative.
7. The detailed laws of a commandment are not to be counted among the commandments.
8. A negative commandment excluding a particular case from its commandment is not to be included among the negative commandments.
9. The enumeration is not to be based on the number of times a particular negative or positive injunction is repeated in Scripture, but instead is to be based upon the nature of the action prohibited or enjoined.
10. Acts prescribed as preliminary to the performance of a commandment are not to be counted.
11. The different elements that go together to form one commandment are not to be counted separately.
12. The successive stages in the performance of a commandment are not to be counted separately.

13. Where a certain commandment has to be performed on more days than one, it is not to be counted once for each day.
14. The modes of punishment are to be counted as positive commandments.

Classification of *Mitzvot* According to Chafetz Chayyim

The Chafetz Chayyim classified the commandments in his book entitled, *Sefer Ha Mitzvot Hakatzar.* In addition to the sixty positive commandments, as enumerated by Maimonides (see the previous section), the Chafetz Chayyim adds these positive commandments (note that numbers in parentheses correspond to the enumeration of the commandments in Maimonides' *Book of Commandments*):

1. (21) Revering the sanctuary.
2. (37) Priests defiling themselves for deceased relatives.
3. (79) Sanctifying the firstborn.
4. (80) Redeeming the firstborn.
5. (81) Redeeming the firstling of an ass.
6. (82) Breaking the neck of the firstling of an ass.
7. (95) Revocation of vows
8. (133) The dough offering.
9. (141) Canceling claims in the sabbatical year.
10. (144) The first of the fleece to be given to the priest.
11. (148) Releasing a dam when taking its nest.
12. (188) The extinction of Amalek.
13. (189) Remembering the nefarious deeds of Amalek.
14. (194) A thief to restore the stolen article.
15. (199) Restoring a pledge to a needy owner.
16. (200) Paying wages on time.
17. (201) An employee is to be allowed to eat of the produce among which he is working.
18. (202) Unloading a tired animal.
19. (203) Assisting the owner in lifting up his burden.
20. (204) Returning lost property to its owner.
21. (245) Rebuking the sinner.
22. (250) The law of buying and selling.
23. (248) The law of inheritance.

The following is the classification of the negative commandments that are applicable today, as presented by the Chafetz Chayyim:

1. (1) Believing in, or ascribing deity to, any but God.
2. (2) Making images for the purpose of prayer.
3. (3) Making an idol for others to worship.
4. (4) Making figures of humans.
5. (5) Bowing down to idols.
6. (6) Worshipping idols.
7. (7) Handing over some of our offspring to the Molech.
8. (8) Practicing the sorcery of *ob*.
9. (9) Practicing the sorcery of *yidde'oni*.
10. (10) Studying idolatrous practices.
11. (11) Erecting a pillar around which people will assemble to honor.
12. (12) Making figured stones upon which to prostrate ourselves.
13. (14) Swearing by an idol.
14. (15) Summoning people to idolatry.
15. (16) Seeking to persuade an Israelite to worship idols.
16. (17) Loving the person who seeks to mislead one into idolatry.
17. (18) Relaxing one's aversion to the misleader.
18. (19) Saving the life of the misleader
19. (22) Benefiting from ornaments that have adorned an idol.
20. (25) Increasing our wealth from anything connected with idolatry.
21. (26) Prophesying in the name of an idol.
22. (27) Prophesying falsely.
23. (28) Listening to the prophecy of one who prophesies in the name of an idol.
24. (30) Adopting the habits and customs of unbelievers.
25. (31) Practicing divination.
26. (32) Regulating our conduct by the stars.
27. (33) Practicing the art of the soothsayer.
28. (34) Practicing sorcery.
29. (35) Practicing the art of the charmer.
30. (36) Consulting a necromancer who uses the *ob*.
31. (37) Consulting a sorcerer who uses the *yido'a*.
32. (38) Seeking information from the dead.
33. (39) Women wearing men's clothing.
34. (40) Men wearing women's clothing.
35. (41) Imprinting any marks on our bodies.
36. (42) Wearing a garment of linen and wool.
37. (43) Shaving the temples of our heads.

38. (44) Shaving the beard.
39. (45) Making the cuttings in our flesh.
40. (46) Settling in the land of Egypt.
41. (47) Accepting opinions contrary to those taught in the Torah.
42. (50) Showing mercy to idolaters.
43. (52) Intermarrying with the heretics.
44. (57) Destroying fruit trees during war.
45. (59) Forgetting what Amalek did to us.
46. (60) Blaspheming the Great Name.
47. (61) Violating a *shevuat bittui.*
48. (62) Violating a *shevuat shav.*
49. (63) Profaning the Name of God.
50. (65) Breaking down houses of worship.
51. (66) Leaving the body of a criminal hanging overnight after execution.
52. (78) Any unclean person entering the levitical camp.
53. (83) Making oil like the oil of anointment.
54. (85) Making incense like that used in the Sanctuary.
55. (101) Slaughtering the mother and her young on the same day.
56. (108) Redeeming the firstling of a clean beast.
57. (155) Delaying payment of vows.
58. (157) Infringing any oral obligation, even if undertaken without an oath.
59. (158) A priest marrying a *zonah.*
60. (159) A priest marrying a *chalalah.*
61. (160) A priest marrying a divorced woman.
62. (166) A common priest defiling himself for any dead person except those prescribed in Scripture.
63. (171) Tearing out our hair for the dead.
64. (172) Eating any unclean animal.
65. (173) Eating any unclean fish.
66. (174) Eating any unclean fowl.
67. (175) Eating any swarming winged insect.
68. (176) Eating anything that swarms upon the earth.
69. (177) Eating any creeping thing that breeds in decayed matter.
70. (178) Eating living creatures that breed in seeds or fruit.
71. (179) Eating any swarming thing.
72. (180) Eating *nevelah* (i.e., an animal that dies without the involvement of another animal).
73. (181) Eating *terefah* (i.e., animal that is torn by another animal).
74. (182) Eating a limb of a living creature.

75. (183) Eating *gid hanasheh* (an animals' hind, including the sciatic nerve).
76. (184) Eating blood.
77. (185) Eating the fat of a clean animal.
78. (186) Cooking meat in milk.
79. (187) Eating meat cooked in milk.
80. (189) Eating bread made from the grain of the new crop (according to some rabbinic authorities).
81. (190) Eating roasted grain of the new crop (according to some rabbinic authorities).
82. (191) Eating fresh ears of grain (according to some rabbinic authorities).
83. (192) Eating *orlah* ("uncircumcised fruit").
84. (193) Eating *kilai hakerem*.
85. (194) Drinking *yain nesech*.
86. (195) Eating and drinking to excess.
87. (196) Eating on Yom Kippur.
88. (197) Eating *chametz* (leaven) during Passover.
89. (198) Eating anything containing leaven during Passover.
90. (199) Eating leaven after the middle of the fourteenth of Nisan.
91. (200) Leaven being seen in our homes during Passover.
92. (201) Possessing leaven during Passover.
93. (215) Sowing *kilayim* (two different kinds of seeds).
94. (216) Sowing grain or vegetables in a vineyard.
95. (217) Mating animals of different species.
96. (218) Working with two different kinds of animals together.
97. (219) Preventing a beast from eating the produce amidst which it is working.
98. (230) Demanding payments for debts after the sabbatical year (according to some rabbinic authorities).
99. (231) Withholding a loan to be canceled by the sabbatical year (according to some rabbinic authorities).
100. (232) Failing to give charity to our needy brethren.
101. (234) Demanding payment from a debtor known to be unable to pay.
102. (235) Lending at interest.
103. (236) Borrowing at interest.
104. (237) Participating in a loan at interest.
105. (238) Oppressing an employee by delaying a payment of his wages.
106. (239) Taking a pledge from a debtor by force.

107. (240) Keeping a needed pledge from its owner.
108. (241) Taking a pledge from a widow.
109. (242) Taking in pledge food utensils.
110. (243) Abducting an Israelite.
111. (244) Stealing money.
112. (245) Committing robbery.
113. (246) Fraudulently altering land boundaries.
114. (247) Usurping our debts.
115. (248) Repudiating our debts.
116. (249) Swearing falsely in repudiating a debt.
117. (250) Wronging one another in business.
118. (251) Wronging one another by speech.
119. (252) Wronging a proselyte by speech.
120. (253) Wronging a proselyte in business.
121. (256) Dealing harshly with fatherless children and widows.
122. (262) Afflicting one's espoused Hebrew bondmaid.
123. (265) Planning to acquire another's property.
124. (266) Coveting another's possessions.
125. (267) A hired laborer eating growing crops.
126. (268) A hired laborer putting of the harvest in his own vessel.
127. (269) Ignoring lost property.
128. (270) Leaving a trapped person.
129. (271) Cheating in measurements and weights.
130. (272) Keeping false weights and measures.
131. (273) A judge committing unrighteousness.
132. (274) A judge accepting gifts from litigants.
133. (275) A judge favoring a litigant.
134. (276) A judge deterred by fear from giving a just judgment.
135. (277) A judge deciding in favor of a poor man through pity.
136. (278) A judge perverting judgment against a person of evil repute.
137. (280) A judge perverting the justice due to proselytes or orphans.
138. (281) A judge listening to one of the litigants in the absence of another.
139. (284) Appointing an unlearned judge.
140. (285) Bearing false witness.
141. (286) A judge receiving a wicked person's testimony.
142. (287) A judge receiving testimony from a litigant's relative.
143. (288) Convicting on the testimony of a single witness.
144. (289) Killing a human being.
145. (297) Neglecting to save an Israelite in danger of his life.
146. (298) Leaving obstacles on public or private domain.

147. (299) Giving misleading advice.
148. (300) Inflicting excessive corporal punishment.
149. (301) Bearing tales.
150. (302) Hating one another.
151. (303) Putting one to shame.
152. (304) Taking vengeance on one another.
153. (305) Bearing a grudge.
154. (306) Taking the entire bird's nest.
155. (312) Differing from traditional authorities.
156. (313) Adding to the written or oral law.
157. (314) Detracting from the written or oral law.
158. (315) Cursing a judge.
159. (317) Cursing an Israelite.
160. (318) Cursing parents.
161. (319) Smiting parents.
162. (320) Working on the Sabbath.
163. (321) Journeying on the Sabbath.
164. (323) Working on the first day of Passover.
165. (324) Working on the seventh day of Passover.
166. (325) Working on Atzeret.
167. (326) Working on Rosh Hashanah.
168. (327) Working on the first day of Sukkot.
169. (328) Working on Shemini Atzeret.
170. (329) Working on Yom Kippur.
171. (330) Having intercourse with one's mother.
172. (331) Having intercourse with one's father's wife.
173. (332) Having intercourse with one's sister.
174. (333) A man having intercourse with the daughter of one's father's wife if she be his sister.
175. (334) Having intercourse with one's son's daughter.
176. (335) Having intercourse with one's daughter's daughter.
177. (336) Having intercourse with one's daughter.
178. (337) Having intercourse with a woman and her daughter.
179. (338) Having intercourse with a woman and her son's daughter.
180. (339) Having intercourse with a woman and her daughter's daughter.
181. (340) Having intercourse with one's father's sister.
182. (342) Having intercourse with one's mother's sister.
183. (342) Having intercourse with the wife of one's father's brother.
184. (343) Having intercourse with one's son's wife.
185. (344) Having intercourse with one's brother's wife.

186. (345) A man having intercourse with a sister of his wife during the latter's lifetime.
187. (346) Having intercourse with a menstruant.
188. (347) Having intercourse with another man's wife.
189. (348) Men lying with beasts.
190. (349) Women lying with beasts.
191. (350) A man lying carnally with a male.
192. (351) A man lying carnally with his father.
193. (352) A man lying carnally with his father's brother.
194. (353) Intimacy with a kinswoman.
195. (354) A *mamzer* (child born of a forbidden marriage) having intercourse with a Jewess.
196. (355) Having intercourse without marriage.
197. (356) Remarrying one's divorced wife after she has remarried.
198. (357) Having intercourse with a woman subject to a Levirate marriage.
199. (360) A man who is incapable of procreating marrying a Jewess.
200. (361) Castration.

3

PERFORMANCE OF *MITZVOT*

Much attention has been paid to the spiritual and psychological aspects related to the performance of commandments. Throughout rabbinic literature there are references to the manner and spirit in which the performance of *mitzvot* ought to be carried out. The following is a brief survey of some of the more salient concepts related to the rabbinic attitude toward the performance of commandments.

What Are the Rabbinic Terms *Simcha Shel Mitzvah* and *Hiddur Mitzvah?*

The ancient rabbis wanted to make sure that the commandments were never to be seen as heavy burdens, but rather as great opportunities to nourish the soul by catering to its need to serve God. Therefore, they said, *mitzvot* ought never to be carried out mechanically but instead with energy and great enthusiasm. The rabbis coined two important terms related to the way in which a Jew was to observe the commandments. The phrase, *simcha shel mitzvah* literally means, "the joy of the commandment." It was meant to emphasize that the commandments ought to be performed with a joyous and uplifted heart rather than with a feeling of oppressive or burdensome duty. The pleasure in performing a commandment was so important that one important rabbinic sage declared that the joy in carrying out a *mitzvah* was even more acceptable to God than the *mitzvah* itself. A *mitzvah* was never to be postponed but should always be performed at the earliest possible moment. If the time for performing a *mitzvah* had not yet arrived (the *mitzvot* of the festivals, for example), we should await it with happy anticipation as one awaits an honored guest.

21

"Be strong as a leopard, light as an eagle, fleet as a hart, and mighty as a lion, to do the will of your Father who is in heaven" (Antigonos of Socho, *Ethics of Our Fathers,* 5:20).

In addition to fulfilling commands with a joyous heart, the rabbis also emphasized the *adornment* of a commandment (*hiddur mitzvah,* in Hebrew). Here, the rabbis suggested that it was important in showing one's love for performing commandments to adorn them and go beyond the call of duty in fulfilling them. So, for example, they suggested that when building and decorating a *sukkah* that one ought to use and design the most beautiful of decorations. Similarly, when writing a Torah scroll, the scribe was required to write it in the finest script and with clear ink so that it would be always a delight to look at. The Talmud (*Bava Kamma* 9b) suggested that Jews spend an extra third of the cost of a *mitzvah* on its adornment. *Hiddur mitzvah* required the highest degree of personal involvement in the performance of any religious act. Through the adornment of the commandments, Jewish people have demonstrated, not only their regard for them, but the expression of their aesthetic appreciation to the greater glory of God.

What Is the Meaning of the Rabbinic Term *Chivvuv Mitzvah?*

Chivvuv mitzvah (love of the *mitzvah*) refers to exemplary conduct whereby a person performs a *mitzvah* with unbounding love, beauty, and dignity. The example that is often given with regard to this concept is the person who, in buying something to perform a particular commandment, would not bargain over the price but rather would pay at once whatever was the asking price. This was done to show that love of God was greater than attachment to material goods.

The ideal of *chivvuv mitzvah* was also regarded as fulfilled whenever a person showed a readiness to perform a commandment personally even when Jewish Law permitted its delegation to others. For example, when the Bible says that the Israelites, when leaving Egypt, carried the unleavened bread and bitter herbs on their shoulders rather than placing them on their beasts of burdens, the rabbis comment that this they did to show their love for performing the commandments personally.

Finally, there have been instances described when people kissed the *sukkah* when entering and leaving it, as well as the four species, as a way of manifesting their great love for these *mitzvot.*

What Is the Term *Zerizut,* and How Does It Relate to the Performance of Commandments?

The term *zerizut* means "alertness." According to the rabbis, a person's attitude toward performing a commandment is indicated by the alertness he or she exhibits when the time comes for its performance. As it says in the Book of Psalms, "I have hastened and not delayed in the observance of Your commandments *(Psalm* 119:60)."

Thus, a commandment that can be performed at any time of the day should be carried out as early as possible. That is why it is meritorious for a circumcision to be performed in the morning rather than in the afternoon, because one always hastens to perform a commandment with alertness (Code of Jewish Law, *Yoreh De'ah* 274, 1).

What Is the Meaning of the Term *Bizui Mitzvah?*

A commandment may not be treated with disrespect *(bizui mitzvah).* There are a variety of ways in which one might show a lack of respect for a *mitzvah.* For example, using a sacred object for a secular purpose is a form of being disrespectful in performing a *mitzvah.* Thus, it is expressly forbidden to count money using the light of a *hanukkiah.* This shows great disrespect for the *mitzvah.*

A second example of disrespect is to attend to one's own affairs before fulfilling a *mitzvah.* Thus, for example, if a person eats before reciting the morning prayers, it is considered a sign of disrespect to God and His commandments.

Finally, one must guard against the disrespectful treatment of an object with which a *mitzvah* has once been performed, such as old *tzizit,* and so forth. This applies especially to objects that are in themselves sacred, such as *tefillin* or a Torah scroll. When these become old and worn, they must not be thrown away but rather should be buried in order to prevent their desecration.

What Is the Concept of *Mitzvah Habbah Be'averah?*

A Jew must also be especially careful not to perform a *mitzvah* with the fruits of sin *(mitzvah habaah averah).* The rabbis say: "If a person has stolen wheat and has ground, kneaded and baked it, and set apart the *challah,* how can he recite a blessing over it. It would not be a blessing, but rather blasphemy!" (Talmud *Sanhedrin* 6b).

What Are the Terms *Kavanah* and *Lishmah,* and How Do They Relate to the Performance of Commandments?

Too much stress on the *performance* of the commands could quite naturally result in pure mechanical behavior in which acts are performed without proper feelings and devotion. To that end, the rabbis instituted the concept of *kavanah,* meaning "direction" or "proper concentration." *Kavanah* refers to the need for correct thoughts and application of the mind before one performs a commandment. Undoubtedly, this is one of the reasons why a blessing is recited before performing a *mitzvah.* The blessing is intended to offer praise to God and remind the participant of the importance of the sanctified act.

A similar idea to *kavanah* is that of *lishmah,* meaning "for its own sake." That is to say, the commandment ought to be carried out without any ulterior motive and without expectation of a reward.

4

REASONS FOR THE COMMANDMENTS: *TA'AMAY HAMITZVOT*

The search for reasons for the commandments springs from a tendency to transcend mere obedience to them by investing them with some intrinsic meaning. The Torah itself offers reasons for some of the commandments. For example, in the Book of Exodus (23:9) there is a commandment that states that one ought not to oppress a stranger, for the Israelites know the heart of a stranger, seeing that they were strangers in the land of Egypt. Here we see that the alien was to receive the same treatment as the native Israelite, who obviously knew from firsthand experience what it was like to be treated as an alien while spending four centuries under Egyptian oppression.

In early rabbinic tradition, there were a few rabbis who favored offering explanations for doing the commandments, which included the enabling of the Jews to acquire merit and to strengthen their level of holiness. For the most part, though, there was little detailed rationalization of the commandments in rabbinic sources. Most rabbinic authorities believed that the yoke of the commandments was to be cherished without the necessity to probe the reasons behind them, and that their basic purpose was to refine the character of people.

Jewish religious philosophers, especially in the medieval period, began to probe for the purpose and meaning of the commandments. Most of their investigation was generally conducted independently of any definitive study of the commandments. It is difficult to ascertain with certainty the reasons that prompted the Middle Age scholars to steadfastly begin to explore commandments. Some have suggested that one cause may have been apologetic. That is to say, with rabbinic leaders being confronted with anti-Semitic attacks, they felt that an intelligent reply would reduce the weight of the misrepresentation.

The following section surveys some of the important philosophers and thinkers who paved the way for a comprehensive series of rationales for the commandments.

Hellenistic Literature

The need for a rational explanation of the commandments was expressed for the first time in the Hellenistic period, a time when the Jewish people were profoundly influenced by Greek culture. The explanation was motivated by a desire to present Judaism to the pagan world as a legislation intended to produced a people of the highest virtue. For example, in the Letter of Aristeas, the dietary laws (*kashrut*) and other commandments, including the wearing of a prayer shawl and the affixing of a *mezuzah* to one's doorpost, were explained as having the purpose of awakening holy thoughts and forming character.

Philo

Philo, a first-century philosopher whose Greek writings focused primarily on the Five Books of Moses, offered one of the first systematic treatises for the reasons behind the commandments. He categorized the commandments into the following four categories: beliefs, virtuous emotions, actions symbolizing beliefs, and actions symbolizing virtues. In his explanation of various rationales for the commandments, he often used the allegorical method of interpretation.

Saadia Gaon

This medieval philosopher was Judaism's first thinker to divide the commandments into those that are an obligation because they are required by reason (called *sichliyot* in Hebrew) and those given through revelation (called *shimiyyot* in Hebrew). The latter, he said, must be accepted for no other reason than that they were proclaimed by God, although on occasion he was able to explain their usefulness.

In his attempt to offer rationales for the commandments of reason, Saadia often pointed out the deleterious effects of the so-called negative commands. For example, the prohibition of stealing undermined the economic basis of a society. With regard to the less understandable laws of the

Jewish diet, Saadia, in his *Book of Beliefs and Opinions,* stated that they were initiated in order to combat animal worship.

Bachya ibn Pakuda

This medieval philosopher combined Saadia's division of the *mitzvot* with his division of "duties of the members of the body" (*chovot ha-evarim*) and "duties of the hearts (*chovot ha-levavot*). The so-called "duties of the members of the body" are of two kinds: duties obligatory by virtue of reason and duties neither prohibited nor rejected by reason (e.g., the prohibition of eating milk and meat together). The "duties of the hearts," on the other hand, are of an intellectual and attitudinal kind, such as belief in God and trust and love in Him. One main difference between this philosopher and Saadia lies in the fact that the former does not attempt to explain the "revelational laws" in terms of their usefulness. For Bachya, the laws with no apparent reason are simply expressions of spirituality and reverence intended to bring people closer to God.

Judah HaLevi

This important medieval philosopher classified the *mitzvot* under these three headings: rational laws (*sichliyot*), which he also termed psychic laws (*nafishiyot*), and which had to do with belief in God and justice; governmental laws (*minhagiyot*), having to do with the functioning of a society; and revelational laws (*shimiyot*), or divine laws (*elohiyot*), whose function was to elevate the Jew to commune with God. Prophecy was the manifestation of the highest level of the divine laws.

Abraham ibn Ezra

He distinguished between laws that are instilled in the human heart prior to revelation (*pikkudim*) and laws that prescribe symbolic acts reminding us of such matters as creation (e.g., the exodus from Egypt and observance of the Sabbath). He also speaks of commandments that he calls "obscure" (*mitzvot ne'elamot*), which have no clear-cut rationale. With regard to some of the latter commandments, ibn Ezra attempts to explain them as prohibitions against acts that are contrary to nature (e.g., cooking a goat in its mother's milk). Others he explains as serving useful purposes. For example, the separation of the leper from the community was commanded by God as a health measure, while the Jewish Laws of the diet were meant to prevent serious injury to a person's body and soul.

Maimonides (RaMBaM)

Perhaps the greatest Jewish philosopher to have ever lived was Maimonides. He did not distinguish between the so-called "rational" and the "revelational" laws. In his opinion, all of the commandments set forth in the Five Books of Moses had useful purposes and rationales. According to Maimonides, the two overall purposes of the Torah were the welfare of the soul and the welfare of the body.

One of his important works was the *Sefer HaMitzvot,* the *Book of Commandments,* in which Maimonides brings together the 613 biblical commandments, listing them under the categories of "positive" and "negative" and adding his own commentary whenever he felt it necessary.

Nachmonides (RaMBaN)

This Spanish rabbi and scholar maintained that there was a reason for each one of the commandments. In his opinion, the commandments are all for the good of humanity, either to keep people from something that might be hurtful, to remove them from bad habits, to teach them mercy and justice, or to constantly remind them of the dependability of God and His miracles. He often used kabbalistic (mystic) teaching in his interpretations.

Moses ben Jacob of Coucy

This French, thirteenth-century scholar stressed the value of Torah study in an orderly fashion. His reputation rests on his most extensive work, called *Sefer Mitzvot Gadol* (SeMaG). This work includes the essence of the Oral Law, arranged in order of commandments and divided into negative and positive. His work is based on Maimonides' *Mishneh Torah,* with a number of differences. For example, unlike Maimonides, he included rabbinic precepts.

Obadiah ben Jacob Sforno

This fourteenth-century, Italian commentator spends a good deal of time explaining the reason for the sacrifices and, as a physician, often uses medical knowledge as well as allegory in his explanations.

Aaron Ha-Levi

A native of Barcelona, Spain, this fourteenth-century philosopher wrote a monumental work called *Sefer HaHinnuch,* the *Book of Education.* In the book, which is primarily intended for youth, he listed all 613 commandments as they occur in the weekly scriptural portions, elucidating each one in a most comprehensive manner.

His exposition of each of the commandments is based on a division into four distinct parts. Part one consists of a discussion of the nature of each commandment, its biblical source, and its rabbinic interpretation. Part two deals with the reason for the *mitzvah.* In part three, the specific laws of the *mitzvah* are cited as derived from the Talmud and various other sources. Part four, the final part, indicates the conditions of each of the *mitzvot* and explains where and when a given command applies, to whom it applies, and what, if any, punishment is due if one violates it.

Moses Mendelssohn

This eighteenth-century German philosopher stated that the goals of the commandments were actions, leading to temporal happiness, and meditation on eternal and historical truths, leading to eternal happiness. He wrote that every ceremony has a specific meaning and relation to the speculative aspect of religion and morality.

5

BIBLICAL REASONS TO OBEY THE COMMANDMENTS

W hy should Jewish people obey the commandments? Jewish tradition has always had a plethora of answers to this question. The Bible suggests a number of reasons to obey God's commandments. The following is a summary of the biblical themes related to observing God's commandments:

Divine Compensation and Punishment

Chapters 11 and 28 of the Book of Deuteronomy are devoted to describing the rewards and punishments that God will bring upon those who obey or disobey Him. The rabbis made the theme central by choosing the following text as part of the second paragraph of the *Shema,* to be said each morning and evening:

> If you will earnestly heed the commandments which I command you this day, to love and serve God with all your heart and soul, then will I favor your land with rain at the proper season—rain in autumn and rain in spring—so that you will have ample harvest of grain and wine and oil. And I will assure grass in the fields for your cattle, and you will eat to contentment.
>
> Be careful lest you are tempted to forsake God and turn to false gods and pray to them. For then the anger of God will be aroused toward you. God will then close up the heavens and there will be no rain and the earth will not yield its produce. You will soon perish from the good land which God is giving to you. (Deuteronomy 11:13–21)

This passage, recited in the traditional daily liturgy as the second section of the *Shema* (Hear O Israel . . .) clearly shows the Torah holding out the

31

reward of an abundant harvest for obeisance to God's *mitzvot.* There are some people who have great difficulty with this section of the Bible, since there are many cases of people who do good and fulfill commandments and yet who suffer, and of bad people who have been known to prosper. Suffice it to say that the Torah had no doubt of the certainty of God's response to obedience and disobedience regarding His commandments.

Human Compensation and Punishment

The Bible clearly expected that many of its commandments would be enforced by the human courts. A biblical judicial process was set in place to cover a variety of aspects of life in which the guilt or innocence of a person would be determined. Here are some examples of punishment for those found guilty of violation of a commandment:

> When men quarrel and one strikes the other with a stone or a fist, and he does not die but has to take to his bed, if then he gets up and walks outdoors upon his staff, the assailant shall go unpunished, except that he must pay for his idleness and his cure. (Exodus 21:18–19)

> When a man opens a pit, or digs a pit and does not cover it, and an ox or an ass falls into it, the one responsible for the pit must make restitution; he shall pay the price to the owner, but shall keep the dead animal. (Exodus 21:33–34)

What the Bible here describes as reason to obey law, namely that you will be punished by the authorities of the Jewish communal courts if you do not, was not only an ancient phenomenon. Throughout the centuries, Jewish people have gone to their own courts in order to resolve disputes.

The Wisdom and Good Teachings of the Commandments

The Bible suggests that we should obey God's commandments because it would be unwise not to. Thus, Moses says this to the Israelites:

> See, I have imparted to you laws and rules, as God has commanded me, for you to abide by in the land which you are about to invade and occupy. Observe them faithfully, for that will be proof of your wisdom and discernment to other peoples, who on hearing of all these laws

will say, "Surely, that great nation is a wise and discerning people."
For what great nation is there that has a god so close at hand as is the
Lord our God whenever we call upon Him? Or what great nation has
laws and rules as perfect as all this Teaching that I set before you this
day? (Deuteronomy 4:5–8)

Here we see that God's laws have been tried and tested, and that it makes
practical sense to follow them because they work in life's experiences. By
following the laws, a person will be happy and succeed at living well.

The Commandments Define the Ethical Life

The Torah affirms that God's commandments are ethical and moral because
God is a moral God, and it explains that the commandments help set for
people the true standard of morality. For example, it states in the Book of
Psalms:

The teaching of God is perfect, renewing life; the decrees of God are
enduring, making the simple wise. The commandments of the Lord
are just, rejoicing the heart; the instruction of God is lucid, making the
eyes light up. The fear of God is pure, abiding forever; the judgments
of God are true, righteous altogether. (Psalm 19:8–10)

The Commandments Are Part
of Our Covenantal Relationship with God

The Jewish promise to obey God is expressed in the covenant (*brit*) that our
ancestors made with God at Mount Sinai. Here, God promised to enter into
a long-term relationship with the children of Israel. This relationship
included giving them a homeland and rewarding them with physical prosperity. The Israelites' side of the bargain was to obey those commandments
that God revealed to them, saying "all that God has commanded, we will
do and we will hear and we will obey" (Exodus 24:7).

The question that modern Jews ask is the following: If our ancestors
voluntarily agreed to enter into God's covenant, why are we obligated by it
as well? Interestingly, Moses had already anticipated this objection when he
spoke to the second generation of Israelites who had not been a part of the
Sinai experience:

God made a covenant with us at Horeb. It was not with our ancestors
that God made this covenant, but with us, the living, every one of us
who is here today. Face to face God spoke to you on the mountain out
of the fire. (Deuteronomy 5:2–4)

From this verse we see that the Israelites were expected to see themselves as
if they themselves had stood at the mountain and obligated themselves to
fulfill the covenant of God. This was also to apply to their descendants for
all generations.

The Commandments Enhance God's Reputation and Honor

The commandments also served as a way of sanctifying God's Name
(reputation) and making it holy and unique. Since God gave the Israelites
commandments as part of the covenantal agreement, the commitment to
follow and obey them reflected, not only upon the Israelites themselves,
but upon God as well. Good behavior, according to the Bible, brought
honor upon God, whereas bad behavior profaned God's Name and
reputation:

You shall faithfully observe My commandments: I am God. You shall
not profane My holy name, that I may be sanctified in the midst of the
Israelite people—I the Lord who sanctify you, I who brought you out
of the land of Egypt to be your God, I am the Lord. (Leviticus
22:31–33)

Therefore, the Bible recommends that Jews do what is right vis-à-vis the
performance of commandments because God's reputation depends upon it.
Sanctifying God's name is therefore a powerful motivation to do what is right.

The Commandments Are a Way to Become
an Extraordinary People

The Hebrew word for "holy" is *kadosh,* which literally means, "to set
apart" or to be like no other. The Torah states that in obeying the *mitzvot,*
the Jewish people become a nation that is unique and set apart from all the
other nations in the world. Since the Israelites agree to obey God's commands, they are called God's treasured people. While this theme permeates
the Bible, there is one especially famous expression of it, which occurred
when the Israelites reach Mount Sinai:

Moses went up to God, and God called to him from the mountain saying, "Thus shall you say to the house of Jacob and declare to the children of Israel: 'You have seen what I did to the Egyptians, how I bore you on eagles' wings and brought you to Me. Now then, if you will obey Me faithfully and keep My covenant, you shall be My most treasured possession among all the nations. Indeed all of the earth is Mine, but you shall be to Me a kingdom of priests and a holy nation.' These are the words that you shall speak to the children of Israel." (Exodus 19:3–6)

This passage defines "holy" as meaning special and unique from among all others. It is important to note that the Israelites are to be God's holy people only if they are obedient to God's commandments.

Obeying Commandments Is the Way for Israelites to Show Their Adoration of God

The Torah describes God as the lover of the Jewish people. Giving them the Torah was a sign of that love. The following biblical passages illustrates God's exteme affection for the Israelites:

For you are a people consecrated to God: of all the peoples on earth God chose you to be His treasured people. It is not because you are the most numerous of peoples that God set His heart on you and chose you. Indeed, you are the smallest of peoples; but it was because God loved you and kept the oath He made to your ancestors that God freed you with a mighty hand and rescued you from the house of bondage, from the power of Pharaoh, king of Egypt.

Know, therefore, that only the Lord your God is God, the steadfast God who keeps His gracious covenant to the thousandth generation of those who love Him and keep His commandments, but who instantly retaliates with destruction against those who reject Him— never slow with those who reject Him, but paying them back instantly. Therefore, observe faithfully the Instruction, the laws, and the norms with which I charge you today. (Deuteronomy 7:6–11)

Perhaps the most graphic description of God's love for Israel can be found in the Book of the Prophet Hosea, who transforms the Sinai covenant into a marriage contract between God and the Israelites:

And I will wed you forever: and I will betroth you with righteousness and justice, and with goodness and mercy, and I will wed you with faithfulness. Then you shall be devoted to God. (Hosea 2:21–22)

These very same words of consecration are used each morning when traditional Jews wrap part of the *tefillin* (phylacteries) around their hands. In this way they renew daily the marital relationship established between God and the Israelites.

6

RABBINIC REASONS TO OBEY THE COMMANDMENTS

There is considerable rabbinic discussion throughout Jewish history as to why the Jewish people ought to obey the commandments. Many rabbis reaffirmed the reasons that the Bible gave but also added some of their own. Here is a brief summary of the rabbinic rationales for observing and obeying the commandments:

Commandments Help to Improve and Perfect People

The purpose of the commandments according to some rabbinic authorities was to make people pure and refined. This point of view can be illustrated in this selection from *Midrash Tanchuma,* "Shemini":

> What does God care whether a man kills an animal in the proper Jewish way and eats it, or whether he strangles the animal and eats it? Will the one benefit Him, or the other injure Him? Or what does God care whether a man eats kosher or non kosher animals? "If you are wise, you are wise for yourself, but if you scorn, you alone shall bear it" (Proverbs 9:12). So you learn that the commandments were given only to refine God's creatures, as it says, "God's word is refined. It is a protection to those who trust in Him" (2 Samuel 22:31). (ed. Buber, 15b)

Commandments Preserve the World

Unlike the previous explanation of the *mitzvot* as ways to purify humanity, other rabbinic sources observed that the commandments were given by

God to the people in order to help continue the very existence of the world itself. Here is an example from the Midrash *Deuteronomy Rabbah*, "Nitzavim" (8:5), to illustrate this point: "God said, 'If you read the Law, you do a kindness, for you help to preserve My world, since if it were not for the Law the world would again become without form and void.'"

The Commandments Establish Israel's National Identity

The Bible stated several times that the Israelites are not to do what the other nations surrounding them were doing. This was the Bible's way of negatively defining the Israelite identity.

In rabbinic times, the identity of the Jews became even more important, in part because the Jewish people were scattered throughout many different countries. Obeying commandments was a way of staying affiliated with the Jewish people and its peoplehood: "If it were not for My law which you accepted, I should not recognize you, and I should not regard you more than any of the idolatrous nations of the world" (Midrash *Exodus Rabbah*, "Ki Tissa," 47:3).

The Commandments Have the Potential to Beautify

Rabbinic literature discusses the artistic and aesthetic values in the covenantal relationship between God and the Jewish people. Obeisance to the commandments helps to make Israel beautiful and attractive in the eyes of God. Finding beauty in each other helps to reinforce the covenantal relationship between God and Israel. It is as if the jewelry and perfumes with which Israel decorates herself for God, her lover, are the commandments themselves:

> "You are beautiful, my love" (Song of Songs 1:15). You are beautiful through the commandments, both positive and negative. You are beautiful through loving deeds, beautiful in your house with the heave offerings and tithes; beautiful in the field through the commandments about gleaning, the forgotten sheaf and the second tithe[;] . . . beautiful in prayer, the reading of the *Shema. (Song of Songs Rabbah,* 1:15)

In short, the authority of the commandments according to rabbinic sources stemmed from a host of factors, all of which were intended to help the Jewish people transform themselves and the world into the kind of community that God wanted them to become.

7

WOMEN'S OBLIGATION TO PERFORM COMMANDMENTS

Is There a Difference between the Obligation of Men and Women vis-à-vis the Performance of Commandments?

There is virtually no distinction between men and women in the area of moral responsibility covered by the so-called negative commandments. There is a distinction, however, between men and women with regard to positive commandments. Women are obligated according to Jewish Law in virtually all positive commandments that are independent of time, but they are exempt from most, though not all, time-bound positive commandments. There are quite a number of rabbinic reasons given for the latter rabbinic dispensation, including the fact that women are excused from the time-related commandments because of their familial duties and responsibilities. Others believed that women have greater potential for spiritual growth than men because of their less-aggressive nature. Therefore, they need to fulfill fewer commandments in order to achieve spiritual perfection.

What Are the Positive Time-Bound Commandments from Which Women Are Exempt?

Women were exempted from seven time-bound positive commands: the recitation of the prayer *Shema,* the wearing of *tefillin,* the wearing of a prayer shawl, the counting of the omer, hearing the *shofar,* dwelling in the *sukkah,* and taking the *lulav* and *etrog.*

May Women Perform Commandments from Which They Are Exempted?

Virtually all rabbinic authorities agree that women may perform the *mitzvot* from which they have been exempted. Furthermore, their voluntary performance is considered by most authorities to be a meritorious act.

One area of controversy among rabbinic authorities relates to whether women are permitted to recite the appropriate blessings before performing an optional commandment. Before performing a *mitzvah,* one must recite: "Blessed are You, Adonai Our God, Ruler of the universe who has sanctified us through commandments and commanded us to . . ." The ending of the phrase depends on the specific *mitzvah*. The phrase "and commanded us" presents a problem in the case of optional commandments for women. Rabbenu Tam, a twelfth-century rabbinic authority, interpreted the phrase as referring to the collective obligation of the Jewish people and ruled that women, as part of the collective, could recite the blessing. Maimonides, on the other hand, interpreted the phrase as referring to individual obligation in the specific *mitzvah* and ruled that women could not recite the blessing when performing an optional commandment. Since the custom of Ashkenazic Jewry has been to follow Rabbenu Tam, Ashkenazic women recite blessings on optional *mitzvot*.

8

THE BAR MITZVAH AND THE BAT MITZVAH: SOME HISTORICAL BACKGROUND

At thirteen, one is ready to fulfill commandments.
Ethics of Our Fathers 5:23

What Is the Meaning of Bar/Bat Mitzvah?

The words *Bar* and *Bat Mitzvah* literally mean the "son and daughter of the commandment." Whereas the word *bat* is a Hebrew word meaning "daughter," the word *bar* is an Aramaic word meaning "son." The Aramaic word *bar* is the equivalent of the Hebrew word *ben*, meaning "son."

What Event Do the Bar and Bat Mitzvah Mark in Jewish Life?

Becoming a Bar or Bat Mitzvah represented Judaism's recognition that a young man or woman had reached the age when he or she was responsible for the performance of *mitzvot*, religious commandments. The individual was no longer considered a minor or child in Jewish Law but rather an adult with all of the religious responsibilities and privileges associated

41

with it. For boys, this age was thirteen according to his Hebrew birthday, while for girls the age was twelve.

What Is the Origin of the Bar Mitzvah?

The origin of the Bar Mitzvah ceremony is shrouded in mystery and debate. The Bible never mentions the Bar Mitzvah ceremony, nor does it give any indication that when a child reached the age of thirteen he or she became an adult. In fact, when a particular age is mentioned in the Bible as a requirement or test for total participation in the activities of the Israelite community, the age is twenty, not thirteen. In Exodus 30:14 we read of a census that was taken among the Israelites when only those twenty years and older were to be counted in the census. In Leviticus 27:1–5, the valuation of individuals for the redemption of vows to God was determined by age. Persons between the ages of five and twenty were grouped together in valuation, giving some indication that maturity comes at the age of twenty.

The Talmud (major source for the rabbinic interpretation of the law) is also silent with regard to a Bar Mitzvah ceremony at the age of thirteen, clearly indicating that a special occasion as we know it today was unknown in talmudic times. The Talmud, however, does mention the term *Bar Mitzvah* twice. Both times it refers to any Jewish person, not necessarily a boy at age thirteen, who observes the commandments. When referring to a thirteen-year-old boy, the Talmud uses the term *bar onshin* ("one who is subject to punishment"). This indicates that a child in talmudic times became liable for any wrongdoing that he might commit at age thirteen.

The clearest recognition of thirteen as the age when a child was considered to be a fully responsible member of the community is in the following statement from the Mishnah, the early part of the Talmud, that "at age thirteen one becomes obliged to fulfill the commandments" (Antigonos of Socho, *Ethics of Our Fathers*, 5:21).

There is a wide array of opinions concerning the reason for the choice of the thirteenth year as the age of performing *mitzvot*. Some authorities ascribe it to foreign influences present in ancient Israel in the first century B.C.E. Still others feel that it may be a throwback to puberty rites that were practiced by many different peoples. Almost every culture in today's world has some kind of initiation rite that marks a child's entrance into puberty.

When Did the "Modern" Bar Mitzvah Ceremony Begin?

One of the first Jewish scholars to use the term *Bar Mitzvah* in the same sense of which it is spoken today was Mordecai ben Hillel, a thirteenth-century German rabbi. Most of the references to the Bar Mitzvah appear after this date.

It was on the Sabbath after a boy's thirteenth birthday that the Bar Mitzvah too place. The child was called to the Torah for the first time in his life, often for the *maftir aliyah* (the honor of being called to the Torah to recite the Torah blessings, with the additional honor of chanting a portion from one of the Books of the Prophets, called a *haftarah*). When the child finished his *aliyah* (literally "going up," refers both to going up to the Torah and reciting the Torah blessings), the father would rise and say, "Blessed is God who has freed me from the responsibility for this boy." The text of this blessing, which is found in a midrash, or homiletical interpretation of the Bible (*Genesis Rabbah* 63:10), symbolizes the fact that from that day onward, the parent is no longer responsible for the child's misdeeds and the child is now required to bear total responsibility for his own actions. This was then followed by a meal of celebration (called a *seudat mitzvah* or *mitzvah* meal), at which the Bar Mitzvah typically would deliver a Bible-related talk (called a *devar Torah*) to show what he had learned.

Although it is likely that the Bar Mitzvah ceremony has known many changes and gone through many stages since it first emerged in Jewish religious life, the basic idea has remained. A boy enters fully into the religious heritage of the Jewish people and has the privilege and responsibility of fulfilling God's commandments.

What Is the Origin of the Bat Mitzvah Ceremony?

Beginning in the second or the third century c.e., young Jewish women at age twelve assumed legal responsibility for the performance of *mitzvot*. As with the age of thirteen for boys, twelve likely corresponded to the age of the onset of puberty. Girls, however, were subject to fewer religious commandments than the boys. They were exempted from a whole series of time-bound, positive commandments on the assumption that their domestic duties at home took precedence.

Many centuries passed before the Bat Mitzvah ceremony as we know it today appeared on the scene. The first known Bat Mitzvah in North America (more than seventy years ago) was that of Judith Kaplan Eisenstein, daughter of Rabbi Mordecai Kaplan, the founder of the Reconstructionist movement. The Bat Mitzvah was held at a Sabbath service on a Saturday. Over the years, the Bat Mitzvah ceremony was adopted by Reform, Conservative, and Reconstructionist synagogues.

What Is a *"Mitzvah* Meal" (*Seudat Mitzvah*), and How Does It Relate to the Bar and Bat Mitzvah?

The festive meal that follows a Bar or Bat Mitzvah is called a religious meal, or *seudat mitzvah* in Hebrew. It was intended as an opportunity to celebrate the joy of this life-cycle event and was expected to take on an aura of sanctity. There seems, however, to have been a tendency, both in the past and in the present, for families to make very elaborate celebrations. These were never in the spirit of Jewish Law, which favored modesty and humility. Already back in 1595 in Cracow, Poland, a communal tax was placed on the Bar Mitzvah feast in order to keep it within the bounds of good taste.

Most rabbis today continue to work to enhance the spiritual aspects of this so-called *mitzvah* meal. The inclusion of blessings before and after the meal, spirited Israel dancing and Jewish music, and the arrangement in advance to give the leftover food to a food bank are some of the suggested ways of investing this meal with deeper Jewish feeling and spirit.

What Is an Adult Bar or Bat Mitzvah?

Since it is never too late to celebrate a Bar or Bat Mitzvah, many synagogues today sponsor Bar and Bat Mitzvah classes as part of their adult studies program. The program generally included a commitment of a year or more of adult Jewish studies, culminating in a group, adult Bar or Bat Mitzvah experience in which class members lead the service and chant a *haftarah.*

When a person reaches the age of eighty-three, there is a beautiful custom in some congregations that allows a person the opportunity of celebrating another Bar or Bat Mitzvah. It often provides a wonderful opportunity for family, relatives, and friends to celebrate an important life's milestone for a second time. Recently, Judith Kaplan Eisenstein, America's first known Bat Mitzvah, celebrated her eighty-third birthday with her second Bat Mitzvah, this time on the afternoon of the Sabbath.

What Is the Connection between a *Mitzvah* and Becoming a Bar or Bat Mitzvah?

Becoming a Bar or Bat Mitzvah means becoming subject to the commandments and responsible for carrying them out. It means that a Bar or Bat Mitzvah ought to take on ways of living and thinking and seeing the world from the perspective of God. Reaching the age of *mitzvot* is an important time of choice for every Bar and Bat Mitzvah. Seriously choosing to be commanded and accepting new responsibilities as a Jew now becomes their responsibility.

What Is a Bar or Bat Mitzvah Project?

Many congregational schools today require every Bar and Bat Mitzvah student to complete what is often called a *mitzvah* project. The project is intended to have students research and begin to experience and perform a whole series of different commandments, thus familiarizing them with the range of possibilities. The following is a cross section of some of the *mitzvah* assignments listed by category that some congregational schools have adopted for use with their Bar and Bat Mitzvah students.

Learning

1. Find a biblical verse or quotation from Jewish sources. Write that selection down, giving its origin. Explain it in your own words and illustrate it with either your own illustration or pictures that you cut out.

2. Read a Jewish book and write a book report summarizing its main points. Explain how this book relates to Judaism and tell what you learned about Jews or Judaism from it.

3. Create your own Jewish Family Scrapbook, which should include your own family tree.

4. If you were planning a trip to Israel, list seven places you would want to visit and explain why you would want to visit them. Pinpoint the places on a map of Israel.

5. Visit a place of Jewish interest (Jewish museum, etc.) with your family and write a report on your reactions to what was there and what you learned from the experience.

Prayer

1. Attend two non-Sabbath services (e.g., Passover, Rosh Chodesh) or two daily services. Write a report on how they differ from a typical Sabbath service.

2. Lead your family in the Friday evening Sabbath rituals. Write a report on your experience.

3. Learn the *Havdalah* service and lead it for a minimum of three months.

Holiday Celebration

1. Fast for a full day on one of the Jewish fast days. Explain the meaning of the particular fast day.

2. Write an original holiday song, including words and melody.

3. Do a Jewish holiday project in music, photography, or art that is related to the meaning of the theme of that particular holiday.

Tzedakah (Acts of Kindness)

1. Make a family *tzedakah* box for charity and contribute to it each week.

2. Research Maimonides' "Eight Steps of Charity" (*Mishneh Torah*). Explain in your own words how Maimonides understands the concept of charity in its various forms.

3. Make a list of the Jewish agencies in your local area that collect *tzedakah*. Write a brief report on how the funds are used.

4. Choose a *tzedakah* hero and research this person. Tell why, in your opinion, you consider this person to be a hero.

Gemilut Chasadim: Deeds of Kindness

1. "Adopt" an elderly Jewish person or shut-in and contact this person on a regular basis.

2. Volunteer to be a friend to, and help and/or work with, a handicapped child or adult.

3. Get involved in the Jewish organization Mazon, which helps the hungry.

4. Participate with your family in a clothing drive for the needy.

5. Encourage your local bakeries and caterers to channel leftover foods to a food bank.

6. Adopt the *tzedakah* habit of buying an extra item of food each time you go shopping for distribution to the needy.

9

THE TEN COMMANDMENTS

Sociologically, if not religiously, the Ten Commandments are the most significant element in the Bible. Often we hear people reducing the Judeo-Christian tradition to the observance of the Ten Commandments. These few brief commands—only 120 words in all—cover the entire gamut of human conduct, not only of outer actions but also of the inner thoughts of the heart. This section of the book is intended to provide some insights into the nature of the Ten Commandments and the Jewish traditional treatment of them.

What Are the Ten Commandments, Where Do They Appear in the Bible, and When Are They Read in the Synagogue?

The Ten Commandments are a series of sayings that represent a summary of universal duties that are binding upon all of humanity. They cover the whole religious and moral life, affirming the existence of God and prohibiting idolatry and the profane use of the divine name. They stress the observance of the Sabbath and the reverence due to one's parents. They forbid murder, theft, false testimony, and predatory desires.

Primarily contained in the Book of Exodus (20:2–17), the Ten Commandments reappear in a somewhat modified form in the Book of Deuteronomy (5:6–21), where the Sabbath is based upon the deliverance from Egypt instead of God's resting on the seventh day from the work of creation, and the word "desire" is used in place of the word "covet."

According to a talmudic statement (*Berakhot* 12a), the Ten Commandments were recited in the Jerusalem Temple as part of the daily liturgy, before the prayer *Shema*. On account of the heretics, however, who asserted that only the Ten Commandments were divinely ordained, the custom was abolished outside the Land of Israel.

Today the Ten Commandments are included as additional readings in Reform, Conservative, Orthodox and Reconstructionist prayerbooks. Perhaps this ambivalent status of including them as a supplementary reading arose from the fear that it might be considered that the Ten Commandments were the sole essence of Judaism and that other commandments could be discarded. The Ten Commandments are also read as part of the regular weekly portions (twice a year in the portions *Yitro* [Exodus 19–20] and *Va'etchanan* [Deuteronomy 5]) and on the festival of Shavuot. It is customary for the congregation to rise when the Ten Commandments are being read.

Why Have the Ten Commandments Also Been Called the "Decalogue," "The Ten Things," and "The Ten Words"?

In Jewish tradition, the Ten Commandments have been called the Ten Things (*aseret hadevarim* in Hebrew) or Ten Speakings (*aseret hadibrot* in Hebrew). The Greek term *Decalogue*, which was first used by a Greek Church Father, Clement of Alexandria in 200 c.e., is a literal rendering of the biblical, *aseret hadevarim*. The reason is that the first of the Ten, "I am the Lord Your God," has been considered a statement of belief rather than a commandment per se.

Were the Ten Commandments Always Identified with Exodus 20:1–14 and Its Parallel in Deuteronomy 5:6–18?

While in prevailing Jewish and Christian traditions, the Ten Commandments have always been identified with the books of Exodus (20:1–14) and Deuteronomy (5:6–18), there have been dissident opinions that hold that the words inscribed on the tablets were not those of these chapter but were from another "Decalogue," and most likely the ritual prescriptions of Exodus 34:14–26. This assumption was first put forward by fifth-century writers. The theory is based on the fact that the section in Exodus has an introduction that sets it into a convenantal framework (verses 10 through 13), a conclusion in which Moses is bidden to write the commandments down, and a report that in fact, Moses did write them on tablets (versus 27 and 28). Furthermore, these passages also contain a concise set of rules dealing with idolatry, mixed marriage, Passover, firstborn and firstfruits, the Sabbath, other Jewish festivals, and prohibitions against offering blood and boiling a goat in its mother's milk.

Since, however, the whole weight of postbiblical tradition identifies the Ten Commandments as the words contained in Exodus 20 (and repeated in

Deuteronomy 5), it is generally held today that they must, indeed, be the words that the tablets contained.

What Are the Divisions of the Ten Commandments?

The divisions of the commandments themselves are not at all certain. There are thirteen sentences in the accepted Jewish version of the Ten Commandments (seventeen in the Christian), but it is difficult to ascertain with certainty from the text itself what comprises the first commandment, the second, and so forth, for while there are thirteen *mitzvot* to be found in the text, their allocation to Ten Commandments can be made in a variety of ways. Thus, there are different traditions. The prevailing Jewish tradition appears to be as follows:

First Commandment: "I am the Lord Your God, who brought you out of the land of Egypt, out of the house of bondage" (Exodus 20:2).

Second Commandment: "You shall have no other gods beside Me. You shall not make for yourself any graven image, nor any manner of likeness, of any thing that is in heaven above, or that is in the earth beneath, or that is in the water under the earth. You shall not bow down to them, nor serve them, for I, the Lord Your God, am a jealous God, visiting the iniquity of the fathers upon the children unto the third and fourth generation" (Exodus 20:3–6).

Third Commandment: "You shall not take the name of the Lord Your God in vain; for the Lord will not hold him guiltless that takes His name in vain" (Exodus 20:7).

Fourth Commandment: "Remember the Sabbath, to keep it holy. Six days you shall labor, and do all your work; but the seventh day is a sabbath unto the Lord Your God, in it you shall not do any manner of work, you, nor your son, nor your daughter, nor your man-servant, nor your maid-servant, nor your cattle, nor your stranger that is within your gates; for in six days the Lord made heaven and earth, the sea, and all that in them is, and rested on the seventh day. Wherefore the Lord blessed the sabbath day, and made it holy" (Exodus 20:8–11).

Fifth Commandment: "Honor your father and your mother, that your days may be long upon the land which the Lord God gives you (Exodus 20:12).

Sixth Commandment: "You shall not murder" (Exodus 20:13).

Seventh Commandment: "You shall not commit adultery" (Exodus 20:13).

Eighth Commandment: "You shall not steal" (Exodus 20:13).

Ninth Commandment: "You shall not bear false witness against your neighbor (Exodus 20:13).

Tenth Commandment: "You shall not covet your neighbor's house, nor his wife, his manservant, his maidservant, nor his ox, nor his ass, nor anything that is your neighbor's" (Exodus 20:14).

This is the Jewish division of the Ten Commandments. However, such writers as Philo, as well as the Jewish Publication Society's translation of the Bible, the Greek Church Fathers, and most Protestant churches (except the Lutherans), consider the first of the Ten Commandments to be: "I am the Lord Your God, who brought you out of the land of Egypt, out of the house of bondage. You shall have no other gods before Me" (verses 2 and 3). That is to say, God's very existence and God's relation to Israel, in addition to the prohibition of worshipping other gods, are seen as belonging together, while the prohibition of idolatry forms the second commandment.

Yet another division is used in the Roman Catholic and Lutheran churches. This follows the written text of Torah scrolls and combines versus 2 through 6 into one commandment; that is, it includes the prohibition against idolatry in the first commandments, and further, it divides the last phrase (verse 14 in the Jewish and verse 17 in the Christian versions) into two parts:

Ninth Commandment: "You shall not covet your neighbor's house . . ."

Tenth Commandment: "You shall not covet your neighbor's wife . . ."

Is There a Logical Structure to the Ten Commandments?

A dual structure can be seen in the Ten Commandments. Commandments one through four deal with man's relationship to God, while commandments six through ten deal with man's relation to man. The fifth command, that of honoring one's parents, forms a sort of bridge between the two groups.

While the Bible itself provides no indication of how the "words" of the commandments were distributed on the actual stone tablets, it is generally assumed that they stood five on one tablet and five on the other. Some commentators (*Mechilta, Yitro* 8) have seen a correlation between the five commandments opposite each other on each of the two tablets. So for example, murder is an injury to God in whose image man is, apostasy is equivalent to marital infidelity, stealing will lead to a false oath, the Sabbath violator attests falsely that God did not create the world in six days and rest on the seventh, and the person who covets his fellow person's wife will end by fathering a child who rejects his true parent and honors another.

Some commentators viewed the commandments as ranging in descending order from Divine matters to human matters and within each group from higher to lower values. In this scenario, duties to God come first, the obligation to worship God alone precedes that of treating His Name with reverence, and both precede the symbolic piety of Sabbath rest. Respect for parental authority naturally follows respect for God. The purely ethical commandments are arranged in a hierarchal form: life, the family, right of possession, reliability of public statements. The last commandment, the ban on desires arising from jealousy, deals with what is most ethically sensitive and protects against the infringing of the other ethical commandments.

The philosopher Abraham ben Chiyya, after placing the first commandment apart as comprehending all the others, divided the other nine according to the commands of **thought, speech, and action** and according to relations between man and God, man and his family, man and man, reaching the following classification.

RELATIONS BETWEEN	MAN AND GOD	MAN AND FAMILY	MAN AND MAN
Thought	Second Command: "Thou shalt have no other God"— fear of God.	Fifth Command: "Honor thy father and thy mother."	Tenth Command: "Thou shalt not covet."
Speech	Third Command: "Thou shalt not take the name of the Lord in vain."	Sixth Command: "Thou shalt not murder," especially one's family.	Ninth Command: "Thou shalt not bear false witness."
Action	Fourth Command: "Remember the Sabbath Day."	Seventh Command: "Thou shalt not commit adultery."	Eighth Command: "Thou shalt not steal."

How Did the Rabbinic Authorities View the Problem of the Two Different Versions of the Ten Commandments and the Layout of Them on the Two Stone Tablets?

For the most part, the problem of the two different versions of the Ten Commandments (i.e., Exodus 20 and Deuteronomy 5) did not constitute any difficulty for the Rabbis. For example, they maintained that "remember the Sabbath day" (Exodus 20:8) and "observe the Sabbath day" (Deuteronomy 5:12) as well as each of the other variations in the two versions were uttered simultaneously (Talmud *Shavuot* 20b).

According to the Talmud (Bava Kamma 55a), the omission of the words "that it may go well with you" (Deuteronomy 5:16) from the Fifth Commandment in the first version was because the initial tablets were destined to be broken.

There were different opinions regarding the arrangement of the commandments on the two tablets. The prevailing opinion was that the first five were written on one tablet and the second five on the second tablet. Others held that each tablet contained the entire Ten Commandments, and still others were of the opinion that the entire Ten Commandments were written on both sides of both tablets. One commentator (Talmud *Shabbat* 104a) was even of the opinion that the letters of the words of the Ten Commandments were incised right through the stone tablets.

What Rabbinic Legends Are Related to the Ten Commandments?

The teachers of the Talmud emphasized the eternal significance of the Ten Commandments by means of metaphor, parable, and poetic imagery. The following is a brief summary of the Ten Commandments as understood in rabbinic imagery.

1. The two stone tablets upon which the Ten Commandments were written were prepared by God on the eve of creation, before human beings were created. In this way, the commandments would always be independent of time and place.

2. The two stone tablets were hewn from God's own sapphire Throne of Glory and were therefore of unimaginable worth and preciousness.

3. The Ten Commandments were heard, not only by all of the Israelite community, but by all of humanity. God divided His speech up into seventy different languages so that all people would understand His message.

4. Each commandment, as it was spoken from atop Mount Sinai, filled the world with sweet aroma, helping to revive even the dead souls of the netherworld.

5. All people, even the souls of unborn generations, were assembled at Sinai to hear the Ten Commandments.

6. When God spoke the words of the Ten Commandments, no creature made a sound: the birds, the oxen, even the ocean itself did not roar. All of Nature was enwrapped in breathless silence at the sound of God's voice speaking the Ten Commands.

7. The fourth commandment, remember the Sabbath day (Exodus 29:8) and observe the Sabbath day (Deuteronomy 5:12), was spoken by God in one single utterance. This was something impossible for the human tongue to utter or the human ear to hear.

8. When the Israelites received the commandments, God clothed them in the radiance of His majesty, including His royal crowns. R. Simeon ben Yochai suggested that God even gave them weapons on which the Divine Name was engraved, so that the angel of death could have no power over them.

9. God waited several months after the exodus from Egypt to give the Ten Commandments to the Israelites. He did this because the Israelites needed time to convalesce after their many years in slavery.

10. When the Israelites left Egypt, there were some people who had been injured by their hard labor. Not wanting to give commandments to the Israelites who were in pain, God gave a sign to the angels, who descended from heaven and healed all of the sick.

11. Before God gave the Israelites the Ten Commandments, He went to all of the other nations, asking each of them whether they would accept the Torah. Each nation in turn refused, stating that to accept commandments such as "not stealing" or "not committing adultery" would be too hard for them. Finally, God came to the Israelites, who immediately volunteered by saying, "*Na'aseh ve'nishma*—we will obey and we will hear" (Exodus 24:7).

10

NOTABLE MITZVAH QUOTATIONS

Throughout Jewish literature there have been a variety of interesting comments and statements related to the concept of the *mitzvah* in Jewish tradition. Here is a cross-section of sixty of them culled from Jewish literature over the ages.

1. Live by the commandments; do not die by them (Talmud *Sanhedrin* 74a).

2. Six hundred and thirteen commandments were given to Moses: 365 negative, corresponding to the days of the year, and 248 positive, corresponding to the number of joints in the human body (Talmud *Makkot* 23b).

3. A commandment is to the Torah what a lamp is to the sun (Midrash *Psalms* 17:7).

4. He who loves *mitzvot* is not sated with *mitzvot* (Midrash *Devarim Rabbah* 2:23).

5. Rabbi Eleazer ben Shammua said: "The man who fears God, delights greatly in God's commandments" (Psalm 112:1). "In His commandments, not in the reward of His commandments" (Talmud *Avodah Zarah* 192).

6. Moses taught us six hundred and eleven *mitzvot*, the numerical value of the word Torah. God Himself taught us the first two commandments in the Decalogue—a total of six hundred and thirteen (*Pesikta Rabbati* 22:3).

7. Have you already performed all the *mitzvot* and only this is left? (Midrash *Eichah Rabbah* 1:3).

8. All the *mitzvot* which the children of Israel perform in this world, come and testify in their favor in the World-to-Come (Talmud *Avodah Zarah* 2).

9. He who sits and does not sin is rewarded as if he had performed a *mitzvah* (Talmud *Kiddushin* 39).

10. May my lot be among those who die as they go forth to perform a *mitzvah* (Talmud *Shabbat* 118).

11. "This is my God and I will glorify Him" (Exodus 15:2)—glorify Him by observing His commandments finely: by making a fine sukkah, a fine synagogue, and so forth (Talmud *Shabbat* 133).

12. If you have observed a few *mitzvot*, you will end by observing many (Talmud *Shabbat* 133).

13. The commandments of the Torah should be performed in a two-fold manner: by the body and by the mind (*kavanah*) (*Zohar* I:72a).

14. Would that they give up discussing Me, and observe instead My *mitzvot* (Jerusalem Talmud *Chagigah* 1:7).

15. God says: "I am Your guardian. Pay Me by observing My *mitzvot*" (Midrash *Vayikra Rabbah* 28:3).

16. Every person should perform a *mitzvah* in the manner he expects a sage to perform it (Mishnah *Pesachim* 54).

17. Just as a childless man or woman is called barren, so the knowledge of Torah without the observance of its commandments is called barren. Not the research is the main thing, but the performance; not the theory, but the practice (*Zohar* IV:218a).

18. What difference does it make to God whether one kills the animal at the throat or at its back? But the commandments were given to purify the people (*Tanchuma Shemini*, 5).

19. We read: "She [namely, the Torah] is more precious than rubies, and all things you can desire are not to be compared to her" (Proverbs 3:15). Things which you desire are not to be compared to Torah, but *mitzvot* desired by God are comparable in importance. We read further (Proverbs 8:11): "For wisdom is better than rubies, and all things desirable [even by God] are not to be compared to her." How is this contradiction to be explained? If the *mitzvah* can be performed by a person other than the student of Torah, he should not desist from his studies (Talmud *Moed Katan* 9).

20. Not every person is able to combine in equal proportions the will and the intention to perform a *mitzvah* in perfection. It is for this reason that we pray in the words of the Psalmist (90:17): "And let the graciousness of the Lord be upon us; establish also upon us the work of our hands; yea the work of our hands establish You it" (*Zohar* II:93b).

21. He who wishes to prevail for God and His commandments should not make the endeavor with an empty hand. He should spend on the task according the substance of his possessions (*Zohar* II:128a).

22. The good deeds which a person performs in this world are transformed into threads of light in the other world, and the hosts in Heaven spin them into a garment to clothe him in the after-life (*Zohar* II:229b).

23. He who performs a *mitzvah* extends the boundaries of heaven (*Zohar* III:113a).

24. It is well to spend an extra third to perform a *mitzvah* in a more satisfactory manner (Talmud *Bava Kamma* 9).

25. Every person should perceive himself as being half good and half evil. By performing one more good act, he becomes a *tzaddik* (righteous person). By performing one more evil act, he becomes a man of wickedness (Talmud *Kiddushin* 40).

26. Rav said: "Let a man always occupy himself diligently with the study of the Torah and the performance of the Commandments even if it be not for their own sake, for out of performance not for its own sake, comes performance for its own sake" (Talmud *Pesachim* 50b).

27. Rav Nachman prepared a good table for each of the three Sabbath meals. Rav Judah gave his entire mind to his prayer. Rav Chuna bar Joshua never went bare-headed. Rav Sheshet never went without *tefillin*. Rav Nachman never went without *tzitzit*. Abbaye never failed to serve wine when a student had finished a volume. Rabba never retired to slumber without searching for merits among his disciples (Talmud *Shabbat* 117).

28. Rabbi Judah the Prince said: "A man should be as careful about a light commandment as about a more serious one, since he does not know how they are to be rewarded, nor which has in it for him the issues of life" (Antigonos of Sochos, *Ethics of Our Fathers*, 2:1).

29. He who does a moral act associates himself with God in His creative work (Talmud *Shabbat* 10a).

30. Rabbi Simeon ben Eleazar said: "Greater is he who acts [namely, who is pious] from love than he who acts from fear of God" (Talmud *Sotah* 31a).

31. A person is respected on High according to the manner in which he performs all positive commandments in fear and in love (*Tikkune Zohar*, p. 70, p. 175b).

32. To the statement: "If it [ceremonial observance] has become an empty thing in your life, if it has become meaningless to you," the Rabbis said: "Know that the fault lies in you, not in it" (Jerusalem Talmud *Pe'ah*, ch. 1).

33. Rabbi Simlai said: "Moses gave to Israel six hundred and thirteen commandments. David came and comprehended them in eleven (Psalm 15).

"Isaiah came and comprehended them in six: 'He that walks righteously, and speaks uprightly, he that despises the gain acquired by oppression, that shakes out his hands from holding of bribes, that stops his ears from hearing of blood, and shuts his eyes from looking upon evil, he shall dwell on high' (Isaiah 33:15).

"Micah came and comprehended them in three: 'He has told you, O man, what is good and what God requires of you—only to do justice, love mercy and walk humbly with your God' (Micah 6:8).

"Isaiah further comprehended them in two: 'Observe justice and do righteousness' (Isaiah 56:1).

"Amos came and comprehended them in one: 'Seek me and live' " (Amos 5:4).

"Another finds the one comprehensive word in *Habakkuk:* 'The righteous man shall live by his faithfulness' (*Habakkuk* 2:4)" (Talmud *Makkot* 24a).

34. From Psalm 111:10: "The first principle of wisdom is the fear [i.e., reverence] of God: all those who do them [the commandments of God] have good understanding," Rabbi deduces: "It is not said: 'who learn them' but 'who do them'; and who do them for their own sake. Whoever does a commandment not for its own sake [from other than a religious motive], it were better for him that he had never been created" (Talmud *Berakhot* 17a).

35. Rabbi Yochanan ben Zakkai said: "You cannot say, 'These commandments appeal to my reason and I shall observe them; those are but futile performances and I do not care to keep them.' We do not know why death makes unclean and why water with the ashes of the red heifer makes clean. It is a decree of the Sovereign King of Kings. God says: 'I have prescribed a statute for you; I have issued a decree to you. You have no right to transgress My decree, for it is written (Numbers 19:2) "This is the statute of the law" ' " (*Tanchuma Buber*, "Chukkat," 26).

26. Rav taught that "the *mitzvot* were given only for the purpose of disciplining and refining people through their observance."

"What concern is it to God," he continued, "whether the animal is slaughtered in one fashion or another? Know that these laws were given solely as disciplining measures with which to refine those who adhere to them" (Midrash *Bereshit Rabbah* 44:1).

37. The means through which Israel gains the good for which God created the universe are the commandments. If Adam would have kept his one commandment, then he would have immediately attained this goal. Since he did not, numerous commandments are required (*Derech HaShem* 1:2:2, 1:3:6, and *Or HaShem* 2:2:5).

38. One of the foundations of our faith is the affirmation that the commandments were given for all times (Maimonides, *Thirteen Principles of Faith*, 9).

39. The most difficult commandments are not those which involve our relationship with God. Rather, they are those which are required to main-

tain an orderly society. It is not God who makes the commandments difficult, but man's moral weakness (*Sefer Chasidim* 567).

40. Every commandment serves to make us more holy and Godly (*Mechilta* to Exodus 22:30).

41. When Israel is occupied with the Torah and commandments, they master their desire and are not mastered by it (Talmud *Avodah Zarah* 5b).

42. As the lily dies with its scent, so Israel will not die so long as it executes the commands, and does good deeds (*Canticles Rabbah*, 2:6).

43. The Israelites are fair and acceptable to God only when they fulfill the commandments of the Torah. It is like a king who said to his wife, "Deck yourself with all of your ornaments that you may be acceptable to me." So God says to Israel, "Be distinguished by the commandments so that you may be acceptable to me." As it says, "Fair are you, my beloved, when you are acceptable to me" (*Sifre Deuteronomy* "Va'etachanan").

44. Rabbi Abba bar Ḳahana said: "Do not sit and weigh the commandments of the Torah. Do not say, 'Because there is greater reward for this command, I will do it, and because there is only a small reward for that command, I will not do it.' What has God done. He has not revealed to people the particular reward for each particular command, in order that they might do all the commands with integrity.

"The matter is like a king who hired laborers, and brought them into his garden. He hid and did not reveal what was the reward for working in the garden, so that they might not neglect that part of the work for which the reward was small, and go and do that part for which the reward was great. In the evening he summoned them all, and said, 'Under which tree did you work?' The first answered, 'Under this one.' The king said, 'That is a pepper tree; its reward is one gold piece.'

"He said to the next, 'Under which tree did you work?' He said, 'Under that one.' The king said, 'It is a white flower tree; its reward is half a gold piece.' He asked a third, 'Under which tree did you work?'' He said, 'Under this one.' The king replied, 'That is an olive tree; its reward is 200 zuzim.' The laborers said to him, 'Ought you not to have told us the tree under which the reward was the greatest?' The king replied, 'If I had done that, how could all of my garden have been tilled?' Even so, God has not revealed the commandments, except for two—one the heaviest of the heavy, the other, the lightest of the light, viz. Exodus 20:12, 'Honor your father and your mother,' and Deuteronomy 22:7, 'You shall let the mother bird go.' For both the reward is the same, namely, long life (Midrash *Deuteronomy Rabbah*, "Ki Tetze," 6:2).

45. Antigonos of Sicho, a discipline of Simeon the Just, used to say, "Be not like servants who minister to their master upon the condition of

receiving a reward; but be like servants who minister to their master without the condition of receiving a reward, and let the fear of Heaven be upon you" (Antigonos of Socho, *Ethics of Our Fathers*, 1:3).

46. The zealous hasten to fulfill the commandments, as it is said, "And Abraham rose up early in the morning to fulfill God's command" (Genesis 2:3) (*Sifra* 58c).

47. Rabbi Joshiah said: Just as you must not allow the *matzah* to get sour, so you must not let the commandment get sour by delay. If a commandment comes your way, do it at once (*Mechilta Pischa*, "Bo," 9).

48. "On this day Israel came to Mount Sinai" (Exodus 19:1). Why on *this* day? Because, when you learn Torah, let not its commandments seem old to you, but regard them as though the Torah were given *this* day. Hence it says, "On *this* day," and not, "On that day" (*Sifre Deuteronomy*, "Va'etchanan," 33).

49. Rabbi Chanina said: It is finer to do what is commanded than to do the same thing when it is not commanded (Talmud *Kiddushin* 31a).

50. Rabbi Elisha ben Abuyah said: If a person causes another to do a commandment, the Scripture regards him as if he had done it himself (*Avot de Rabbi Natan*, v. 1, xxix, 39b).

51. When a shepherd pastures his flock behind a synagogue and hears the *shofar* on Rosh HaShanah, then, if he has *kavanah* (proper concentration), he has fulfilled the commandment to hear the *shofar* [even though he was not in the synagogue itself]. But if he did not have *kavanah*, he has not fulfilled his duty. All depends on whether the man directed his heart or not (Tosefta *Rosh Hashanah* 3:6).

52. Unlike other distinguished rabbis, Rabbi Israel Salanter would often pour only a small quantity of water over his hands for the ritual of washing before the meal, even though the law recommends that as much water as possible ought to be used. Those who witnessed Rabbi Israel's conduct were amazed that he was content with the minimum requirements of the law. "Yes," the rabbi said. "I know that it is a *mitzvah* to use a good deal of water, but have you noticed that the poor servant girl has to bring in the water from the well outside in the bitter cold? I am not anxious to perform special acts of piety at the expense of the poor girl's toil" (chasidic folktale).

53. Once Rabbi Levi Yitchak of Berditchev stayed in a hut at the top of a mountain on the eve of sukkot. Tossing and turning in his bed all through the night, he longed for the morning when he could carry out the *mitzvah* of taking the *lulav* and *etrog*. When morning arrived, he quickly put on his clothes and ran down the mountain in order to get to the synagogue as quickly as was humanly possible (chasidic folktale).

54. Rabbi Yehudah said in the name of Rav: "It is prohibited for a person to eat anything until he feeds his animal, because the verse first says, 'And I will provide grass in the fields for your animals' (Deuteronomy 11:15) and only afterwards does it say, 'and you shall eat and be satisfied' (Deuteronomy 11:15)" (Talmud *Gittin* 62a).

55. Rabbi Nachman bar Yitzchak said: We do not make *mitzvot* into bundles [i.e. performing two or more at the same time] (Talmud *Pesachim* 102b).

56. Rabbi Elazar said: People on a mission to perform commandments will not be harmed, neither on the way there nor on the way back (Talmud *Pesachim* 8b).

57. Rabbi Yochanan said: "Among the dead—I am released" (Psalm 88:6)—when a person dies, that person is free from the obligation of performing *mitzvot* (Talmud *Shabbat* 151b).

58. Hillel used to say: The more one eats, the more one excretes. The more fat one puts on, the more food for the worms and maggots. But the more *mitzvot*, the more well being for the body (*Avot de Rabbi Natan*, A:28).

59. A stolen *lulav* is unfit for *mitzvah* use, as are stolen *hadasim, aravot*, and *etrogim* (Mishnah *Sukkah* 3:1, 2, 3, 5).

60. "Why should I fear in the time of trouble? It is because of the sins around my heels" (Psalms 49:6). Blessed be the Name of the Holy One, blessed be He, Who gave the Torah to the Israelites, the Torah which has 613 *mitzvot* in it, some easy, some difficult. And because there are easy ones to which people pay no attention, throwing them under their heels, it is for that reason that David is afraid on the Day of Judgment. So he says, "Master of the Universe, I am not afraid of the difficult commandments. Rather I am afraid of the easy *mitzvot*. Perhaps I violated one of them, and I cannot even remember if I did or not, because it was so easy. And You have clearly said, 'Be as careful of easy commandments as of the difficult ones.'" It is for this reason that David said, "Why should I fear in the time of trouble? It is because of the sins around my heels" (*Tanchuma Ekev* 1).

11

THE 613 COMMANDMENTS BY MOSES MAIMONIDES

As has been previously stated, there are 613 commandments in the Torah, according to rabbinic tradition. There are 365 negative ones that tell people what they cannot do, and 248 positive ones, that tell people what to do. The list that follows was set forth by Maimonides in his *Book of Commandments* (*Sefer HaMitzvot*). Note numbers for the biblical sources are cited after the listing of each of the positive and negative commandments.

The 613 Commandments as Enumerated in *Sefer Ha-Mitzvot*

Positive Commandments

The Jew is required to (1) believe that God exists and to (2) acknowledge God's unity; to (3) love, (4) fear, and (5) serve God. The Jew is also instructed to (6) cleave to God (by associating with and imitating the wise) and to (7) swear only by God's name. One must (8) imitate God and (9) sanctify God's name.

The Jew must (10) recite the *Shema* each morning and evening and (11) study the Torah and teach it to others. The Jew should bind *tefillin* on the (12) head and (13) the arm. The Jew should make (14) *tzitzit* for the garments and (15) fix a *mezuzah* on the door. The people are to be (16) assembled every seventh year to hear the Torah read and (17) the king must write a special copy of the Torah for himself. (18) Every Jew should have a Torah scroll. One should (19) praise God after eating.

The Jews should (20) build a Temple and (21) respect it. It must be (22) guarded at all times and the (23) Levites should perform their special duties in it. Before entering the Temple or participating in its service the priests

(24) must wash their hands and feet; they must also (25) light the candelabrum daily. The priests are required to (26) bless Israel and to (27) set the shewbread and frankincense before the Ark. Twice daily they must (28) burn the incense on the golden altar. Fire shall be kept burning on the altar (29) continually and the ashes should be (30) removed daily. Ritually unclean persons must be (31) kept out of the Temple. Israel (32) should honor its priests, who must be (33) dressed in special priestly raiment. The priests should (34) carry the Ark on their shoulders, and the holy anointing oil (35) must be prepared according to its special formula. The priestly families should officiate in (36) rotation. In honor of certain dead close relatives the priests should (37) make themselves ritually unclean. The high priest may marry (38) only a virgin.

The (39) *tamid* sacrifice must be offered twice daily and the (40) high priest must also offer a meal-offering twice daily. An additional sacrifice (*musaf*) should be offered (41) every Sabbath, (42) on the first of every month, and (43) on each of the seven days of Passover. On the second day of Passover (44) a meal offering of the first barley must also be brought. On *Shavuot* a (45) *musaf* must be offered and (46) two loaves of bread as a wave offering. The additional sacrifice must also be made on (47) Rosh Hashanah and (48) on the Day of Atonement when the (49) Avodah must also be performed. On every day of the festival of (50) Sukkot a *musaf* must be brought as well as on the (51) eighth day thereof.

Every male [and female] Jew should make (52) pilgrimage to the Temple three times a year and (53) appear there during the three pilgrim Festivals. One should (54) rejoice on the Festivals. On the 14th of Nisan one should (55) slaughter the paschal lamb and (56) eat of its roasted flesh on the night of the 15th. Those who were ritually impure in Nisan should slaughter the paschal lamb on the (57) 14th of Iyar and eat it with (58) *matzah* and bitter herbs. Trumpets should be (59) sounded when the festive sacrifices are brought and also in times of tribulation.

Cattle to be sacrificed must be (60) at least eight days old and (61) without blemish. All offerings must be (62) salted. It is a *mitzvah* to perform the ritual of (63) the burnt offering, (64) the sin offering, (65) the guilt offering, (66) the peace offering, (67) and the meal offering.

Should the Sanhedrin err in a decision its members (68) must bring a sin offering which offering must also be brought (69) by a person who has unwittingly transgressed a *karet* prohibition [i.e., one which, if done deliberately, should incur *karet*]. When in doubt as to whether one has transgressed such a prohibition a (70) "suspensive" guilt offering must be brought.

For (71) stealing or swearing falsely and for other sins of a like nature, a guilt offering must be brought. In special circumstances the sin offering (72) can be according to one's means.

One must (73) confess one's sins before God and repent for them. A (74) man or (75) woman who has a seminal issue must bring sacrifice; a woman must also bring a sacrifice (76) after childbirth.

A leper must (77) bring a sacrifice after he [or she] has been cleansed.

One must (78) tithe one's cattle. The (79) firstborn of clean [i.e., permitted] cattle are holy and must be sacrificed. firstborn children must be (80) redeemed. The firstling of the ass must be (81) redeemed; if not (82) its neck has to be broken.

Animals set aside as offerings (83) must be brought to Jerusalem without delay and (84) may be sacrificed only in the Temple. Offerings from outside the land of Israel (85) may also be brought to the Temple.

Sanctified animals (86) which have become blemished must be redeemed. A beast exchanged for a offering (87) is also holy. The priests should eat (88) the remainder of the meal offering and (89) the flesh of sin and guilt offerings; but consecrated flesh which has become (90) ritually unclean or (91) which was not eaten within its appointed time must be burned.

A Nazirite must (92) let his hair grow during the period of his separation. When that period is over he must (93) shave his head and bring his sacrifice.

A person must (94) honor one's vows and one's oaths which a judge can (95) annul only in accordance with the law.

Anyone who touches (96) a carcass or (97) one of the eight species of reptiles becomes ritually unclean; food becomes unclean by (98) coming into contact with a ritually unclean object. Menstruous women (99) and those (100) lying-in after childbirth are ritually impure. A (101) leper, (102) a leprous garment, and (103) a leprous house are all ritually unclean. A man having (104) a running issue is unclean, as is (105) semen. A woman suffering from (106) running issue is also impure. A (107) human corpse is ritually unclean. The purification water (*mei niddah*) purifies (108) the unclean, but it makes the clean ritually impure. It is a *mitzvah* to become ritually clean (109) by ritual immersion. To become cleansed of leprosy one (110) one must follow the specified procedure and also (111) shave off all of one's hair. Until cleansed the leper (112) must be bareheaded with clothing in disarray so as to be easily distinguishable.

The ashes of (113) the red heifer are to be used in the process of ritual purification.

If a person (114) undertakes to give one's own value to the Temple, one must do so. Should a person declare (115) an unclean beast, (116) a house, or (117) a field as a donation to the Temple, one must give their value in money as fixed by the priest. If one unwittingly derives benefit from Temple property (118) full restitution plus a fifth must be made.

The fruit of (119) the fourth year's growth of trees is holy and may be eaten only in Jerusalem. When you reap your fields you must leave (120) the corners, (121) the gleanings, (122) the forgotten sheaves, (123) the misformed bunches of grapes and (124) the gleanings of the grapes for the poor.

The firstfruits must be (125) separated and brought to the Temple and you must also (126) separate the great heave offering (*terumah*) and give it to the priests. You must give (127) one tithe of your produce to the Levites and separate (128) a second tithe which is to be eaten only in Jerusalem. The Levites (129) must give a tenth of their tithe to the priests.

In the third and sixth years of the seven-year cycle you should (130) separate a tithe for the poor instead of a second tithe. A declaration (131) must be recited when separating the various tithes and (132) when bringing the firstfruits to the Temple. The first portion of the (133) dough must be given to the priest.

In the seventh year (*shemittah*) everything that grows is (134) ownerless and available to all; the fields (135) must lie fallow and you may not till the ground. You must (136) sanctify the Jubilee [50th] year and on the Day of Atonement in that year (137) you must sound the *shofar* and set all Hebrew slaves free. In the Jubilee year all land is to be (138) returned to its ancestral owners and, generally, in a walled city (139) the seller has the right to buy back a house within a year of the sale.

Starting from entry into the land of Israel, the years of the Jubilee must be (140) counted and announced yearly and septennially.

In the seventh year (141) all debts are annulled but (142) one may exact a debt owed by a foreigner.

When you slaughter an animal you must (143) give the priest his share as you must also give him (144) the first of the fleece. When a person makes a *cherem* (a special vow) you must (145) distinguish between what belongs to the Temple (i.e., when God's name was mentioned in the vow) and between what goes to the priests. To be fit for consumption, beast and fowl must be (146) slaughtered according to the law and if they are not of a domesticated species (147) their blood must be covered with earth after slaughter.

Set the parent bird (148) free when taking the nest. Examine (149) beast, (150) fowl, (151) locusts and (152) fish to determine whether they are permitted for consumption.

The Sanhedrin should (153) sanctify the first day of every month and reckon the years and the seasons.

You must (154) rest on the Sabbath day and (155) declare it holy at its onset and termination. On the 14th of Nisan (156) remove all leaven from your ownership and on the night of the 15th (157) relate the story of the exodus from Egypt; on that night (158) you must also eat matzah. On the (159) first and (160) seventh days of Passover you must rest. Starting from the first day of the first sheaf (16th of Nisan) you shall (161) count 49 days. You must rest on (162) Shavuot and on (163) Rosh Hashanah; on the Day of Atonement you must (164) fast and (165) rest. You must also rest on (166) the first and (167) the eighth day of Sukkot during which festival you shall (168) dwell in booths and (169) take the four species. On Rosh Hashanah (170) you are to hear the sound of the *shofar.*

Every male should (171) give half a shekel to the Temple annually. You must (172) obey a prophet and (173) appoint a king. You must also (174) obey the Sanhedrin; in the case of division, (175) yield to the majority. Judges and officials shall be (176) appointed in every town and they shall judge the people (177) impartially. Whoever is aware of evidence (178) must come to court to testify. Witnesses shall be (179) examined thoroughly and, if found to be false, (180) shall have done to them what they intended to do to the accused.

When a person is found murdered and the murderer is unknown the ritual of (181) decapitating the heifer must be performed.

Six cities of refuge should be (182) established. The Levites, who have no ancestral share in the land, shall (183) be given cities to live in.

You must (184) build a fence around your roof and remove potential hazards from your home.

Idolatry and its appurtenances (185) must be destroyed, and a city which has become perverted must be (186) treated according to the law. You are instructed to (187) destroy the seven Canaanite nations, and (188) blot out the memory of Amalek, and (189) to remember what they did to Israel.

The regulations for wars other than those commanded in the Torah (190) are to be observed and a priest should be (191) appointed for special duties in times of war. The military camp must be (192) kept in a sanitary condition. To this end, every soldier must be (193) equipped with the necessary implements.

Stolen property must be (194) restored to its owner. Give (195) charity to the poor. When a Hebrew slave goes free the owner must (196) give him gifts. Lend to (197) the poor without interest; to the foreigner you may (198) lend at interest. Restore (199) a pledge to its owner if he needs it. Pay the worker his wages (200) on time; (201) permit him to eat of the produce with which he is working. You must (202) help unload an animal when necessary, and also (203) help load human or beast [of burden]. Lost property (204) must be restored to its owner. You are required (205) to reprove the sinner but you must (206) love your neighbor as yourself. You are instructed (207) to love the proselyte. Your weights and measures (208) must be accurate.

Respect the (209) wise; (210) honor and (211) revere your parents. You should (212) perpetuate the human species by marrying (213) according to the law. A bridegroom is to (214) rejoice with his bride for one year. Male children must (215) be circumcised. Should a man die childless, his brother must either (216) marry his widow or (217) release her (*chalitza*). He who violates a virgin must (218) marry her and may never divorce her. If a man unjustly accuses his wife of premarital promiscuity (219) he shall be flogged, and may never divorce her. The seducer (220) must be punished according to the law. The female captive must be (221) treated in accordance with her special regulations. Divorce can be executed (222) only by means of a written document. A woman suspected of adultery (223) has to submit to the required test.

When required by the law (224) you must administer the punishment of flogging and you must (225) exile the unwitting homicide. Capital punishment shall be by (226) the sword, (227) strangulation, (228) fire, or (229) stoning, as specified. In some cases the body of the executed (230) shall be hanged, but it (231) must be brought to burial the same day.

Hebrew slaves (232) must be treated according to the special laws for them. The master should (233) marry his Hebrew maidservant or (224) redeem her. The alien slave (235) must be treated according to the regulations applying to him.

The applicable law must be administered in the case of injury caused by (236) a person, (237) an animal or (238) a pit. Thieves (239) must be punished. You must render judgment in cases of (240) trespass by cattle, (241) arson, (242) embezzlement by an unpaid guardian and in claims against (243) a paid guardian, a hirer, or (244) a borrower. Judgment must also be rendered in disputes arising out of (245) sales, (248) inheritance and (246) other matters generally. You are required to (247) rescue the persecuted even if it means killing the oppressor.

TEXTUAL SOURCES FOR POSITIVE COMMANDMENTS

1. Exodus 20:2
2. Deuteronomy 6:4
3. Deuteronomy 6:13
4. Deuteronomy 6:13
5. Exodus 23:25;
   Deuteronomy 11:13;
   (Deuteronomy 6:13, 13:15)
6. Deuteronomy 10:20
7. Deuteronomy 19:20
8. Deuteronomy 28:9
9. Leviticus 22:32
10. Deuteronomy 6:7
11. Deuteronomy 6:7
12. Deuteronomy 6:8

13. Deuteronomy 6:8
14. Numbers 15:38
15. Deuteronomy 6:9
16. Deuteronomy 31:12
17. Deuteronomy 17:18
18. Deuteronomy 31:19
19. Deuteronomy 8:10
20. Exodus 25:8
21. Leviticus 19:30
22. Numbers 18:4
23. Numbers 18:23
24. Exodus 30:19
25. Exodus 27:21
26. Numbers 6:23
27. Exodus 25:30
28. Exodus 30:7
29. Leviticus 6:6
30. Leviticus 6:3
31. Numbers 5:4
32. Leviticus 21:8
33. Exodus 28:2
34. Numbers 7:9
35. Exodus 30:31
36. Deuteronomy
    18:6-8
37. Leviticus 21:2-3
38. Leviticus 21:13
39. Numbers 28:3
40. Leviticus 6:13
41. Numbers 28:9
42. Numbers 28:11
43. Leviticus 23:26
44. Leviticus 23:10
45. Numbers 28:26-27
46. Leviticus 23:17
47. Numbers 29:1-2
48. Numbers 28:26-27
49. Leviticus 16
50. Numbers 29:13
51. Numbers 29:36
52. Exodus 23:14
53. Exodus 34:23;
    Deuteronomy 16:16
54. Deuteronomy 16:14
55. Exodus 12:6
56. Exodus 12:8
57. Numbers 9:11
58. Numbers 9:11 Exodus 12:8
59. Numbers 10:10; 10:9
60. Leviticus 22:27
61. Leviticus 22:21
62. Leviticus 2:13
63. Leviticus 1:2
64. Leviticus 6:18
65. Leviticus 7:1
66. Leviticus 3:1
67. Leviticus 2:1; 6:7
68. Leviticus 4:13
69. Leviticus 4:27
70. Leviticus 5:17-18
71. Leviticus 5:15, 21-25;
    19:20-21
72. Leviticus 5:1-11
73. Numbers 5:6-7
74. Leviticus 15:13-15
75. Leviticus 15:28-29
76. Leviticus 12:6
77. Leviticus 14:10
78. Leviticus 27:32
79. Exodus 13:2
80. Exodus 22:28;
    Numbers 18:15
81. Exodus 34:20
82. Exodus 13:13
83. Deuteronomy 12:5
84. Deuteronomy 12:14
85. Deuteronomy 12:26
86. Deuteronomy 12;15
87. Leviticus 27:33
88. Leviticus 8:9
89. Exodus 29:33
90. Leviticus 7:19

91. Leviticus 7:17
92. Numbers 6:5
93. Numbers 6:18
94. Deuteronomy 23:24
95. Numbers 30:3
96. Leviticus 11:8, 24
97. Leviticus 11:29–31
98. Leviticus 11:34
99. Leviticus 15:19
100. Leviticus 12:2
101. Leviticus 13:3
102. Leviticus 13:51
103. Leviticus 14:44
104. Leviticus 15:2
105. Leviticus 15:16
106. Leviticus 15:19
107. Numbers 19:14
108. Numbers 19:13, 21
109. Leviticus 15:16
110. Leviticus 14:2
111. Leviticus 14:9
112. Leviticus 13:45
113. Numbers 19:2–9
114. Leviticus 27:2–8
115. Leviticus 27:11–12
116. Leviticus 27:14
117. Leviticus 27:16, 22–23
118. Leviticus 5:16
119. Leviticus 19:24
120. Leviticus 19:9
121. Leviticus 19:9
122. Deuteronomy 24:19
123. Leviticus 19:10
124. Leviticus 19:10
125. Exodus 23:19
126. Deuteronomy 18:4
127. Leviticus 27:30; Numbers 18:24
128. Deuteronomy 14:22
129. Numbers 18:26
130. Deuteronomy 14:28
131. Deuteronomy 26:13
132. Deuteronomy 26:5
133. Numbers 15:20
134. Exodus 23:11
135. Exodus 34:21
136. Leviticus 25:10
137. Leviticus 25:9
138. Leviticus 25:24
139. Leviticus 25:29–30
140. Leviticus 25:8
141. Deuteronomy 15:3
142. Deuteronomy 15:3
143. Deuteronomy 18:3
144. Deuteronomy 18:4
145. Leviticus 27:21, 28
146. Deuteronomy 12:21
147. Leviticus 17:13
148. Deuteronomy 22:7
149. Leviticus 11:2
150. Deuteronomy 14:11
151. Leviticus 11:21
152. Leviticus 11:9
153. Exodus 12:2; Deuteronomy 16:1
154. Exodus 23:12
155. Exodus 20:8
156. Exodus 12:15
157. Exodus 13:8
158. Exodus 12:8
159. Exodus 12:16
160. Exodus 12:16
161. Leviticus 23:35
162. Leviticus 23
163. Leviticus 23:24
164. Leviticus 16:29
165. Leviticus 16:29, 31
166. Leviticus 23:35
167. Leviticus 23:42
168. Leviticus 23:42
169. Leviticus 23:40
170. Numbers 29:1

171. Exodus 30:12–13
172. Deuteronomy 18:15
173. Deuteronomy 17:15
174. Deuteronomy 17:11
175. Exodus 23:2
176. Deuteronomy 16:18
177. Leviticus 19:15
178. Leviticus 5:1
179. Deuteronomy 13:15
180. Deuteronomy 19:19
181. Deueronomy 21:4
182. Deuteronomy 19:3
183. Numbers 35:2
184. Deuteronomy 22:8
185. Deuteronomy 12:2; 7:5
186. Deuteronomy 13:17
187. Deuteronomy 20:17
188. Deuteronomy 25:19
189. Deuteronomy 25:17
190. Deuteronomy 20:11–12
191. Deuteronomy 20:2
192. Deuteronomy 23:14–15
193. Deuteronomy 23:14
194. Leviticus 5:23
195. Deuteronomy 15:8;
     Leviticus 25:35–36
196. Deuteronomy 15:14
197. Exodus 22:24
198. Deuteronomy 23:21
199. Deuteronomy 24:13;
     Exodus 22:25
200. Deuteronomy 24:15
201. Deuteronomy 23:25–26
202. Exodus 23:5
203. Deuteronomy 22:4
204. Deuteronomy 22:1; Exodus
     23:4
205. Leviticus 19:17
206. Leviticus 19:18
207. Deuteronomy 10:19
208. Leviticus 19:36
209. Leviticus 19:32
210. Exodus 20:12
211. Leviticus 19:3
212. Genesis 1:28
213. Deuteronomy 24:1
214. Deuteronomy 24:5
215. Genesis 17:10;
     Leviticus 12:3
216. Deuteronomy 25:5
217. Deuteronomy 25:9
218. Deuteronomy 22:29
219. Deuteronomy 22:18–19
220. Exodus 22:15–23
221. Deuteronomy 21:11
222. Deuteronomy 24:1
223. Numbers 5:15–27
224. Deuteronomy 25:2
226. Exodus 21:20
227. Exodus 21:16
228. Leviticus 20:14
229. Deuteronomy 22:24
230. Deuteronomy 21:22
231. Deuteronomy 21:23
232. Exodus 21:2
233. Exodus 21:8
234. Exodus 21:8
235. Leviticus 25:46
236. Exodus 21:18
237. Exodus 21:28
239. Exodus 21:37–22:3
240. Exodus 22:4
241. Exodus 22:5
242. Exodus 22:6–8
243. Exodus 22:9–12
244. Exodus 22:13
245. Leviticus 25:14
246. Exodus 22:8
247. Deuteronomy 25:12
248. Numbers 27:8

Prohibitions

It is (1) forbidden to believe in the existence of any but the One God.

You may not make images (2) for yourself or (3) for others to worship or for (4) any other purpose.

You must not worship anything but God either in (5) the manner prescribed for Divine worship or (6) in its own manner of worship.

Do not (7) sacrifice children to Molech.

You may not (8) practice necromancy or (9) resort to "familiar spirits" neither should you take idolatry or its mythology (10) seriously.

It is forbidden to construct a (11) pillar or (12) dais even for the worship of God or to (13) plant trees in the Temple.

You may not (14) swear by idols or instigate an idolator to do so, nor may you encourage or persuade any (15) non-Jew or (16) Jew to worship idols.

You must not (17) listen to or love anyone who disseminates idolatry nor (18) should you withhold yourself from hating him [or her]. Do not (19) pity such a person. If somebody tries to convert you to idolatry (20) do not defend that person or (21) conceal the fact.

It is forbidden to (22) derive any benefit from the ornaments of idols. You may not (23) rebuild what has been destroyed as a punishment for idolatry nor may you (24) gain any benefit from its wealth. Do not (25) use anything connected with idols or idolatry. It is forbidden (26) to prophesy in the name of idols or prophesy (27) falsely in the name of God. Do not (28) listen to the one who prophesies for idols and do not (29) fear the false prophet or hinder his execution.

You must not (30) imitate the ways of idolaters or practice their customs; (31) divination, (32) soothsaying, (33) enchanting, (34) sorcery, (35) charming, (36) consulting ghosts or (37) familiar spirits and (38) necromancy are forbidden. Women must not (39) wear male clothing nor men [clothing] (40) of women. (41) Do not tattoo yourself in the manner of the idolaters.

You may not wear (42) garments made of both wool and linen nor may you shave [with a razor] the sides of (43) your head or (44) your beard. Do not (45) lacerate yourself over your dead.

It is forbidden to return to Egypt to (46) dwell there permanently or to (47) indulge in impure thoughts or sights. You may not (48) make a pact with the seven Canaanite nations or (49) save the life of any member of them. Do not (50) show mercy to idolaters, (51) permit them to dwell in the land of Israel or (52) intermarry with them. A Jewish woman may not (53) marry an Ammonite or Moabite even if he converts to Judaism but should refuse [for reasons of genealogy alone] (54) a descendant of Esau or (55) an

Egyptian who are proselytes. It is prohibited to make (56) peace with the Ammonite or Moabite nations.

The (57) destruction of fruit trees even in times of war is forbidden as is wanton waste at any time. Do not (58) fear the enemy and do not (59) forget the evil done by Amalek.

You must not (60) blaspheme the Holy Name, (61) break an oath made by it, (62) take it in vain or (63) profane it. Do not (64) test Adonai, [who is] God.

You may not (65) erase God's name from the holy texts or destroy institutions devoted to Divine worship. Do not (66) allow the body of one hanged to remain so overnight.

Be not (67) lax in guarding the Temple.

The high priest must not enter the Temple (68) indiscriminately; a priest with a physical blemish may not (69) enter there at all or (70) serve in the sanctuary and even if the blemish is of a temporary nature, he may not (71) participate in the service there until it has passed.

The Levites and the priests must not (72) interchange in their functions. Intoxicated persons may not (73) enter the sanctuary or teach the Law. It is forbidden for (74) non-priests, (75) unclean priests or (76) priests who have performed the necessary ablution but are still within the time limit of their uncleanness to serve in the Temple. No unclean person may enter (77) the Temple or (78) the Temple Mount.

The altar must not be made of (79) hewn stones nor may the ascent to it be by (80) steps. The fire on it may not be (81) extinguished nor may any other but the specified incense be (82) burned on the golden altar. You may not (83) manufacture oil with the same ingredients and in the same proportions as the anointing oil which itself (84) may not be misused. Neither may you (85) compound incense with the same ingredients and in the same proportions as that burnt on the altar. You must not (86) remove the staves from the Ark, (87) remove the breastplate from the ephod or (88) make any incision in the upper garment of the high priest.

It is forbidden to (89) offer sacrifices or (90) slaughter consecrated animals outside the Temple. You may not (91) sanctify, (92) slaughter, (93) sprinkle the blood of or (94) burn the inner parts of a blemished animal even if the blemish is (95) of a temporary nature and even if it is (96) offered by Gentiles. It is forbidden to (97) inflict a blemish on an animal consecrated for sacrifice.

Leaven or honey may not (98) be offered on the altar, neither may (99) anything unsalted. An animal received as the hire of a harlot or as the price of a dog (100) may not be offered.

Do not (101) kill an animal and its young on the same day.

It is forbidden to use (102) olive oil or (103) frankincense in the sin offering or (104), (105), in the jealousy offering (*sotah*). You may not (106) substitute sacrifices even (107) from one category to the other. You may not (108) redeem the firstborn of permitted animals. It is forbidden to (109) sell the tithe of the herd or (110) sell or (111) redeem a field consecrated by the *cherem* vow. When you slaughter a bird for a sin offering you may not (112) split its head.

It is forbidden to (113) work with or (114) shear a consecrated animal. You must not slaughter the paschal lamb (115) while there is still leaven about; nor may you leave overnight (116) those parts that are to be offered up or (117) to be eaten.

You may not leave any part of the festive offering (118) until the third day or any part of the (119) the second paschal lamb or (120) the thanksgiving offering until the morning.

It is forbidden to break a bone of (121) the first or (122) second paschal lamb or (123) to carry their flesh out of the house where it is being eaten. You must not (124) allow the remains of the meal offering to become leaven. It is also forbidden to eat the paschal (125) raw or sodden or to allow (126) an alien resident, (127) an uncircumcised person or an (128) apostate to eat of it.

A ritually unclean person (129) must not eat of holy things nor may (130) holy things which have become unclean be eaten. Sacrificial meat (131) which is left after the time limit or (132) which was slaughtered with wrong intentions must not be eaten. The heave offering must not be eaten by (133) a non-priest, (134) a priest's sojourner or hired worker, (135) an uncircumcised person, or (136) an unclean priest. The daughter of a priest who is married to a non-priest may not (137) eat of holy things.

The meal offering of the priest (138) must not be eaten, neither may (139) the flesh of the sin offerings sacrificed within the sanctuary or (140) consecrated animals which have become blemished. You may not eat the second tithe of (141) corn, (142) wine, or (143) oil or (144) unblemished firstlings outside Jerusalem. The priests may not eat the (145) sin-offerings or the trespass-offerings outside the Temple courts or (146) the flesh of the burnt-offering at all. The lighter sacrifices (147) may not be eaten before the blood has been sprinkled. A non-priest may not (148) eat of the holiest sacrifices and a priest (149) may not eat the firstfruits outside the Temple courts.

One may not eat (150) the second tithe while in a state of impurity or (151) in mourning; its redemption money (152) may not be used for anything other than food and drink.

You must not (153) eat untithed produce or (154) change the order of separating the various tithes.

Do not (155) delay payment of offerings—either freewill or obligatory—and do not (156) come to the Temple on the pilgrim festivals without an offering.

Do not (157) break your word.

A priest may not marry (158) a harlot, (159) a woman who has been profaned from the priesthood, or (160) a divorcee; the high priests must not (161) marry a widow or (162) take one as a concubine.

Priests may not enter the sanctuary with (163) overgrown hair of the head or (164) with torn clothing; they must not (165) leave the courtyard during the Temple service. An ordinary priest may not render himself (166) ritually impure except for those relatives specified, and the high priest should not become impure (167) for anybody in (168) any way.

The tribe of Levi shall have no part in (169) the division of the land of Israel or (170) in the spoils of war.

It is forbidden (171) to make oneself bald as a sign of mourning for one's dead.

A Jew may not eat (172) unclean cattle, (173) unclean fish, (174) unclean fowl, (175) creeping things that fly, (176) creatures that creep on the ground, (177) reptiles, (178) worms found in fruit or produce or (179) any detestable creature.

An animal that has died naturally (180) is forbidden for consumption as is (181) a torn or mauled animal. One must not eat (182) any limb taken from a living animal. Also prohibited is (183) the sinew of the thigh (*gid hanefesh*) as is (184) blood and (185) certain types of fat (*chelev*). It is forbidden (186) to cook meat together with milk or (187) eat of such a mixture. It is also forbidden to eat (188) of an ox condemned to stoning (even should it have been properly slaughtered).

One may not eat (189) bread made of new corn or the new corn itself, either (190) roasted or (191) green, before the *omer* offering has been brought on the 16th of Nisan. You may not eat (192) *orlah* or (193) the growth of mixed planting in the vineyard. Any use of (194) wine libations to idols is prohibited, as is (195) gluttony and drunkenness. One may not eat anything on (196) the Day of Atonement. During Passover it is forbidden to eat (197) leaven (*chametz*) or (198) anything containing a mixture of such. This is also forbidden (199) after the middle of the 14th of Nisan [the day before Passover]. During Passover no leaven may be (200) seen or (201) found in your possession.

A Nazirite may not drink (202) wine or any beverage made from grapes; he may not eat (203) grapes, (204) dried grapes, (205) grape seeds or (206) grape peel. He may not render himself (207) ritually impure for his dead nor may he (208) enter a tent in which there is a corpse. He must not (209) shave his hair.

It is forbidden (210) to reap the whole of a field without leaving the corners for the poor; it is also forbidden to (211) gather up the ears of corn that fall during reaping or to harvest (212) the misformed clusters of grapes, or (213) the grapes that fall or to (214) return to take a forgotten sheaf.

You must not (215) sow different species of seed together or (216) corn in a vineyard; it is also forbidden to (217) crossbreed different species of animals or (218) work with two different species yoked together.

You must not (219) muzzle an animal working in a field to prevent it from eating.

It is forbidden to (220) till the earth, (221) to prune trees, (222) to reap [in the usual manner] produce or (223) fruit which has grown without cultivation in the seventh year (*shemittah*). One may also not (224) till the earth or prune trees in the Jubilee year, when it is also forbidden to harvest [in the usual manner] (225) produce or (226) fruit that has grown without cultivation. One may not (227) sell one's landed inheritance in the land of Israel permanently or (228) change the lands of the Levites or (229) leave the Levites without support.

It is forbidden to (230) demand repayment of a loan after the seventh year; you may not, however (231) refuse to lend to the poor because that year is approaching. Do not (232) deny charity to the poor or (233) send a Hebrew slave away empty-handed when he finishes his period of service. Do not (234) dun your debtor when you know that he [or she] cannot pay. It is forbidden to (235) lend to or (236) borrow from another Jew at interest or (237) participate in an agreement involving interest either as a guarantor, witness, or writer of the contract.

Do not (238) delay in the payment of wages.

You may not (239) take a pledge from a debtor by violence, (240) keep a poor person's pledge when he [or she] needs it, (241) take any pledge from a widow or (242) from any debtor if he [or she] earns a living from it.

Kidnapping (243) a Jew is forbidden.

Do not (244) steal or (245) rob by violence. Do not (246) remove a land marker or (247) defraud.

It is forbidden (248) to deny receipt of a loan or a deposit or (249) to swear falsely regarding another person's property.

You must not (250) deceive anybody in business. You may not (251) mislead a person even (252) verbally or (253) do him [or her] injury in trade.

You may not (254) return or (255) otherwise take advantage of a slave who has fled to the land of Israel from his master, even if his master is a Jew.

Do not (256) afflict the widow or the orphan. You may not (257) misuse or (258) sell a Hebrew slave; do not (259) treat him cruelly or (260) allow a heathen to mistreat him. You must not (261) sell your Hebrew maidservant or, if you marry her, (262) withhold food, clothing, and conjugal rights from her. You must not (263) sell a female captive or (264) treat her as a slave.

Do not covet (265) another person's possessions even if you are willing to pay for them. Even (266) the desire alone is forbidden.

A worker must not (267) cut down standing corn during one's work or (268) take more fruit than one can eat.

One must not (269) turn away from a lost article which is to be returned to its owner nor may you (270) refuse to help a person on an animal which is collapsing under its burden.

It is forbidden to (271) defraud with weights and measures even (272) to possess inaccurate weights.

A judge must not (273) perpetrate injustice, (274) accept bribes or be (275) partial or (276) afraid. He [or she] may (277) not favor the poor or (278) discriminate against the wicked; he [or she] should not (279) pity the condemned or (280) pervert the judgment of strangers or orphans.

It is forbidden to (281) hear one litigant without the other being present. A capital case cannot be decided by (282) a majority of one.

A judge should not (283) accept a colleague's opinion unless he [or she] is convinced of its correctness; it is forbidden to (284) appoint as a judge someone who is ignorant of the law.

Do not (285) give false testimony or accept (286) testimony from a wicked person or from (287) relatives of a person involved in the case. It is forbidden to pronounce judgment (288) on the basis of the testimony of one witness.

Do not (289) murder.

You must not convict on (290) circumstantial evidence alone.

A witness (291) must not sit as a judge in capital cases.

You must not (292) execute anybody without due proper trial and conviction.

Do not (293) pity or spare the pursuer.

Punishment is not to be inflicted for (294) an act committed under duress.

Do not accept ransom (295) for a murderer or (296) a manslayer.

Do not (297) hesitate to save another person from danger and do not (298) leave a stumbling block in the way or (299) mislead another person by giving wrong advice.

It is forbidden (300) to administer more than the assigned number of lashes to the guilty.

Do not (301) tell tales or (302) bear hatred in your heart. It is forbidden to (303) shame a Jew, (304) to bear a grudge or (305) to take revenge.

Do not (306) take the dam when you take the young birds.

It is forbidden to (307) shave a leprous scale or (308) remove other signs of that affliction. It is forbidden (309) to cultivate a valley in which a slain body was found and in which subsequently the ritual of breaking the heifer's neck (*eglay arufah*) was performed.

Do not (310) suffer a witch to live.

Do not (311) force a bridegroom to perform military service during the first year of his marriage. It is forbidden to (312) rebel against the transmitters of the tradition or to (313) add or (314) detract from the precepts of the law.

Do not curse (315) a judge, (316) a ruler or (317) any Jew.

Do not (318) curse or (319) strike a parent.

It is forbidden to (320) work on the Sabbath or (321) walk further than the permitted limits (*eruv*). You may not (322) inflict punishment on the Sabbath.

It is forbidden to work on (323) the first or (324) the seventh day of Passover, on (325) Shavuot, on (326) Rosh Hashanah, on the (327) first and (328) eighth (*Shemini Atzeret*) days of Sukkot and (329) on the Day of Atonement.

It is forbidden to enter into an incestuous relationship with one's (330) mother, (331) stepmother, (332) sister, (333) half-sister, (334) son's daughter, (335) daughter's daughter, (336) daughter, (337) any woman and her daughter, (338) any woman and her son's daughter, (339) any woman and her daughter's daughter, (340) father's sister, (341) mother's sister, (342) paternal uncle's wife, (343) daughter-in-law, (344) brother's wife and (345) wife's sister.

It is also forbidden to (346) have sexual relations with a menstruous woman.

Do not (347) commit adultery.

It is forbidden for (348) a man or (349) a woman to have sexual intercourse with an animal.

Homosexuality (350) is forbidden, particularly with (351) one's father or (352) uncle.

It is forbidden to have (353) intimate physical contact (even without actual intercourse) with any of the women with whom intercourse is forbidden.

A *mamzer* may not (354) marry a Jewish woman.

Prostitution (355) is forbidden.

A divorcee may not be (356) remarried to her first husband if, in the meanwhile, she has married another.

A childless widow may not (357) marry anybody other than her late husband's brother.

A man may not (358) divorce a wife whom he married after having raped her or (359) after having slandered her.

A eunuch may not (360) marry a Jewish woman.

Castration (361) is forbidden.

You may not (362) elect as king anybody who is not of the seed of Israel.

The king may not accumulate an excessive number of (363) horses, (364) wives, or (365) wealth.

TEXTUAL SOURCES FOR PROHIBITIONS

1. Exodus 20:3
2. Exodus 20:4
3. Leviticus 19:4
4. Exodus 20:20
5. Exodus 20:5
6. Exodus 20:5
7. Leviticus 18:21
8. Leviticus 19:31
9. Leviticus 19:31
10. Leviticus 19:4
11. Deuteronomy 16:21
12. Leviticus 20:1
13. Deuteronomy 16:21
14. Exodus 23:13
15. Exodus 23:13
16. Deuteronomy 13:12
17. Deuteronomy 13:9
18. Deuteronomy 13:9
19. Deuteronomy 13:9
20. Deuteronomy 13:9
21. Deuteronomy 13:9
22. Deuteronomy 7:25
23. Deuteronomy 13:17
24. Deuteronomy 13:18
25. Deuteronomy 7:26
26. Deuteronomy 18:20
27. Deuteronomy 18:20
28. Deuteronomy 13:3, 4
29. Deuteronomy 18:22
30. Leviticus 20:23
31. Leviticus 19:26;
    Deuteronomy 18:10
32. Deuteronomy 18:10
33. Deuteronomy 18:10–26
34. Deuteronomy 18:10–11
35. Deuteronomy 18:10–11
36. Deuteronomy 18:10–11
37. Deuteronomy 18:10–11
38. Deuteronomy 18:10–11
39. Deuteronomy 22:5
40. Deuteronomy 22:5
41. Leviticus 19:28
42. Deuteronomy 22:11
43. Leviticus 19:27
44. Leviticus 19:27
45. Deuteronomy 16:1; 14:1;
    Leviticus 19:28
46. Deuteronomy 17:16
47. Numbers 15:39
48. Exodus 23:32;
    Deuteronomy 7:2
49. Deuteronomy 20:16
50. Deuteronomy 7:2
51. Exodus 23:33
52. Deuteronomy 7:3
53. Deuteronomy 23:4
54. Deuteronomy 23:8
55. Deuteronomy 23:8
56. Deuteronomy 23:7
57. Deuteronomy 20:19

58. Deuteronomy 7:21
59. Deuteronomy 25:19
60. Leviticus 24:16;
    Exodus 22:27
61. Leviticus 19:12
62. Exodus 20:7
63. Leviticus 22:32
64. Deuteronomy 6:16
65. Deuteronomy 12:4
66. Deuteronomy 21:23
67. Numbers 18:5
68. Leviticus 16:2
69. Leviticus 21:23
70. Leviticus 21:17
71. Leviticus 21:18
72. Numbers 18:3
73. Leviticus 10:9–11
74. Numbers 18:4
75. Leviticus 22:2
76. Leviticus 21:6
77. Numbers 5:3
78. Deuteronomy 23:11
79. Exodus 20:25
80. Exodus 20:26
81. Leviticus 6:6
82. Exodus 30:9
83. Exodus 30:32
84. Exodus 30:32
85. Exodus 30:37
86. Exodus 25:15
87. Exodus 28:28
88. Exodus 28:32
89. Deuteronomy 12:13
90. Leviticus 17:3–4
91. Leviticus 22:20
92. Leviticus 22:22
93. Leviticus 22:24
94. Leviticus 22:22
95. Deuteronomy 17:1
96. Leviticus 22:25
97. Leviticus 22:21

98. Leviticus 2:11
99. Leviticus 2:13
100. Deuteronomy 23:19
101. Leviticus 22:28
102. Leviticus 5:11
103. Leviticus 5:11
104. Numbers 5:15
105. Numbers 5:15
106. Leviticus 27:10
107. Leviticus 27:26
108. Numbers 18:17
109. Leviticus 27:33
110. Leviticus 27:28
111. Leviticus 27:28
112. Leviticus 5:8
113. Deuteronomy 15:19
114. Deuteronomy 15:19
115. Exodus 34:25
116. Exodus 23:10
117. Exodus 12:10
118. Deuteronomy 16:4
119. Numbers 9:13
120. Leviticus 22:30
121. Exodus 12:46
122. Numbers 9:12
123. Exodus 12:46
124. Leviticus 6:10
125. Exodus 12:9
126. Exodus 12:45
127. Exodus 12:48
128. Exodus 12:43
129. Leviticus 12:4
130. Leviticus 7:19
131. Leviticus 19:6–8
132. Leviticus 7:18
133. Leviticus 22:10
134. Leviticus 22:10
135. Leviticus 22:10
136. Leviticus 22:4
137. Leviticus 22:12
138. Leviticus 6:16

139. Leviticus 6:23
140. Deuteronomy 14:3
141. Deuteronomy 12:17
142. Deuteronomy 12:17
143. Deuteronomy 12:17
144. Deuteronomy 12:17
145. Deuteronomy 12:17
146. Deuteronomy 12:17
147. Deuteronomy 12:17
148. Deuteronomy 12:17
149. Exodus 29:33
150. Deuteronomy 26:14
151. Deuteronomy 26:14
152. Deuteronomy 26:14
153. Leviticus 22:15
154. Exodus 22:28
155. Deuteronomy 23:22
156. Exodus 23:15
157. Numbers 30:3
158. Leviticus 21:7
159. Leviticus 21:7
160. Leviticus 21:7
161. Leviticus 21:14
162. Leviticus 21:15
163. Leviticus 10:6
164. Leviticus 10:6
165. Leviticus 10:7
166. Leviticus 21:1
167. Leviticus 21:11
168. Levticus 21:11
169. Deuteronomy 18:1
170. Deuteronomy 18:1
171. Deuteronomy 14:1
172. Deuteronomy 14:7
173. Leviticus 11:11
174. Leviticus 11:13
175. Deuteronomy 14:19
176. Leviticus 11:41
177. Leviticus 11:44
178. Leviticus 11:42
179. Leviticus 11:43
180. Deuteronomy 14:21
181. Exodus 22:30
182. Deuteronomy 12:23
183. Genesis 32:33
184. Leviticus 7:26
185. Leviticus 7:23
186. Exodus 23:19
187. Exodus 34:26
188. Exodus 21:28
189. Leviticus 23:14
190. Leviticus 23:14
191. Leviticus 23:14
192. Leviticus 19:23
193. Deuteronomy 22:9
194. Deuteronomy 32:38
195. Leviticus 19:26;
     Deuteronomy 21:20
196. Leviticus 23:29
197. Exodus 13:3
198. Exodus 13:20
199. Deuteronomy 16:3
200. Exodus 13:7
201. Exodus 12:19
202. Numbers 6:3
203. Numbers 6:3
204. Numbers 6:3
205. Numbers 6:4
206. Numbers 6:4
207. Numbers 6:7
208. Leviticus 21:11
209. Numbers 6:5
210. Leviticus 23:22
211. Leviticus 19:9
212. Leviticus 19:10
213. Leviticus 19:10
214. Deuteronomy 24:19
215. Leviticus 19:19
216. Deuteronomy 22:9
217. Leviticus 19:19
218. Deuteronomy 22:10
219. Deuteronomy 25:4

220. Leviticus 25:4	261. Exodus 21:8
221. Leviticus 25:4	262. Exodus 21:10
222. Leviticus 25:5	263. Deuteronomy 21:14
223. Leviticus 25:5	264. Deuteronomy 21:14
224. Leviticus 25:11	265. Exodus 20:17
225. Leviticus 25:11	266. Deuteronomy 5:18
226. Leviticus 25:11	267. Deuteronomy 23:26
227. Leviticus 25:23	268. Deuteronomy 23:25
228. Leviticus 25:33	269. Deuteronomy 22:3
229. Deuteronomy 12:19	270. Exodus 23:5
230. Deuteronomy 15:2	271. Leviticus 19:35
231. Deuteronomy 15:9	272. Deuteronomy 25:13
232. Deuteronomy 15:7	273. Leviticus 19:15
233. Deuteronomy 15:13	274. Exodus 23:8
234. Exodus 22:24	275. Leviticus 19:15
235. Leviticus 25:37	276. Deuteronomy 1:17
236. Deuteronomy 23:20	277. Leviticus 19:15;
237. Exodus 22:24	Exodus 23:3
238. Leviticus 19:13	278. Exodus 23:6
239. Deuteronomy 24:10	279. Deuteronomy 19:13
240. Deuteronomy 24:12	280. Deuteronomy 24:17
241. Deuteronomy 24:17	281. Exodus 23:1
242. Deuteronomy 24:10	282. Exodus 23:2
243. Exodus 20:13	283. Exodus 23:2
244. Leviticus 19:11	284. Deuteronomy 1:17
245. Leviticus 19:13	285. Exodus 20:16
246. Deuteronomy 19:14	286. Exodus 23:1
247. Leviticus 19:13	287. Deuteronomy 24:16
248. Leviticus 19:11	288. Deuteronomy 19:15
249. Leviticus 19:11	289. Exodus 20:13
250. Leviticus 25:14	290. Exodus 23:7
251. Leviticus 25:17	291. Numbers 35:30
252. Exodus 22:20	292. Numbers 35:12
253. Exodus 20:20	293. Deuteronomy 25:12
254. Deuteronomy 23:16	294. Deuteronomy 22:26
255. Deuteronomy 23:17	295. Numbers 35:31
256. Exodus 22:21	296. Numbers 35:32
257. Leviticus 25:39	297. Leviticus 19:16
258. Leviticus 25:42	298. Deuteronomy 22:8
259. Leviticus 25:43	299. Leviticus 19:14
260. Leviticus 25:53	300. Deuteronomy 25:2–3

301. Leviticus 19:16
302. Leviticus 19:17
303. Leviticus 19:17
304. Leviticus 19:18
305. Leviticus 19:18
306. Deuteronomy 22:6
307. Leviticus 13:33
308. Deuteronomy 24:8
309. Deuteronomy 21:4
310. Exodus 22:17
311. Deuteronomy 24:5
312. Deuteronomy 17:11
313. Deuteronomy 13:1
314. Deuteronomy 13:1
315. Exodus 22:27
316. Exodus 22:27
317. Leviticus 19:14
318. Exodus 21:17
219. Exodus 21:15
320. Exodus 20:10
321. Exodus 16:29
322. Exodus 35:3
323. Exodus 12:16
324. Exodus 12:16
325. Leviticus 23:21
326. Leviticus 23:25
327. Leviticus 23:35
328. Leviticus 23:36
329. Leviticus 23:28
330. Leviticus 18:7
331. Leviticus 18:8
332. Leviticus 18:9
333. Leviticus 18:11

334. Leviticus 18:10
335. Leviticus 18:10
336. Leviticus 18:10
337. Leviticus 18:17
338. Leviticus 18:17
339. Leviticus 18:17
340. Leviticus 18:12
341. Leviticus 18:13
342. Leviticus 18:14
343. Leviticus 18:15
344. Leviticus 18:16
345. Leviticus 18:18
346. Leviticus 18:19
347. Leviticus 18:20
348. Leviticus 18:23
349. Leviticus 18:23
350. Leviticus 18:22
351. Leviticus 18:7
352. Leviticus 18:14
353. Leviticus 18:6
354. Deuteronomy 23:3
355. Deuteronomy 23:18
356. Deuteronomy 24:4
357. Deuteronomy 25:5
358. Deuteronomy 22:29
359. Deuteronomy 22:19
360. Deuteronomy 23:2
361. Leviticus 22:24
362. Deuteronomy 17:15
363. Deuteronomy 17:16
364. Deuteronomy 17:17
365. Deuteronomy 17:17

12

SELECTED COMMANDMENTS AND THEIR RATIONALE

This section of the book surveys selected commandments and their rationale as presented by various rabbinic commentators. The commandments are divided by category, and were chosen based upon the fact that most of them are still applicable today. Commandments in each category are presented in the order in which they appear in the Torah. The rationale section, entitled "Commentators," is preceded by several statements illuminating various laws or customs associated with each particular commandment. Many of the statements are based on rabbinic interpretation and are intended to help further define the understanding of the commandment. Each commandment section will conclude with a section entitled, "If You Want to Learn More," where, various references for further study of the commandment are presented.

Section I: God

1. Belief in the Existence of God

"I the Lord am your God who brought you out of the land of Egypt, the house of bondage." (Exodus 20:2).

i. This *mitzvah* obligates every Jew to believe in the existence of God.

ii. Belief in God is one of the fundamental principles of our faith, and the first principle of Maimonides' *Thirteen Principles of Faith*.

iii. Without a belief in the existence of God, an understanding of the Torah and the observance of its commandments are impossibilities.

iv. Any Israelite who does not believe that God exists is considered an apostate and does not merit a portion in the World-to-Come.

v. This commandment has no set time for its fulfillment, since people are required to live with this concept all the days of their life.

vi. A Jew is prohibited from uttering even a single word that might be interpreted by others as an indication that other "gods" exist.

Commentators

Nachmonides.

Nachmonides views the first commandment as a preface to the others. In order to explain the reason why it was needed, he offers the following comparison. He compares God to a king who conveys to his subjects that before he gives them his laws and statutes, they first must have total faith and belief in him as their sovereign ruler. Similarly, belief in One God is the prerequisite for the acceptance of all of the other commandments.

Next, Nachmonides notes that each of the Ten Commandments is addressed to the individual in the second person singular rather than the second person plural. He states that the reason for this is to show that each and every individual must bear the responsibility for his or her own actions, and must not follow the majority when the majority is in the wrong.

Finally, Nachmonides explains the reason why the first commandment begins with the phrase, "I am the Lord Your God who brought you up out of Egypt." This is to teach people that there is not a thing in this world (including the miraculous deliverance from Egypt) that can take place or occur unless God wills it to happen so.

Ibn Ezra.

Ibn Ezra, like Nachmonides, questions why the first commandment mentions God as the Redeemer from Egypt rather than the Creator of the Universe. Surely, the creation of the world was a greater miracle than that of the exodus from Egypt? Therefore, God's ability to create the world should have been mentioned in the first commandment. Ibn Ezra answers by saying that, unlike the creation of the world, which no one witnessed, the exodus was an event that generations of people witnessed in their lifetimes. Thus people who have witnessed first hand the exodus from Egypt will be much more likely to believe in a personal God who becomes involved with people in their time of need.

Hinnuch.

He states that the reason why God as the liberator of the Israelites from Egypt is stated in the first commandment is to ensure that the Israelites will always be reminded that their freedom did not occur by chance, but rather by the Hand of God. Thus we are constantly reminded that God fulfills all of His promises that He made to our ancestors, and that God will continue His watchful eye over His people.

Maimonides.

He states that this first commandment in which Israelites were commanded to believe in God is of the very essence of Judaism. Indeed, without a firm belief in the existence of God, the observance of God's commandments would be an impossibility. Thus, this first commandment is the most fundamental of fundamentals and pillar of all sciences to know that there is a first cause (i.e., God) that brings into existence all existing things.

If You Want to Learn More

See Talmud *Shabbat* 88b; Talmud *Sanhedrin* 99a; Maimonides, *Book of Commandments,* positive commandment 1; *Code of Jewish Law, Orach Chayyim,* ch. 61; *Sefer HaHinnuch (mitzvot* 25, 26).

2. Prohibition of Making a Graven Image

"You shall not make for yourselves a graven image, nor any manner of likeness, of any thing that is heaven above, or that is in the earth beneath, or that is in the water under the earth. You shall not bow down to them or serve them." (Exodus 20:5).

i. This commandment, the second of the Ten Commandments, is directed against idolatry and forbids one to bow down to images and sculptures.

ii. The biblical injunction against idolatry included the prohibition of making an idol, worshipping an idol and worshipping God with pagan rites.

iii. In the Talmud a whole tractate, *Avodah Zarah,* is devoted to the details of idolatry.

iv. Idolatry was considered by the ancient rabbis as one of the three cardinal sins, for which one is enjoined to suffer martyrdom rather than transgress (the other two are incest and murder).

v. According to the Talmud (*Horayot* 8a), the *mitzvah* of the prohibition of idolatry was so important that its fulfillment was equivalent to the fulfillment of all the commandments of the Torah.

vi. In ancient times the penalty for knowingly worshipping an idol was death by stoning.

vii. According to the Jewish law codes, Jewish people were forbidden to use libation wine (i.e., wine involved in idolatry rites). As a precautionary measure this prohibition was extended to include any wine that was prepared by a Gentile. Such wine was expressly forbidden for Jewish consumption.

viii. By rabbinic law (Talmud *Avodah Zarah* 12a), a person is forbidden to bend down before an idol in order to remove a thorn lodged in his foot or in order to pick up coins which he has dropped in front of the idol "because it would look as though he were bowing down to the idol; he must first sit down, and then extract the thorn or pick up the coins."

Commentators

Or HaChayyim.

The author was concerned that the commandment prohibiting belief in another god should not have been necessary to have been stated, since the first of the Ten Commandments clearly states, "I am the Lord Your God." He provides the following answer: the stating of the commandment "you shall not have another God before Me" makes it perfectly clear that "the Lord Your God" is not one deity supreme among many other gods, but rather that He is the One and the Only God, and there are no others. The *Or HaChayyim* further states that it is entirely possible that a person could acknowledge God's supremacy but still feel the need to use an intermediary such as an idol in order to help in communicating with the One God. Such an intermediary, says the Or HaChayyim, is, based on the commandment of "you shall not make for yourself a graven image," totally forbidden.

Targum Jonathan.

This Aramaic translator of the Bible stated that the first of the Ten Commandments ("I am God . . .") established the duty to acknowledge God, whereas the second commandment demands recognition of God's singularity and forbids the presentation of God in any form of sculptured image.

Nachmonides.

Nachmonides is concerned with the definition of what constitutes the worshipping of an idol. He describes three different manifestations of idolatry. (a) The worshipping of human beings who are regarded as one's heroes is idolatry in its most primitive form, as are (b) the adoration of celestial bodies or any person "born under a lucky star," or (c) the attempt to foretell the future by attempting to communicate with the dead.

Recanti.

Much like the *Or HaChayyim,* Recanti believed that the second of the Ten Commandments was presented to keep people from erring and believing that God Himself was working through intermediaries (i.e., lesser gods) that were permitted to be worshipped.

Maimonides.

He states that the acceptance of idolatry is tantamount to repudiating the whole Torah, as well as the Prophets and everything that they were commanded. He further states that by this prohibition, the Jewish people are not only forbidden to make images for purposes of worship, but that there is no difference between making them themselves or directing others to make them. Furthermore, whoever violates this negative commandment is subject to the punishment of whipping, even if that person does not worship it. Finally, Maimonides also believes that the prohibition against making an idol is an integral part of the doctrine of the unity and incorporeality of God (i.e., that God is One, and that God is all spirit with no body).

Rebbe of Kotsk.

This chasidic rabbi takes the commandment less literally than some of his fellow commentators. He states that the prohibition against idolatry includes the prohibition against making idols out of the *mitzvot.* He states that we ought never to imagine that the chief purpose of a commandment is its outer form (i.e., the doing); rather, the purpose is the inward meaning (i.e., the devotion and spirit with which it is done).

If You Want to Learn More

See Talmud *Sanhedrin* 60b, 61a, 62b; Talmud *Avodah Zarah* 43b, 54a; Maimonides, *Book of Commandments,* negative commandments 2, 5, 6, 10, 14; Maimonides, *The Guide of the Perplexed,* pt. 1, sect. 36; *Code of*

Jewish Law, Yoreh De'ah, 139–152; *Sefer HaHinnuch,* commandments 27–29, 86, 214.

3, 4. Hallowing God's Name and the Prohibition against Profaning It

"You shall not profane My holy name, but I will be hallowed among the children of Israel" (Exodus 20:7, Leviticus 22:32).

i. The assertion that a person, with all of his limitations and faults, can hallow God, and that God requires man to hallow His name, is known in rabbinic literature as *kiddush HaShem* (sanctification of God's name).

ii. The commandment of hallowing God's name was originally directed to the priesthood, who, as guardians of the Sanctuary, were warned in this manner to fulfill their duties to God. Later, the obligation to sanctify God's name was extended to the "kingdom of priests"—the whole Jewish people.

iii. The most extreme form of hallowing God's name is martyrdom—the instance of a Jew's faith being so strong that he or she is wiling to forgo the privilege of living, if necessary, in order to prevent the desecration of God's name. It was during the war against the Romans that *kiddush HaShem* became associated with martyrdom.

iv. The rabbis decreed that only with regard to three cardinal sins—the heinous transgressions of idolatry, incest, and murder—should a person prefer to make the supreme sacrifice rather than be forced into submission. If a person were coerced to violate any other *mitzvah,* the rabbis said that he should spare himself from death and violate the law.

v. The opposite of the sanctification of God's name is *chillul HaShem,* the profanation of God's name. Any immoral act has been regarded as a *chillul HaShem.*

Commentators

Maimonides.

He classifies the concept of profaning God's name under three categories:

a. When force is being used to make a Jew violate a law with the alternative of being put of death, he should choose transgression rather than death. The exceptions to the rule are when the transgressions involve idol worship, unchastity, or murder.
b. If a Jew is not being compelled forcefully to sin but does so anyway out of sheer spite, this is considered *chillul HaShem.*

c. If a highly moral person of flawless character commits a wrong, even a minor one, he is profaning the name of God.

Hinnuch.

He states that the Jewish people were born to be the servants of God. No servant is a true and authentic one unless he or she is dedicated to God with all of his or her body and soul. This is the way to sanctify God's name. Furthermore, whoever is not willing to give up his life for God can never be a good servant. If it is a fact that men lay down their lives for their masters, then how much more should this be so in obedience to the command of the King of Kings!

Saadia Gaon.

He believed that desecration of God also related to the beliefs and faith of a person. For Saadia, a person who even has doubts about the efficacy of religion and faith in God is a desecrator of God's holy name.

Sforno.

He states that we have witnessed the perfection of God's actions in the world. Since man was made in God's image, man ought to reciprocate, like God, with perfect action. In order to achieve this we must sanctify, and never desecrate, God's holy name.

Nehama Leibowitz.

She says that the command of hallowing God's name raises an interesting and important question. How is it conceivable for moral man, who is molded of dust and ashes, to profane the holiness of God, who is Himself the supreme source of sanctity? Man's own aspirations to holiness are but an imitation of the Divine holiness. It is strange, she says, that man himself, who is so far removed from holiness, should be commanded to sanctify God's name. Her answer relates to the distinction between the essential holiness of God, which transcends place and time, and the holiness of God's name (i.e., the recognition of God and God's holiness). The positive commandment, to sanctify God's name in the midst of the children of Israel, and the negative one, of not profaning God's name, imply recognition of God's sovereignty over people and the acknowledgment that people have been created for the sake of God's name.

If You Want to Learn More

See Talmud *Shavuot*, 21a, 25b; Talmud *Shabbat* 120a; Talmud *Yoma* 86a; Talmud *Megillah* 23b; Maimonides, *Book of Commandments,* positive commandment 9, negative commandments 61–63; *Sefer HaHinnuch,* commandments 30, 227, 295, 296; *Code of Jewish Law, Yoreh De'ah,* 157, 236; Nehama Leibowitz, *Studies in the Book of Exodus.*

5. Prohibition of Taking God's Name in Vain

"You shall not take the Lord your God in vain" (Exodus 20:7).

i. This is the third of the Ten Commandments, and forbids us from dishonoring God by invoking God's name to attest what is untrue.

ii. Oaths during talmudic times were taken by holding the Scroll of the Torah in one's hand and swearing by God (Talmud *Shevuot* 38b).

iii. There are four types of oaths in rabbinic law (c.f. Talmud *Shevuot* 21a, 25b, 39a) that are considered as examples of "taking God's name in vain":

a. *Shevua'at sheker*: This is simple perjury.

b. *Shevu'at shav*: In this kind of superfluous oath, which uses the name of God, a person makes a vow that he knows in advance he cannot fulfill or swears to a fact that is obvious (e.g., "I swear that this stone is a stone").

c. *Shevu'at ha-pikadon*: This is an oath to the effect that one does not possess an object that rightfully belongs to someone else when, in fact, the object is in his possession. If such a person had taken the false oath intentionally, he had to pay the rightful owner the complete original value of the object in addition to one-fifth of the value. Additionally, he had to bring an offering of young doves. If, however, the person had not realized that he had sworn falsely, the rabbis did not consider him as guilty.

d. *Shevu'at ha-edut*: This is a false oath that a potential witness takes to the effect that he knows nothing about the litigation, and therefore cannot offer testimony, when in fact he could testify.

Commentators

Hinnuch.

The Hinnuch states that since God is an everlasting God and people are mortal, when a person swears an oath in the name of God, that person is swearing by that which is eternal. Thus, a person is expected to keep a vow made in God's name (even though there may always be external forces working against him) as a way of continuing to affirm, and be reminded of, God's existence as being eternal and enduring. It is, therefore, always important to swear an oath to God with awe and reverence for Him.

Ibn Ezra.

He states that there are many who believe that taking God's name in vain is a somewhat minor *mitzvah* in comparison to that of murder, adultery, or stealing. However, he believes that violating it is an even great transgression than violating those commandments that follow. His reasoning is as follows: since a person does not usually make a habit of committing the sins of murder, stealing, or adultery, such a person must wait for an opportunity to sin. In addition, one is generally afraid of being caught after committing such heinous crimes. Taking an oath in God's name, however, can become habitual, to the extent that a person may even swear that he did not do so. As such, therefore, it bears explicit punishment for the violator to plainly see—namely, that God will not hold guiltless those who take His name in vain.

Ibn Ezra sums up the seriousness of taking God's name in vain as follows: just as God's Name is true, so should a person's word be true. Thus, if a person does not keep his word, it is tantamount to repudiating God's name and reputation.

Keli Yakar.

This commentator holds that when a person takes God's name in vain, he is upsetting the balance of all of nature because every living thing has a part of God in it. The Keli Yakar compares a person who takes God's name in vain to one who shakes a tree trunk. When one shakes the trunk, the branches and tree leaves will also begin to shake and may even fall off.

Cassuto.

He does not take the phrase, "taking God's name in vain," to refer to a false utterance but rather to refer to the misuse of God's holy name to describe that which is not God. He explains, therefore, that this commandment is to be interpreted to extend to not using God's name for any valueless purpose, not just for a false oath. Cassuto sees such worthless purposes in connection with which the gentiles mention the name of their gods, such as incantations, divination, and the like.

If You Want to Learn More

See Talmud *Shavuot* 21a, 25b; Talmud *Berakhot* 33a; Maimonides, *Book of Commandments* negative commandments 61, 62; *Code of Jewish Law, Yoreh De'ah,* 236; Cassuto, *A Commentary on the Book of Exodus; Sefer HaHinnuch,* commandment 30.

6. Belief in the Oneness of God

Hear O Israel, the Lord our God, the Lord is One (Deuteronomy 6:4).

i. This commandment, enunciating the principle of monotheism, sounds the key note of all of Judaism and has been its watchword and confession of faith throughout the ages.

ii. God is unique; He is unlike any other and therefore has no likeness.

iii. To say that God is One is to say that God cannot be divided or fragmented. It naturally follows that God cannot be a physical being, since physical beings can be divided.

iv. For centuries the words of this commandment (i.e., "Hear O Israel . . .") have been said aloud on countless occasions when Jews sanctified God's name through their death.

v. The Jewish people continue to say the words of this commandment during morning and evening prayer services throughout the year. The words are also affixed to their doorposts in receptacles called *mezuzot* and inscribed on parchment in their phylacteries, called *tefillin.*

vi. Any Jew who is ordered to violate the commandment of the belief in the Oneness of God by committing idolatry must be ready to sacrifice his or her life rather than consent to do so.

Commentators

Maimonides.

For Maimonides, this commandment provided the second principle in his *Thirteen Principles of Faith*: "I believe with perfect faith that God is One. There is no unity that is in any way like His. He alone is our God—He was, He is and He will be."

Maimonides expands upon this principle of faith by stating that God is the cause of everyone, and His unity is absolutely unique. Since God's power is infinite and continuous it cannot be associated with anything physical. And since God cannot be physical, there can be no physical qualities separating Him from another similar being. Therefore, there can be, states Maimonides, only one God. Maimonides goes on to say that there are five types of nonbeliever, including a person who admits that the world has a master but says that there are two or more gods.

Nachmonides.

He holds that the purpose of this commandment pronouncing the Oneness of God is to convey the important message of religious commitment. Commitment to the Oneness of God is so important that any person who does not believe in God's Oneness nullifies all other religious commitments.

Hinnuch.

The Hinnuch states that all civilized people must intellectually acknowledge God's Oneness since it is the core element of the faith of all people. He further states that if any person does not acknowledge God's Oneness, it is as though that person denied the main principle of God's existence. Interesting also is the Hinnuch's statement that this commandment is among those that apply in every place and time and for both man and woman.

Rashbam.

His concern relates to the fact that there are people who believe in lesser gods along with their belief in the One God. Thus he emphatically states that one has violated the commandment of belief in God's Oneness if one has faith in the power of gods of lesser status, especially those involved in black magic and sorcery.

Ba'al Ha-Turim.

He was concerned that a person might be confused by the many manifestations of God and God's character traits, thus being led to believe that perhaps there is more than one God. He thus states that believing in God's Oneness means that although God may sometimes appear as a strict and stern judge, and at other times as a merciful and compassionate parent, that He is really one and the same God.

If You Want to Learn More

See Talmud *Berakhot* 6a, 13a, 15a, 33b; Talmud *Sanhedrin* 74a; Maimonides, *Book of Commandments,* positive commandments 2, 3; *Sefer*

Mitzvot Gadol, positive commandments 2, 3; *Sefer HaHinnuch,* commandments 417, 418; *Code of Jewish Law, Orach Chayyim,* ch. 61.

7. Love of God

"You shall love God with all your heart, with all your soul and with all of your might" (Deuteronomy 6:5).

i. The love for God is one of the first instances in human history that such a commandment was demanded in any religion.

ii. The meaning of the love of God in rabbinic literature is generally interpreted as a longing to be near God and a striving to reach God's holiness, in the same manner as a person will pursue any object for which he feels a strong passion. God must be given undivided allegiance, and some rabbis take the words "with all your might" to mean that one should love God with the heart's last drop of blood and give up one life's for God, should He require it. Others interpret "with all your might" as meaning "whatever treatment God metes out to a person" (Talmud *Berakhot* 54a).

iii. The duty to love God presupposes a reciprocal relationship, for God has loved Israel since the days of the patriarchs. Love can help motivate people to do God's will.

iv. The Midrash (*Sifre Deuteronomy* 32) holds that the best expression of love for God occurs when people conduct themselves in such a manner as to make God beloved by others. It is the attention to God's commandments and their performance with proper devotion that shows one's love for God.

v. The Prophets Hosea, Jeremiah, and Isaiah saw God and the Israelites in a love relationship, where God metaphorically was portrayed as the groom and the people of Israel as God's bride. Bliss is in store for the bride who deserves the love of her bridegroom but severe consequences will result if the bride (Israel) betrays the trust of her bridegroom (God) (see Hosea 2; Jeremiah 2, 3, 31:2–6; and Isaiah 49:14–54:8).

vi. Love of God is another one of the commandments that can be done everywhere and anywhere, wherever the opportunity for performing commandments exists.

Commentators

Recanti.

He identifies the concept of love with the Hebrew word *chesed,* meaning "kindly and merciful." Since people were made in God's image, loving God is an aid to being merciful and kind to their fellow human beings.

Or HaChayim.

The author states that we must love God because God chose the Israelite people to be His treasured and chosen nation and demands their love.

Bachya ibn Pakuda.

He was one of a few commentators who believed that the love of God could be achieved only if one divorced himself from worldly pursuits.

> "What does the love of God consist of? The soul's complete surrender of its own accord to the Creator in order to cleave to His supernal light. . . . Then it will become totally preoccupied with God's service and have no place for any other thought, sending forth not even one of the limbs of its body on any other service but that drawn to by God's will; loosening the tongue but to make mention of God and praise God out of love of God and longing for God" (*Duties of the Heart*).

Maimonides.

Maimonides attempts to answer the question of how love, which is not under the control of a person's will, can be the subject of a commandment. He understands the *mitzvah* of loving God as meaning to dwell upon and contemplate God's commandments (certainly an activity under the control of a persons' will), in order that a person might obtain a conception of God and, in doing so, attain absolute joy. One obtains a conception of God through the study of God's Torah and God's creation. Furthermore, Maimonides states that one who loves God and reaches a stage of absolute joy will be so moved as to call upon the foolish and ignorant to seek the truth.

Chayim Luzzatto.

He attempts to answer the question that some might have of how the command to love God can apply to a person who has never seen God. Luzzatto explains "loving God with all your heart" as follows: since the Torah speaks in the language of humans and depicts a God who has feelings, anger and desire, love and hate, it naturally follows that a person must also be described as loving or hating God, for whoever sets God always before him and is exclusively concerned with doing God's pleasure and observing

God's commandments will be called God's lover. The love of God is, therefore, not a separate commandment but an underlying principle of all of God's commandments. The love itself cannot be the subject of a command.

If You Want to Learn More

See Talmud *Berakhot* 15a, 16a, 33b, 34a, 54a; Talmud *Pesachim* 56a; Talmud *Yoma* 86a; *Sefer Mitzvot Katan,* commandments 2, 3; Maimonides, *Book of Commandments,* positive commandments 2, 3; *Sefer HaHinnuch,* commandments 417, 418.

8. Prohibition against Testing God

"You shall not try the Lord your God as you tried Him in Massah." (Deuteronomy 6:16).

i. This commandment states that a person ought not to test God by questioning God's power or protection. The latter part of the commandment refers to an incident in Exodus 16:2 when the Israelites had left Egypt and were on their way to Sinai. The whole of the congregation complained to Moses and Aaron, wishing that they would have died in Egypt rather than submit to the hunger that they were experiencing. God then decided to provide heavenly food, called manna, to save them from hunger, but the manner in which it was to be given to the Israelites would be a test of their faith and obedience.

ii. This commandment, according to rabbinic interpretation, also demands of a person not to obey God's commandments in order to see if he or she will be rewarded for doing so. There is one exception. Basing their premise on a verse in the Book of Malachi (3:10), the rabbis agreed to the expectations that a person might have that God fulfill His promises. The Prophet Malachi says: "Bring all the tithes to the storehouse, and prove Me now by this, says God: If I will not open for you the window of Heaven and pour you out a blessing." This has been interpreted to mean that if an Israelite sincerely brings his tithes, then he has the right to the reward of God's blessings.

Commentators

Hinnuch.

He states that one should never ask God's Prophets to show signs and miracles at one's every whim. It is God's decision to make as to when He chooses to show miracles, and never the prerogative of the Prophet. For if Prophets did have some ability to display heavenly signs, such Prophets might be open to ridicule on the occasions when they were unable to perform such miracles.

Nachmonides.

He interprets the phrase, "do not try God as you did at Massah" to mean that one should not question whether God is in the midst of you to perform miracles or make your worship of God dependent upon material reward, for the Israelites' intention at Massah was to follow God if they got water through a miracle; otherwise, they would forsake God. This, Nachmonides says, was a great sin. Thus, it is expressly forbidden to try Prophets or God, and God ought never to be worshipped with expectation of receiving a Divine reward.

Maimonides.

He states that this commandment also prohibits the testing of any of God's commandments in order to determine the reward upon their fulfillment. The sole exceptions, he states, are the laws of the tithes and those of *tzedakah* (charity).

Kimchi.

He holds that this commandment also prohibits a person from exposing himself to mortal danger and expecting God to perform a miracle to save him (c.f. 1 Samuel, 16:2, Kimchi).

Saadia Gaon.

He holds that it is forbidden to question whether God is able to accomplish a specific deed, but that it is permissible for a person to ask God for a sign indicating whether he is doing that which is right in God's eyes and thus is worthy of God's blessings and bounty.

If You Want to Learn More

See Talmud *Shabbat* 53b; Talmud *Nedarim* 62a; *Sefer Mitzvot Gadol*, negative commandment 4; *Sefer HaHinnuch*, commandment 424.

9. Walking in God's Ways

"What does God require of you . . . to walk in all of His ways?" (Deuteronomy 10:12).

i. By this *mitzvah* we are commanded to be like God as far as it is in our power.

ii. *Imitatio dei* ("imitation of God") is a theological slogan used by the early Church Fathers. It asks of man (the highest form of animal) to act like God by imitating God's attributes (e.g., be a loving person, a merciful person, and so forth, just as God is a loving and merciful God).

iii. The Talmud (*Sotah* 14a) comments as follows in its interpretation of "walking in God's ways":

> Just as the Holy One, blessed be He, clothes the naked (i.e., Adam and Eve, Genesis 3:21), so should a person clothe the naked; just as the Holy One, blessed be He, visits the sick (i.e., God and Abraham, Genesis 18:3), so should a person visit the sick; just as the Holy One, blessed be He, comforts the mourners (i.e., Isaac, Genesis 25:11), so should a person comfort the mourners; just as the Holy One, blessed be He, buries the dead (i.e., Moses, Deuteronomy 34:6), so should a person bury the dead.

Commentators

Maimonides.

Maimonides interprets the commandment of "walking in God's ways" as one of the fundamental teachings of Judaism. Since man was made in God's image, the supreme duty of all of humankind is to make one's ways like those of God, the Creator and Source of all beings. Maimonides also interprets the precept of "walking in God's ways" as an invitation to avoid extremes. That is to say, a person should avoid being overly angry yet not be indifferent to what is happening, a person should be moderate in his spending, and so forth.

Ibn Ezra.

Ibn Ezra concentrates his interpretation on the very phrase "to walk" (in God's ways), which is a word of action. Thus, for Ibn Ezra, to walk in God's ways means to put God's ways and attributes into deeds of action. Simply believing in God is not sufficient, as God requires the active participation of His creation in the improvement of the world.

Abrabanel.

He states that if a person were to literally "walk" in God's ways, he or she would abstain from food, drink, and all other bodily functions, since God is a God of total spirit. Of course this approach would be life-threatening to people. Therefore, to walk in God's ways must mean to perform one's daily activities in a Godlike manner rather than simply following one's primitive, animal instincts.

If You Want to Learn More

See Talmud *Sukkah* 45b; Talmud *Sotah* 14a; Maimonides, *Book of Commandments,* positive commandment 8.

10, 11. Fearing and Serving God

"You shall fear the Lord your God, and serve Him" (Deuteronomy 10:20).

i. Fear of God has usually been interpreted to mean having a sense of awe and supreme regard for God. In the popular idiom, to say that one has fear of God is usually another way of defining a pious Jew who is convinced that he or she is fulfilling the will of God in performing God's commandments.

ii. The idea that religion is the foundation of all wisdom is frequently expressed by the rabbinic sages of Israel. "Fear of God is the beginning of wisdom" (Psalms 111:10).

iii. "Serving God" has been interpreted in rabbinic literature to mean prayer, because it is through prayer that one serves his God through his heart. That is why prayer has often been called in liturgical writing the service of the heart. (*Sifre* to Deuteronomy 11:13).

iv. Some rabbinic sources say that to "serve God" means to study the Law.

v. The rabbis said that a man is obligated to pray to God three times a day: in the morning, afternoon, and evening. These three prayers were instituted to correspond to the sacrificial offerings in the ancient sanctuary, which took place three times daily.

Commentators

Hinnuch.

He makes several observations regarding the rationale of prayer: prayer is not only a means of acquiring things in life that we desire but it is also a way of acknowledging that there is only One God who can grant us things that we seek and to whom we can turn in prayer to obtain them.

Recanti.

He states that when a person reaches the heights of total commitment to God and that person's love knows no bounds, then he will rise to fear God. For Recanti, fear of God is on a higher plane than the love for God.

Abraham Joshua Heschel.

He states that the beginning of awe is wonder, and that the beginning of wisdom is awe. For Heschel, when a person realizes that God is the foundation of the world, that person will be overwhelmed by a sense of awe and the holiness of God. Thus, Heschel believes that the awe of God is almost equivalent to the word *religion* itself.

Maimonides.

He connects the commandment to believe in the fear and awe of God with punishment, which is an integral part of the faith of Israel. He says that fearing God means that a person ought never to be at ease and self-confident but should always expect God's punishment at all times.

With regard to serving God, Maimonides believes that this means to pray to God with proper devotion (*kavanah,* in Hebrew). For Maimonides, prayer without devotion is no prayer at all, and a person who has prayed undevotedly is under the obligation to recite the prayers again. Maimonides reminds us that pious people waited an hour before saying their prayers and an hour after completing them, in order to always maintain the proper frame of mind.

If You Want to Learn More

See Talmud *Pesachim* 22b; Talmud *Shabbat* 31a, 31b; Maimonides, *Book of Commandments,* positive commandments 4, 5; *Code of Jewish Law, Orach Chayyim,* 89; *Sefer HaHinnuch,* commandments 432, 433; Abraham Joshua Heschel, *Between God and Man,* ch. 5.

12. Cleaving to God

"To God shall you cleave" (Deuteronomy 10:20).

i. Since God has no bodily substance, the only way in which a person can cleave to God is by imitating God's own attributes.

ii. The way to learn God's attributes is by selected knowledgeable and saintly teachers (Talmud *Ketubot* 111b).

iii. The rabbis use the words "To God you shall cleave" as proof that it is one's duty to marry a wise man's daughter, to give one's own daughter in marriage to a wise man, to confer benefits on wise men, and to conduct business with them.

iii. For mystics, the way to cling to God is through the use of the most efficacious meditations during prayer. They interpret the concept of *devekut* (cleaving to God) as the highest step on the spiritual ladder, which is reached after the believer has mastered the attitudes of fear and love of God.

iv. According to Chasidism, *devekut* should be the believer's constant state of mind, even while he is dealing with everyday necessities of life and not only during the high points of prayer and other religious activity.

Commentators

Maimonides.

It is impossible, says Maimonides, for a person to cling to a God who has no body and who is all spirit. Therefore, what must be meant by this commandment is that a person should always seek out and cling to people who are most likely to preach godliness, such as rabbis and judges. One must try to join them in every possible manner of fellowship, including eating, drinking, and business affairs, for it is such wise people who are regarded by Maimonides as being nearest to God.

Nachmonides.

Disagreeing with the rationale of Maimonides, he states that the significance of this commandment is that a person should be so motivated to perform the commandments (a form of clinging to God) and so ready to swear by God's name that he will fulfill his resolution.

Alshech.

Sinners often flee from God in order to escape their guilty conscience. The most effective corrective to this is to cleave to God and to have some of God's virtue become a fabric of their own selves.

Recanti.

Like Maimonides, he, too, believes that clinging to God means to cling to a teacher who lives always by God's teachings. By doing this, a person comes as close as possible to clinging to God.

If You Want to Learn More

See Talmud *Ketubot* 111b; Talmud *Pesachim* 49a; Maimonides, *Book of Commandments,* positive commandment 6; *Sefer HaHinnuch,* commandment 434.

13. Swearing in God's Name

"In God's name you shall swear" (Deuteronomy 10:20).

   i. This commandment is generally understood to mean that when people are required to confirm or deny something, they are to do so only by God's name.

   ii. One must never casually make a vow or promise since God's name is behind it.

   iii. There was rabbinic concern that if oath taking became too frequent an occurrence by any person, that God's name would be used flippantly. Accordingly, the practice of swearing by God's name before a Jewish court of law was slowly phased out and another type of an oath was substituted.

   iv. Rabbinic opinion always considered it commendable to take an oath to serve as a strong motivator in the performance of a commandment.

Commentators

Hinnuch.

Whenever any person speaks out on an important issue, that person should use God's name. In this way a person always becomes accountable to God, and the precept helps strengthen one's faith in God and in God's providence.

Maimonides.

He holds that it is every person's duty to use God's name when taking an oath because this adds to the sanctity and weight of the words and becomes, in a sense, a declaration of faith.

Nachmonides.

He disagrees with Maimonides and states that few people are able to attain the degree of holiness and piety needed in order to invoke God's name with the proper reverence. Therefore, swearing in God's name ought to be avoided whenever possible.

Bachya ibn Asher.

He discusses the impropriety of swearing by God's name. However, he states that at times it may be necessary to do so in order to clearly show the purposeful intention of the oath.

Ibn Ezra.

He contends that one must cling to God not only in deed but also in belief and faith.

If You Want to Learn More

See Talmud *Nedarim* 10b; Talmud *Sanhedrin* 63a, 63b; Maimonides, *Book of Commandments,* positive commandment 7; *Sefer Mitzvot Gadol,* positive commandment 123; *Code of Jewish Law, Yoreh De'ah,* 237; *Sefer HaHinnuch,* commandment 435.

Section II: Torah

1. Wearing a Tallit *(Prayer Shawl)*

"Make fringes in the corners of your garments throughout their generations" (Numbers 15:38).

    i. The wearing of a prayer shawl (*tallit*) in the synagogue is derived from this verse, which bids people to put fringes on the corners of their garments. The *tallit* is worn during the day because the Torah employs the words, "you shall see it."

    ii. Traditionally, a *tallit* is worn by Jewish males thirteen years and older (and some Jewish women who choose to do so) during the morning services. In many Orthodox synagogues it is the custom that only married men wear a *tallit.*

    iii. Once a year, on the evening of Yom Kippur (the Day of Atonement), the *tallit* is worn to add the aura of sanctity to the occasion.

iv. During the reading of the third paragraph of the *Shema* (Numbers 15:37–40), it is traditional to gather the four corners of the *tallit,* called the *tzitzit* or fringes, and kiss them when the Hebrew word, *tzitzit,* is read. Likewise, when called to the Torah, it is customary to touch the first word of the passage to be read with the *tzitzit,* which one then kisses before reciting the Torah blessing.

v. A *tallit* may be made of linen, wool, or silk, and the fringes are generally made of the same material as the *tallit.*

vi. The Torah commands that a thread of *techalet* (blue) be attached to each fringe. This was made from an expensive blue dye that was extracted from an aquatic sea mollusk. The use of this dye ceased during the rabbinic period because the formula for obtaining the exact shade of blue was lost. One can still purchase today fringes with the blue dye, the claim being that a cousin of the extinct aquatic animal has been rediscovered.

vii. In addition to the prayer shawl being worn during actual prayer services, there is a practice among traditional Jewish men to wear a small *tallit,* called a *tallit katan,* under their clothing at all times.

viii. The rabbis, playing on the numerical value of Hebrew letters, arrive at the conclusion that the five letters of the Hebrew word *tzitzit* amount to 600, which, with the 8 threads and the 5 knots on each fringe, make for a total of 613, the exact number of commandments in the Torah.

ix. When putting on a *tallit,* it is customary to recite Psalms 104:1–2: "Bless God, O my soul: God, you are very great. You are clothed in glory and majesty, wrapped in a robe of light; You spread the heavens like a tent cloth." The following blessing is then recited:

בָּרוּךְ אַתָּה יְיָ אֱלֹהֵינוּ מֶלֶךְ הָעוֹלָם אֲשֶׁר קִדְּשָׁנוּ בְּמִצְוֹתָיו
וְצִוָּנוּ לְהִתְעַטֵּף בַּצִּיצִית:

Baruch atah Adonai elohaynu melech ha'olam asher kid-shanu bemitzvotav vetzivanu l'hitatef ba'tzitzit.

Praised are You, Adonai our God, Sovereign of the Universe, who has made us holy with *mitzvot* and instructed us to wrap ourselves with *tzitzit.*

The neckpiece (the "atara" in Hebrew) of the *tallit* is then kissed and the *tallit* is put on.

Commentators

Keli Yakar.

He holds that the blue threads of the fringes are to be a symbolic reminder of the waters of the sea. This teaches people the moral lesson that just as the ocean must stay within certain defined boundaries (otherwise, flooding and disaster may occur), so, too, a Jew must live by the defined bounds of the *mitzvot*.

Nachmonides.

He holds that the blue threads of the *tzizit* are a constant reminder of the blue sky, and the sky is to be a reminder to the Jew of God in the heavens above. Thus, wearing a *tallit* is a reminder that there is a Heavenly Parent above.

Or HaChayyim.

The author contends that just as the *tallit* has four *tzizit* on its four corners, so, too, the Jew is to be reminded that God is omnipresent and rules the four corners of the world.

Alshech.

Interestingly, the Alshech uses the custom of a person tying a string around one's finger as a memory device in his explanation of the rationale for wearing a prayer shawl. He states that when a person mindlessly ties string around his finger, it serves no purpose. However, if one uses string around one's finger as a true reminder, then that string serves a purpose and has an authentic significance. Similarly, one who wears a *tallit* must always be cognizant of the fact that the fringes on the corners are symbolic of commandments. If that be the case, then the prayer shawl will truly serve its real purpose, that of a memory device to perform God's commandments.

Maimonides.

He states that the windings around each of the fringes of the prayer shawl (7, 8, 11, and 13) have the number value of 39, which happens to correspond to the number value of the Hebrew words *Adonai Echad,* meaning "God is One." Thus, when one looks at the fringe one is constantly reminded that God is One God, a fundamental principle of Judaism.

Hinnuch.

He states that this commandment serves to remind people that a person's body and soul belong to God. He bases this upon a symbolic interpretation of the colors blue and white, which are, in the Bible, associated with the fringes of the prayer shawl, The white signifies the body, while the blue thread is symbolic of the soul.

If You Want to Learn More

See Talmud *Menachot* 39a, 39b, 43b, 44a; Talmud *Sukkah* 9a; Maimonides, *Mishneh Torah,* chapter on the Laws of *Tzitzit;* Maimonides, *Book of Commandments,* positive commandment 14; *Code of Jewish Law, Orach Chayyim,* ch. 8; *Sefer HaHinnuch,* commandment 386.

2, 3. Reading the Shema *and Teaching One's Children Torah*

"And you shall teach them diligently to your children, speaking of them when you lie down, and when you rise up" (Deuteronomy 6:7).

i. The prayer the *Shema* ("Hear O Israel, the Lord is Our God, the Lord is One") is the basic declaration of the faith of the Jewish people. It proclaims the oneness and unity of God.

ii. According to rabbinic tradition, the study of the Torah and its transmission to one's children is considered one of the most important commandments. For example, the Mishneh states: "These are the things whose fruits a person enjoys in this world while the capital remains for the person in the world to come: honoring parents, acts of loving-kindness[,] . . . making peace between a person and one's friend. But the study of the Torah surpasses them all" (Talmud *Pe'ah* 1:1).

iii. The *Shema* prayer was always on the lips of Jewish martyrs. For example, Rabbi Akiba endured the greatest torture while his flesh was being torn with iron combs. He purportedly died with the words of this prayer on his lips.

iv. According to the rabbis, when a child is old enough to begin to speak, he ought to be instructed in the teachings of the Torah. (Talmud *Sukkah* 42a) Traditionally, it was the father's responsibility to teach his son Torah, but usually a teacher was hired or students were sent to a local *cheder* (one-room schoolhouse).

v. So great was the importance of teaching one's children Torah that we find the illustrious Chizkiah, King of Judah, carrying his own children on his own shoulders to study the Torah (Talmud *Berakhot* 10b).

Commentators

Saadia Gaon.

He held that the best way to teach Torah was in an attractive manner, which includes the methodology of storytelling.

Abrabanel.

Playing on the Hebrew word *veshinantem* ("you shall teach"), he states that this Hebrew word derives from the word *shnayim,* meaning "two." Thus, Abrabanel reasons that it is only possible to teach Torah if one teaches it over and over again. This is the only way in which it can be truly understood.

Hinnuch.

He holds that the reason why rabbinic tradition stated that the *Shema* must be recited in the morning and in the evening is to allow the worshipper to show his or her acceptance of God's sovereignty every day and night. A person needs to accept God constantly in order to be reminded that God is watching him and will always guard him from committing a sin.

Maimonides.

He states that this commandment, which commands us to teach and learn, is extremely useful, for without wisdom there cannot be any good act or any true and authentic knowledge. Maimonides also associates the study of Torah with the Messianic Age when, he believes, people will be free to study the Torah without any interference whatsoever.

If You Want to Learn More

See Talmud *Kiddushin* 29b, 30a; Talmud *Sanhedrin* 7b, 24a; Talmud *Chullin* 89a; Talmud *Berakhot* 2a, 2b, 4b, 5a, 47b, 63b; Talmud *Shabbat* 119b; Maimonides, *Book of Commandments,* positive commandments 10, 11; *Sefer HaHinnuch,* commandments 419, 420; *Code of Jewish Law, Yoreh De'ah,* 246; *Code of Jewish Law, Orach Chayyim,* 61.

4, 5. Wearing Tefillin (Phylacteries)

"And you shall bind them for a sign on your hand, and they shall be for frontlets between your eyes" (Deuteronomy 6:8).

i. The word *tefillin* is usually translated by the Greek term "phylacteries," which means amulets, but *tefillin* are not amulets. Rather, they are small black leather boxes containing parchment upon which verses speaking of binding on one's arm and forehead are written. (The verses cited are from Exodus 13:9, 13:16, and Deuteronomy 6:8, 11:8.)

ii. Centuries ago, *tefillin* were worn all day and removed at night. Today, *tefillin* are worn during the morning service on weekdays. They are not worn on the Sabbath or festivals. One reason given for this is that *tefillin* are referred to as being an *ot*, a "sign," and since the Sabbath is also a sign of God's covenant with Israel, to wear *tefillin* on that day would be considered superfluous.

iii. The head box of the *tefillin* has the Hebrew letter *shin* inscribed on one side of it and a four-branched *shin* on the opposite side. The letter *shin* stands for *Shaddai*, one of the biblical names of God. When the *tefillin* strap is wrapped around the arm and hand in the correct way, the Hebrew letters in the word *Shaddai* are formed.

iv. *Tefillin* are put on after the *tallit* is put on. The *tefillin* of the arm are always wrapped on one's weaker arm (seven wraps are made around the forearm), and the following blessing is said:

בָּרוּךְ אַתָּה יְיָ אֱלֹהֵינוּ מֶלֶךְ הָעוֹלָם אֲשֶׁר קִדְּשָׁנוּ בְּמִצְוֹתָיו
וְצִוָּנוּ לְהָנִיחַ תְּפִלִּין:

Praised are You, Adonai our God, Ruler of the Universe, who has made us holy by Your *mitzvot* and commanded us to put on *tefillin*.

Next, the *tefillin* of the head are put on and the following blessing recited:

בָּרוּךְ אַתָּה יְיָ אֱלֹהֵינוּ מֶלֶךְ הָעוֹלָם אֲשֶׁר קִדְּשָׁנוּ בְּמִצְוֹתָיו
וְצִוָּנוּ עַל מִצְוַת תְּפִלִּין:

Praised are You, Adonai our God, Ruler of the Universe, who has made us holy by Your *mitzvot* and who gave us the *mitzvah* of *tefillin*.

Finally, the leather straps are wrapped around the hand and middle finger while the words of the Prophet Hosea (2:21–22) are recited:

וְאֵרַשְׂתִּיךְ לִי לְעוֹלָם. וְאֵרַשְׂתִּיךְ לִי בְּצֶדֶק וּבְמִשְׁפָּט וּבְחֶסֶד
וּבְרַחֲמִים: וְאֵרַשְׂתִּיךְ לִי בֶּאֱמוּנָה, וְיָדַעַתְּ אֶת־יְיָ:

Thus says God: I will betroth you to Me forever. I will betroth you
with righteousness, justice, with love and with compassion. I will
betroth you to Me with faithfulness, and you shall love God.

Commentators

Abrabanel.

He comments that the arm and head straps of the *tefillin* are visual reminders that we must bind ourselves and dedicate ourselves to God. This
memory device will keep people on the proper track rather than allow
them to follow their evil inclination.

Recanti.

He states that just as God has chosen the people of Israel to be His unique
and treasured nation, so, too, by inserting the *Shema* prayer in the *tefillin*
boxes we acknowledge our pride in the One and Unique God, thus reminding ourselves to always serve Him with all of our heart and soul.

Hinnuch.

He states that man is composed of flesh and blood, and thus is subject to the
many lusts of his evil inclination. But man also possesses a soul, which can
help deter a person from evilness. Sometimes a person's soul can become
weak, especially when one's bodily lusts overwhelm him. One of the
purposes of the *mitzvah* of wearing *tefillin* is to help guard and protect
one's soul, and to assist it in fighting against the evil inclination of one's
sensual lusts.

Joseph Karo.

The position of the *tefillin* against the heart, symbolizing the seat of a
person's emotions, and against the brain, symbolizing the senses of the

soul, indicates the worshipper's desire for complete self-subjugation to the service of God.

Maimonides.

He quotes Rabbi Eliezer the Great, who said (Talmud *Chullin* 89a) that this verse, "And all of the people of the earth shall see that the name of God is called upon you" (Deuteronomy 28:10), refers to the head *tefillin*. Thus, the observance of this commandment constitutes a proclamation before "the people of the earth" that God's Name is called upon Israel. Maimonides also says that the sanctity of *tefillin* is very great, and as long as the *tefillin* are on the head and arm of a man, he will be modest and God-fearing and will devote his thoughts to truth and righteousness.

If You Want to Learn More

See Talmud *Menachot* 35b, 36a, 42b, 43a; Talmud *Shabbat* 49a, 118b, 130a; Maimonides, *Book of Commandments,* positive commandments 12, 13; *Sefer Mitzvot Gadol,* positive commandments 21, 22; *Code of Jewish Law,* chs. 25–45; *Sefer HaHinnuch,* commandments 421, 422.

6. Affixing a Mezuzah

"And you shall write them upon the doorposts of your home and upon your gates" (Deuteronomy 6:9).

i. This commandment concerns the affixing of a *mezuzah* upon one's doorpost. The *mezuzah* served as the distinctive mark of the Jewish home. It consists of a small roll of parchment on which is written the prayer *Shema* and the two biblical passages concerning the love for God and His precepts (Deuteronomy 6:4–9, 11:13–21).

ii. The parchment is enclosed in a receptacle and fastened in a slanting position to the upper part of the doorpost on the right side of the entrance of each room, with the upper end of the case pointing inward and the lower one outward.

iii. The Hebrew word *Shaddai,* meaning God, is written on the back of the parchment and made visible through a small opening near the top of the case.

iv. Upon entering one's home and leaving it, it is customary to touch the *mezuzah* with the fingers and then kiss the fingers.

v. The attaching of a *mezuzah* to the doorpost is always accompanied with the following blessing:

בָּרוּךְ אַתָּה יְיָ אֱלֹהֵנוּ מֶלֶךְ הָעוֹלָם אֲשֶׁר קִדְּשָׁנוּ בְּמִצְוֹתָיו וְצִוָּנוּ
לִקְבּוֹעַ מְזוּזָה:

Praised are You, Adonai Our God, Ruler of the Universe who has made
us holy by Your *mitzvot* and commanded us to affix a *mezuzah*.

Commentators

Hinnuch.

For the Hinnuch, the *mezuzah* is a visual reminder of God's omnipresence
and the obligation to love God and always have faith in Him.

Recanti.

He holds that the *mezuzah* serves as a protection against evil messengers.
Whenever an evil spirit confronts the name of God which is usually on the
exterior of the *mezuzah,* the spirit will refrain from entering. The Recanti
contends that the word *mezuzah* itself is a combination of the Hebrew
words *mavet* and *zaz,* which mean "Death, remove yourself and go away."

Maimonides.

In contrast to Recanti, Maimonides declares that those who look upon the
mezuzah as an amulet to ward off evil spirits are ignorant, failing to
understand its real purpose which is to keep the Jew constantly aware of the
Divine Oneness and moral duties.

Abrabanel.

He states that there are gates and doorposts that belong to an individual and are
a part of that individual's home, while there are also national gates of the
Jewish national homeland. For Abrabanel, the purpose of the *mezuzah* is to
constantly remind the Jew of the gift of Israel, the Jewish national homeland.

Neil Gillman.

Neil Gillman, quoting one of his students, has expressed a connection
between "speed bumps," which are built to slow cars down in public

parking lots, and the *mezuzah,* which is a sort of speed bump. When a person enters or leaves a home and follows the custom of kissing the *mezuzah,* it allows just enough time for that person to slow down and always be reminded that the home one is entering or leaving is a sanctified one in which God is present.

If You Want to Learn More

See Talmud *Sukkah* 3b; Talmud *Berakhot* 15b; Maimonides, *Book of Commandments,* positive commandment 15; *Code of Jewish Law, Yoreh De'ah,* commandment 285; *Sefer HaHinnuch,* commandment 423.7.

7. *Prohibition against Adding or Subtracting from the Torah*

All these words which I command you, that you shall observe to do, you shall not add thereto nor diminish from it'' (Deuteronomy 13:1; see also Deuteronomy 4:2).

  i. It is entirely possible that this commanded was at first directed to the scribes, warning them to keep the Torah text exactly as they found it, with its mistakes in spelling, duplications, and sometimes almost incomprehensible passages.

  ii. This prohibition also warns against weakening the force of God's commandments by additions or omissions that would dilute its original meaning.

  iii. Special attention by rabbinic authorities was taken of the fact that Deuteronomy 4:2 was phrased in the plural while Deuteronomy 13:1 was phrased in the singular. Thus, the former was understood to be addressed to the leaders of the community, who were warned not to pass off their commandments and laws as equivalent to the Torah itself and to let the community of Israel know at all times which laws were from the Torah and which ones were of rabbinic nature. On the other hand, Deuteronomy 13:1 was seen to address itself to each individual, commanding each person to be complete in his or her own observance.

  iv. Still other authorities understood this negative commandment to prohibit changes in the number of the commandments, totaling 613. For these authorities, it meant that neither the number of commandments nor any of the details of each were to be tampered with.

  v. In time, although the written word of the Torah remained the same, rabbis interpreted the law and expanded upon it according to the needs of the time. Guidelines, of course, were created for each set of interpretations.

By the year 250 c.e., the Mishnah, the first rabbinic interpretation of the Torah, was completed by its editor, Judah the Prince. In the year 500 c.e., the Gemara (the interpretation of the Mishnah), was completed, thus forming what has become known as the Talmud (i.e., the Oral Law).

Commentators

Ibn Ezra.

He said that the purpose of this prohibition of adding or subtracting to the law was to prevent the possible danger of adding some innovation that would constitute a foreign form of illegal worship.

Maimonides.

He states that to add or diminish from the Torah would deny the permanent validity of its truths. Thus the prohibition to never add nor diminish from the Torah was declared.

Radbaz.

He states that this negative commandment relates to the alteration of the actual words of the text of the Torah. If one were to tamper with the text itself, the Torah would never again be the constant and supreme authority of the Jewish people.

Hinnuch.

He states that at the root of this precept lies the reason that God who commands us about the Torah is the very ultimate of perfection. That is to say, all of God's works and commands are wholly perfect and good. Any addition or subtraction to them is thus considered a defect, and in effect detracts from God's own perfection and goodness.

Joseph Karo.

He states that this commandment does not mean that the Torah's enactments could never be added to or modified as new conditions warranted change. They could, in fact, be modified, as long as the modifications were never proclaimed as new revelations on high.

Rashi.

He states in his commentary that Israel was not to invent additions to the laws, nor arbitrarily diminish from them (e.g., using five species on the festival of Sukkot instead of four or placing five fringes on the prayer shawl instead of the four).

If You Want to Learn More

See Talmud *Sanhedrin* 88b; Talmud *Megillah* 14a; Maimonides, *Book of Commandments,* negative commandments 313, 314; *Code of Jewish Law, Orach Chayyim,* 128; *Sefer HaHinnuch,* commandments 454, 455.

8. Blessing God for Our Food

"And you shall eat, and be satisfied and bless the Lord your God" (Deuteronomy 8:10).

i. This biblical verse is the basis for the commandment of reciting the blessing after the meals, which is known in Hebrew as *birkat hamazon.*

ii. The blessings after the meal consist of four blessings. According to a talmudic statement (Talmud *Berakhot* 48b), the first paragraph was composed by Moses, the second by Joshua, the third by Kings David and Solomon, and the fourth by the sages. The first praises God for providing food for all creatures, while the second expresses gratitude for the good land God gave us, for redemption from Egypt, for the covenant of circumcision and for the giving of the Torah. The third asks God to be merciful toward Israel and to restore the ancient Temple, while the fourth expresses thanks to God and includes petitions for Him to fulfill specific desires, such as blessing the house in which one has eaten and sending Elijah the Prophet.

iii. According to the rabbis, the *birkat hamazon* may be recited in any language. It is usually recited in Hebrew, and its recitation is restricted to a meal at which bread is eaten. If no bread is eaten, a special short form of the *birkat hamazon* is recited.

iv. Although the Bible indicates that the blessing after the meal must be recited only after one has been sated after enjoying a complete meal, the rabbis instituted the commandment that one must recite the after the meal blessing following the eating of anything the size of an olive or greater.

v. The duty of inviting the table companions to recite the *birkat hamazon* jointly is based on Psalms 34:4—"Exalt God with me, and let us extol God together."

vi. Some people remove utensils, especially knives, from the table before reciting the blessing after the meal. The reason for this is that one's table has often been compared to an altar, and the altar of the Temple was constructed of stones that were not hewn with tools. Since tools can be used as weapons, it was desirable that one's table should always be associated with peace.

Commentators

Hinnuch.

He asks the following questions: Why would God, the Source of all blessings, need people to bless Him for the food that they have eaten? What does God gain from people reciting these blessings in His honor? The Hinnuch answers that a complete person is one who not only thinks of his own welfare, but one who is concerned with all people. And so, too, it is with God. Praising God at a meal is merely a way of acknowledging that in God resides all blessings and that we must always turn to God for life's gifts and bounty.

Judah HaLevi.

He states that by blessing God, we double our enjoyment of the food.

Maimonides.

He states that the person who enjoys anything (including a meal) without a blessing commits a sacrilege. This is because, in not saying the blessing, a person fails to express his gratefulness to God for his food as well as other past favors to the people as a whole.

Baal Ha-Turim.

He holds to the opinion that a person should not only wait to bless God when one has eaten and has been satisfied, but that a person should eat and be satisfied precisely because a person has blessed God. Thus, for the Baal ha-Turim, the phrase, "and you shall bless," means that blessing ought to be felt before beginning to eat the meal. This prior blessing before the meal is necessary in order to transfer the food from God's possession (i.e., the creator of the food) to the possession of a person. The blessing itself is thus an expression of thankfulness for the transferring of title of the food from God over to man.

Joseph Hertz.

He states that thanking God for one's food raises the satisfaction of a physical craving into the realm of spirit. Eating is transformed into a religious act, and one's table is turned into one's family altar.

Simon Glustrom.

He states that just as a Jew is bidden to recite a blessing before partaking of a meal, so too he is required to praise God after he has been satisfied. Glustrom sees a psychological motivation for the requirement of reciting the blessing after the meal. A person who has eaten a meal is often quite prone to forget the source of his nourishment. This explains the commandment of the grace after the meal, which is even more praiseworthy than the blessing before the meal, since a person is even more likely to walk away from the table and forget to say it.

If You Want to Learn More

See Talmud *Berakhot* 20b, 21a, 48b, 49b; Talmud *Bava Metziah* 114a; Maimonides, *Book of Commandments,* positive commandment 27; *Sefer Mitzvot Katan,* positive commandment 19; *Sefer HaHinnuch,* positive commandment 430; Simon Glustrom, *Language of Judaism* (chapter on *Birkat Hamazon*).

9. Assembling on the Festival of Sukkot Every Seventh Year (Law of Hakhel)

"Gather all the people together, the men and the women and the little ones, and your sojourners" (Deuteronomy 31:12).

i. This *mitzvah,* known as the *mitzvah* of *hakhel* ("assembly"), refers to the people of Israel gathering at the end of every seven year cycle. The purpose of the assembly was that "they may hear and so learn to revere God and to observe faithfully every word of God's teaching (Deuteronomy 31:10–13).

ii. This ceremony is mentioned only once in the entire Talmud (*Sotah* 7:8), but in great detail. According to the description of the ceremony, a Torah scroll was presented to King Agrippa from the High Priest. The king, after pronouncing the appropriate prayer, read from the Book of Deuteronomy (chapters 1–6:10, 11:13–22, and 14:22–28.

iii. In recent years in Israel as well as in the United States there has been a attempt among several religious groups to revive a symbolic form of the *hakhel* ceremony.

Commentators

Nachmonides.

He was puzzled by the fact that the *hakhel* commandment included the attendance of very young children, who obviously would be too young to truly understand the meaning of the proceedings. Nachmonides answers that the attendance of the young is in keeping with rabbinic tradition to begin one's religious training at a young age. A youngster, even if he or she does not fully understand, can begin to ask questions. It is hoped that inspirational answers to the questions will continue to fuel the child's interest in Judaism.

Ibn Ezra.

Ibn Ezra's concern related to the invitation of the strangers to this large assembly. He believed that they may have been invited in an attempt to proselytize them, since there was always the possibility that the reading of the Torah would inspire them.

Hinnuch.

He states that at the root of the commandment of *hakhel* is the listening to the Torah, the spiritual essence of the Jewish people. It is fitting, he says, that all should assemble together at one time in this group experience to hear the words of the Torah. The collective experience of the group, including the performance of the king, would help to inspire the people to have even more of a yearning for knowledge of the Torah.

Keli Yakar.

He sees a symbolic connection between the gathering together of the people at the festival of Sukkot and the joining of the four species (the *etrog, lulav, hadassim,* and *aravot*) used in the festival. This joining symbolizes the importance of national unity of the people of Israel and interest in its social welfare. The gathering was purposefully held at the end of the sabbatical year, when all debts were canceled, in order to emphasize that the difficulties of any nation are often due to the greed of the wealthy who show little deference toward the less fortunate.

If You Want to Learn More

See Talmud *Sotah* 41a; Talmud *Chagigah* 3a; Maimonides, *Book of Commandments,* positive commandment 16; *Sefer HaHinnuch,* positive commandment 612.

10. Writing a Torah Scroll

"Now, therefore, write this song for me" (Deuteronomy 31:19).

i. This is the last and 613th commandment in the Bible. It requires of every Jew to write a Torah scroll, the holiest object in all of Jewish ritual.

ii. According to the rabbinic authorities, even if one had been given a Torah scroll by someone else, that person is nevertheless commanded to write one of his own.

iii. The writing of a Torah scroll must be done in accordance with the many regulations associated with it. Thus, it must be handwritten on parchment from a kosher animal.

Commentators

Maimonides.

Knowing the great difficulty and challenge of writing one's own scroll, he holds that if it is impossible for one to write it himself, one must either purchase one or hire a scribe to write it for him.

Ibn Ezra.

He contends that owning and using a Torah will help a person solve life's many problems that will pose themselves over the years.

Hinnuch.

He states that this commandment does not limit itself to writing or owning a Torah scroll. It also includes the purchase of other religious books, which ought to be a part of every Jewish home library.

If You Want to Learn More

See Talmud *Sanhedrin* 21b; Talmud *Shabbat* 104a; Talmud *Bava Metziah* 85b; Maimonides, *Book of Commandments,* positive commandment 18; *Code of Jewish Law, Yoreh De'ah),* ch. 270; *Sefer HaHinnuch,* commandment 613.

Section III: Temple and the Priests

1. Building a Sanctuary

"Then you shall make a Sanctuary for Me" (Exodus 25:8).

i. The portable sanctuary (in the form of a tent) was set up by Moses in the wilderness to accompany the Israelites on their wanderings. It was known as the *mishkan* (habitation) or the *ohel mo'ed* (tent of meeting).

ii. The *mishkan* consisted of an outer court, enclosed by curtains, and the sanctuary proper, which was divided by a hanging curtain into two chambers. The first chamber contained the table, the *menorah,* and the altar of incense. The second chamber, known as the Holy of Holies, was entered once a year by the High Priest on the Day of Atonement. The Ark of the Covenant, designed to hold the two stone tablets (i.e., containing the Ten Commandments), was the only object placed here.

iii. Four centuries later, King Solomon placed the Ark of the Covenant in the First Temple built in Jerusalem. It was destroyed in the year 586 B.C.E. by the Babylonians, rebuilt some years later, and again destroyed by the Romans in the year 70 A.D. It was during the first century of the common era that small synagogues began to emerge in Israel, taking the place of the great Jerusalem Temple.

Commentators

Maimonides.

He states that the main purpose of the sanctuary was to wean the people of Israel from idolatry and turn their attention toward the One and only God.

Hinnuch.

He was of the opinion that an omnipresent God does not require a specific place in which to reside and shine forth His glory. Rather, the purpose of the sanctuary was, not as a dwelling place for God, but rather as a place where people would come to worship and receive Divine inspiration. Such a holy place would serve to help purify and sanctify the thoughts of all those who gathered to worship there.

Kotzker Rebbe.

The Kotzker Rebbe was once asked: "Where does God dwell?" He replied: "Wherever you let God in." Thus, although God can, and does, dwell anywhere, it is entirely likely that a place such as a sanctuary can best inspire people who worship there to let God into their hearts, minds, and souls.

Ramban.

He believed that the purpose of the sanctuary was to bring God closer to the people so that the people could better be able to feel God's Presence. The worship of the golden calf by the Israelites jeopardized the intimacy of God's relationship with His people. Only after Moses' intercession and the peoples' repentance did God forgive them and ask that a sanctuary be built in which He would dwell.

Abrabanel.

He states that at the outset, God only commanded civil laws and not sacrificial laws. However, after the golden calf was fashioned God had a change of heart, especially when He saw the sinful ways of His people. It was then that God felt constrained to provide an antidote for their spiritual infirmity. The sacrifices that were to take place in God's sanctuary filled this function, each type for a particular offence.

Sforno.

He believed that the command to construct a sanctuary was a sort of afterthought, and that it was required only after the Jewish people fell from God's grace by building the golden calf. The purpose of the sanctuary was to allow the Jewish people entry once again into God's presence.

If You Want to Learn More

See Talmud *Sanhedrin* 16b, 20b; Talmud *Menachot* 110a; Maimonides, *Book of Commandments,* positive commandment 20; *Sefer Mitzvot Gadol,* positive commandment 163; *Sefer HaHinnuch,* commandment 95.

2. *Kindling the Menorah in the Sanctuary*

"Aaron and his sons shall tend the lamp" (Exodus 27:21).

i. This commandment relates to the seven branched candelabrum which was used in the portable sanctuary (*mishkan*) set up by Moses in the wilderness as well as in the Jerusalem Temple.

ii. The priests were obligated to tend the lights of the *menorah* both morning as well as in the evening.

iii. According to tradition, only the center lamp was left burning all day. It was called the western lamp (*ner hama'aravi* in Hebrew) because it was placed next to the branches on the east side.

iv. In synagogues today, the eternal light usually hanging near or atop the Ark has replaced the center lamp of the ancient *menorah*.

Commentators

Maimonides.

Ignoring the details of its manufacture, he holds that the *menorah* was placed in the sanctuary in front of the curtain in order to enhance the glory and splendor of the House of God. For an abode illuminated by a continual light concealed by a curtain makes a deep psychological impact.

Hinnuch.

Like Maimonides, he, too, ignores the details of the *menorah*. Rather, he states that it enhances the glory of the sanctuary through its ability to illuminate. The ultimate idea underlying this is to inculcate awe and humility.

Abrabanel.

Unlike Maimonides and the Hinnuch, Abrabanel seeks meaning in the details of the manufacturing of the *menorah*. He states that the table, the altar of incense, and the *menorah* symbolize that though a person worships God without thought of reward, God will not begrudge a person the reward for his actions. There are two kinds of reward—material (wealth and honor), corresponding to the table and shewbread, and the reward of wisdom and attaining great spiritual heights. The *menorah* symbolized this. The lamp of God is the soul of man. The seven lamps symbolize the seven degrees of wisdom to be found in the Divine law. All the lamps turned inward to the middle one, towards the Holy of Holies, symbolizing that true wisdom must harmonize with the fundamentals of the Torah, housed in the Ark. The *menorah* was to be made of pure gold, implying that wisdom must not be tainted by alien ideas.

Alshech.

He also has an allegorical interpretation of the *menorah*. He says that the *menorah* symbolizes man, who is like a lamp, ready to give light with the help of God, through Torah and good works. It is therefore eighteen handbreadths high, the height of a medium-sized man. Though formed of gross matter, man should make himself pure and free of dross and sin like pure gold. Man can only become a lamp of pure gold through the cleansing and refining effect of suffering. This is what the expression, "beaten work," in the Torah alludes to. The *menorah* was made of one piece and not of separate ones pieced together, symbolizing the unity of all man's parts and meaning that one should not defile the others and be different in quality from the rest.

Keli Yakar.

He says that the *menorah* symbolized the radiance and splendor that enters any person's life who commits to God and to the study of the Torah.

If You Want to Learn More

See Talmud *Arakhin* 16a; Talmud *Zevachim* 19a, 88b, 95a; Maimonides, *Book of Commandments,* positive commandment 33, negative commandments 87, 88; *Sefer HaHinnuch,* commandments 99–101.

3. Priestly Vestments

"And you shall make holy garments [for Aaron]" (Exodus 28:2).

i. The commandments to don priestly garments are addressed exclusively to Aaron or concern him and his sons.

ii. There were three types of priestly clothing worn by them during the Temple service. The vestments of the "ordinary" priest consisted of a coat, breeches, a hat, and a girdle. The vestments of the High Priest (*Kohen Gadol*) consisted of the same four garments worn by the ordinary priest, with the one exception that the High Priest wore a miter and not a hat. In addition, the High Priest wore a breastplate with the name of God placed within it and an *ephod* (apron) attached to the breastplate. He also wore a woolen robe (*me'il*) and a golden diadem (*tzitzit*) on which were inscribed the Hebrew words, *kodesh l'Adonai* ("Holy unto God").

iii. If a priest failed to wear the correct garments, his service was invalidated and he was subject to punishment.

Commentators

Nachmonides:

He compares the garments of the priests to those worn by royalty. Thus, for the Ramban, their function was to enhance the dignity and prestige of the wearer and his sacred office in the eyes of the people.

Benno Jacob.

He discusses the role of clothing in society as conceived in the Torah. God provided Adam and Eve with clothing when He created them. Thus, clothing has, since this time, always constituted the primary distinguishing mark of human society. Accordingly, the commandment to priests to wear these special vestments was intended to consecrate them and sanctify them so that they may be better able to minister to God.

Hinnuch.

He states that the special priestly garments were intended to always remind the priest of his sacred duty to perform in the Temple.

Abrabanel.

He saw a symbolism in each of the four basic garments:

   a. The shirt: This garment was worn next to the body to remind the priest that every act that he performed needed to be pure and holy.
   b. The breeches: These were intended to cover up the private parts.
   c. The girdle: This garment, which held up the priest's breeches, was to remind the priest of his duty to "gird" against the evil which he might encounter.
   d. The hat: This was a reminder of God above.
   e. The *ephod,* worn by the High Priest, symbolized the unity of the Jewish people.
   f. The *me'il* had golden bells around its bottom, which reminded the priest that God hears everything always.
   g. The diadem and the breastplate with God's name symbolized the proclamation of truth.

If You Want to Learn More

See Talmud *Sotah* 48b; Talmud *Zevachim* 19a, 88b; Talmud *Shabbat* 139b; Maimonides, *Book of Commandments,* positive commandment 33, negative commandments 87, 88; *Sefer Mitzvah Gadol,* positive commandment 173; *Sefer HaHinnuch,* commandments 99–101.

4. Burning of Incense in Temple

"On the golden altar the Priest must burn the incense" (Exodus 30:7).

i. The golden altar was the place where the priest burned incense twice a day, once in the morning and once at night.

ii. During the burning of the incense the priest sprinkled incense (made from eleven different ingredients) on the hot, glowing coals.

iii. Sweet incense was used extensively as an element in the Jerusalem Temple worship. Its use was probably due to the worshipper's desire to honor God by offering to Him what he enjoyed himself. It also served to counteract the smell of burning flesh and blood when animal sacrifices were offered in the courts of the *mishkan* and the Temple.

iv. In Judaism today the fragrance of incense and spices has survived only in the ceremony known as Havdalah, which separates the departing Sabbath from the weekday experience. A spice box is passed around for everyone to smell and remember the sweet savor of the spices as a symbol of the fragrance of the day of rest.

Commentators

Hinnuch.

He stated that the purpose of the incense was to have its sweet scent lead the priests to more holy thoughts that would be more conducive for worship.

George Mendenhall.

He suggested that the main function of the incense was to hide the presence of God, for in Leviticus 16:2 it states that God appeared "in a cloud over the cover of the Ark," and in verse 13 it further elaborates, "He shall put the incense on the fire before God, so that the cloud from the incense screens the cover lest he die." According to Mendenhall, the incense was to represent, in the postwilderness days, the pillar of cloud in which God had descended upon the Tent, which had been God's "mask." Thus, the incense was to the Israelites a means of assuring that God could not be seen.

Keli Yakar.

His concern was the reason why the incense offering was made by the priest both in the morning and in the evening. He answered that morning represents the birth of man and evening represents man's death. This is to ensure, metaphorically, that man is born free of guilt and is also free of guilt when he dies and his soul returns to God.

Abrabanel.

He contends that according to one tradition, when pounding the eleven ingredients together to make the incense, the priest worked the rhythm of a unique chant. Doing this work to rhythmic music would result in a better and more evenly united compound of spices.

Maimonides.

He took a very practical view of the burning of the incense, and he believed that since many animals were slaughtered daily in the holy place, the stench of the place would be like that of a slaughterhouse. The sweet smell of the burning incense on the altar was therefore a deterrent to the odor of the animals, thus producing a more respectful ambiance to the sanctuary.

If You Want to Learn More

See Talmud *Menachot* 49b, 50a, 50b; Talmud *Pesachim* 59a; Maimonides, *The Guide of the Perplexed,* pt. 3, sect. 45; Maimonides, *Book of Commandments,* positive commandment 28, negative commandments 81, 85; *Code of Jewish Law, Yoreh De'ah,* 265, sect. 11; *Sefer HaHinnuch,* commandments 103–105; George Mendenhall, *The Tenth Generation,* p. 212.

5. Washing of Hands of the Priests

"And Aaron and his sons shall wash their hands and their feet and the laver" (Exodus 30:19).

i. The washing of the hands and feet of the priests was performed daily, both in the morning and in the evening before they entered the sanctuary.

ii. In modern times, many traditional Jews continue to wash their hands before meals while reciting the special benediction over the washing of the hands:

בָּרוּךְ אַתָּה יְיָ אֱלֹהֵינוּ מֶלֶךְ הָעוֹלָם, אֲשֶׁר קִדְּשָׁנוּ בְּמִצְוֹתָיו,
וְצִוָּנוּ עַל נְטִילַת יָדָיִם.

Praised are You, Adonai our God, who has made us holy by Your *mitzvot* and commanded us to wash our hands.

Commentators

Hinnuch.

He states that the cleansing of the hands by the priests was a way of making great the glory of the Temple, since the priests always washed their hands before performing their divine work.

Nachmonides.

He saw in the washing of the hands both a symbolic act of purification as well as the practical purpose of priests washing their hands (and feet, too) to remove dirt and dust.

Rashi.

He states that the washing of the hands of the priest was their way of sanctifying themselves thus allowing them to proceed in officiating in their holy tasks.

If You Want to Learn More

See Talmud *Sanhedrin* 83b; Talmud *Yoma* 28a, 32b; Talmud *Sanhedrin* 83a; Maimonides, *Book of Commandments,* positive commandment 24; *Sefer HaHinnuch,* commandment 106.

6. Respect for the Sanctuary

"You shall have reverence for my sanctuary" (Leviticus 19:30).

i. The visitation of the Israelites to the sanctuary was an opportunity for the Israelites to commune with God. As such, their behavior had to be respectful.

ii. It was forbidden to dirty the Temple floor or to use the grounds of the Temple as a shortcut in order to reach some other destination.

iii. In ancient times, one would enter the Temple grounds from the right hand side and depart from the left. One always moved toward the exit walking backward, so as to never turn one's back on the Holy of Holies.

iv. Today the synagogue has become the substitute for the ancient Temple sanctuary. Many laws have developed over the years concerning proper synagogue etiquette. All are intended to maintain respectfulness and a feeling of reverential awe for the worshipper.

Commentators

Maimonides.

He states that when a person receives a feeling of awe as a result of the beauty of the Temple, he or she will be more likely to want to carry out God's commandments.

Hinnuch.

He states that proper respect for the sanctuary would help to purify the thoughts of the people and to rectify and perfect the hearts and minds of the people toward God.

Abarbanel.

He says that there is a close correlation between the person who accepts God's commandments and one who stands in awe while in a sanctuary.

If You Want to Learn More

See Talmud *Yevamot* 6b; Talmud *Berakhot* 62b; Maimonides, *The Guide of the Perplexed*, pt. 3, sect. 45; Maimonides, *Book of Commandments*, positive commandment 21; *Code of Jewish Law, Orach Chayyim*, 151; *Sefer HaHinnuch*, commandment 254.

7. Priestly Blessing

"You shall bless the children of Israel and you shall say to them: May God bless you and keep you; may God shine His face on you and be gracious to you. May God lift up His countenance on you and give you peace" (Numbers 6:23–26).

i. The priestly blessing was part of the daily service at the Temple. Each morning and evening the priests raised their hands aloft and pronounced the priestly blessing from a special platform.

ii. Today in traditional synagogues, the priests remove their shoes, wash their hands, and ascend the platform in front of the Ark. Then they face the congregation and with fingers stretched in a symbolic arrangement underneath the prayer shawl covering their face, they repeat the priestly blessing, word for word, after the cantor.

iii. Today in Reform, Conservative, and Reconstructionist synagogues, the pronouncement of the blessings is no longer restricted to the priests. Rabbis now often conclude various ritual occasions, services, or weddings with this blessing.

iv. There is a custom for parents to bless their children every Friday evening. For sons, the blessing is, "May God make you like Ephraim and Menasseh." Daughters are blessed with the formula, "May God make you like Sarah, Rebecca, Rachel, and Leah." For both sons and daughters, the conclusion of the blessing is the priestly blessing (Numbers 6:23–26).

Commentators

Bachya ibn Pekuda.

He states that the first blessing has three words, the second five, and the third seven. This is to remind us of the foundation for all blessings: the three Patriarchs, the Five Books of Moses, and the seven Heavens.

Hinnuch.

He states that at the root of this precept lies the reason that in His great goodness, God desires to bless His people through the ministering servants who stay constantly in the Temple. It is due to their merit that the blessing would take effect for them.

Joseph Hertz.

He comments that the priestly blessing consists of three short verses of three, five, and seven words, respectively. Thus, the blessing mounts by gradual stages from the petition for material blessing and protection to that for divine favor as a spiritual blessing, and in a beautiful climax culminates in the petition for God's most important gift of peace, the welfare in which all material and spiritual well-being is comprehended.

Rashi.

He explains the first part of the threefold blessing as follows: "Keep you" means that plunderers should not come and take your property. He who gives a gift to his slave cannot safeguard it from everyone and if robbers come and take it what benefit has he therefrom? But God both gives and stands guard. Rashi explains the second part of the blessing (i.e., God lifts up His face) to mean that God will remove His anger.

If You Want to Learn More

See Talmud *Ketubot* 24b; Talmud *Berakhot* 20b; Talmud *Chullin* 49a; Talmud *Menachot* 18a; Maimonides, *Book of Commandments,* positive commandment 26; *Code of Jewish Law, Orach Chayyim,* 128; *Sefer HaHinnuch,* commandment 378.

Section IV: Festivals

1. Sanctification of the New Moon

"This month shall be for your the beginning of months; it shall be for you the first month of the year" (Exodus 12:2).

   i. Unlike the secular (Gregorian) calendar, which is solar, the Jewish calendar is both lunar and solar. The months are fixed by the moon's movements around the earth, the years by the earth's revolution around the sun.

   ii. Since the lunar year (354 days) is shorter than the solar year (365 days), a system was devised to coordinate the lunar with the solar year. The method that was adopted utilizes the periodic addition of a "leap month" to make the years more equal in length and ensure that the Jewish festivals always occur at their correct season.

   iii. In biblical times, the first month of the Hebrew calendar was called *Aviv.* It was on the fifteenth of that month—now commemorated as the first day of Passover—that the Israelites achieved freedom from Egyptian slavery. The return from the Babylonian exile, however, occurred in the fall, and that is why Rosh Hashanah, the New Year's festival, is celebrated on the first day of the autumn month of Tishri.

   iv. In ancient times, the determination of the lunar month was facilitated by two eyewitnesses sent by the Jewish Court to look for the new moon. When the court was convinced that their determination was satisfactory, the *Bet Din* (Jewish Court) proclaimed that day to be the new month. The announcement of the new moon was done by signaling from hilltop to hilltop, using small fires. The use of the ram's horn was also used to signal the new month.

   v. In modern times, the new month (*Rosh Chodesh*) is observed in synagogues on the first day of every month in the Hebrew calendar. *Hallel* (psalms of praise) are recited during the morning service, and the Torah reading (Numbers 28:1–15) describes the special sacrificial offerings for each new month in biblical times.

Commentators

Hinnuch.

He states that the root of this precept is that the Israelites should keep the
holy days of God at their proper time. It was important that the festivals,
many of which are connected with agricultural seasons, occur in their
correct season.

Recanti.

His concern related to the reason why the Jewish calendar follows the lunar
system. The answer that he gave was that the moon is the only heavenly
body that renews itself. Since the moon is miraculously renewed by God
each month, it stands to reason that God must have been the creator of the
world as well.

Abrabanel.

He states that the miraculous exodus from Egypt was the most important
Jewish national event, and thus the Bible's insistence that it begin the year.
However, Abrabanel correctly notes that the Jewish people today also
accept the month of Tishri as Rosh Hashanah, the beginning of the new
year. This, he states, is possible, since Tishri commemorates the beginning
of the creation of the world and reminds Jews of the growing things which
they need to sustain them. In the national sense, however, we always begin
the year with the celebration of the Festival of Freedom—Passover.

Ibn Ezra.

Similar in thought to Abrabanel, he has indicated that the people of Israel
have two new years—Nisan and Rosh Hashanah. He answers that Rosh
Hashanah is the agricultural new year, involving produce, firstfruits, and so
forth. The national new year, on the other hand, is related to the historical
event of the exodus from Egypt.

Sforno.

He says that before the exodus from Egypt, time was always at the mercy of
Israel's taskmasters. With this commandment concerning the fixing of the
months, time was now at Israel's own command and the Israelites could set it.

If You Want to Learn More

See Talmud *Rosh Hashanah,* 7a, 18a, 20a; Talmud *Ketubot* 21b; Maimonides, *Book of Commandments,* positive commandment 153; *Sefer HaHinnuch,* commandment 4.

2. Ban on Leaven on Passover

"On the first day [of Passover] you shall put away leaven out of your house" (Exodus 12:15). "In the first month, on the fourteenth day of the month, in the evening, you shall eat unleavened bread" (Exodus 12:18). "Seven days shall there be no leaven found in your houses" (Exodus 12:19).

    i. To prepare for the festival of Passover one is commanded to remove all leaven (*chametz*) from one's home and eat only unleavened bread (*matzah*) during the holiday.

    ii. Jewish Law requires that all leaven must be removed from the home on the fourteenth of the month of Nisan.

    iii. *Chametz* includes any food derived from wheat, spelt, barley, rye, or oats.

    iv. Today, in order to be sure that a Jewish family does not have leaven in its possession, the rabbis instituted the custom of "selling the leaven" (*mechirat chametz*) to a non-Jew for the duration of the festival.

    v. Jewish law demands that all Jewish persons eat *matzah* (unleavened bread) on the first night of Passover. During the rest of the festival, one is encouraged to eat it and certainly forbidden from eating any leaven during all of the festival.

Commentators

Hinnuch.

He states that the eating of *matzah* on Passover is an eternal reminder of the exodus from Egypt. The Israelites left in such haste that they did not allow time for their bread to rise.

Abrabanel.

Like the Hinnuch, he, too, sees the unleavened bread as a reminder of Egyptian slavery. However, he is concerned about why there is a commandment to refrain from even *possessing* any leaven during the festival of Passover. He proposes two answers. One, that if a Jew has leaven in his home during the festival that he might be tempted to eat it. The second reason is a more symbolic one. Leaven, he states, represents one's evil inclination. When the Jews officially began to become a nation after their freedom from Egypt, they were free from all evil inclination (*chametz*). We must always work to remove the *chametz* of evilness from our children's lives so that the future of a Jewish people free from the evil inclination will be ensured.

Bachya ben Asher.

In his allegorical explanation, he compares leaven to stern judgment. Just as leaven expands and spreads out, so, too, does judgment expand and not retreat. Thus, we must remove all leaven from our homes when we celebrate the festival of freedom. This teaches us that life itself must be based on mercy, compassion, and kindness, and not only strict judgment.

Sidney Greenberg.

In a most interesting allegorical explanation, he states the reason that leaven is forbidden to be in a Jew's possession during Passover is that the Egyptians were among the first people to cultivate yeast (i.e., leaven) for purposes of making bread rise. Thus, in this explanation, the desire to remove all leaven from one's home and possession is a symbolic way of removing ourselves from the taskmasters of Egyptian culture by ridding ourselves of the leaven of the Egyptians.

If You Want to Learn More

See Talmud *Pesachim* 5a, 5b, 28b, 120a; Midrash *Rabbah,* "Bo"; Maimonides, *Book of Commandments,* positive commandments 156, 158, negative commandments 197–199, 201; *Code of Jewish Law, Orach Chayyim,* 431–440; *Sefer HaHinnuch,* commandments 9–12, 19, 20, 485.

3. Telling the Story of the Exodus of Egypt to One's Children

"And you shall tell your son on that day" (Exodus 13:8).

i. This commandment refers to the important event of the Passover seder, when, using the book called the Haggadah, families retell the story of the Israelites' exodus from Egypt.

ii. The story of Passover must be told on the level of a child, so that even a very young one is able to comprehend it. According to Jewish Law, if a man has neither children nor a wife, he still must celebrate the seder and ask and answer the questions himself.

Commentators

Hinnuch.

He wonders why a person who has no children must still be required to tell himself the story. The Hinnuch, using principles of educational psychology, states that telling a story aloud (even to oneself) is likely to have greater emotional impact and relevance to a person than if that same person merely thought to himself about the story of the exodus.

Or HaChayyim.

The author states (like Maimonides and the Hinnuch) that one who is childless must recite the story of Passover to himself. Interestingly, the Or HaChayyim states that if a childless person continues each year to relate the story aloud to himself, eventually he will bear children to whom he can tell the story in future years.

Recanti.

In his explanation he relates this commandment of telling the exodus story to the dependability of God in time of crisis. Recanti states that any person who truly believes in God's miraculous power will indeed pass on the story to others. In this way, others will always be convinced that God can and will redeem the Israelite people from future dangers.

If You Want to Learn More

See Talmud *Pesachim* 116b; *Sefer Mitzvot Gadol,* positive commandment 41; *Sefer HaHinnuch,* commandment 21.

4. Going Forth from One's Place on the Sabbath

Let no person go out of his place on the seventh day (Exodus 16:29).

i. This verse is generally rabbinically interpreted to mean that one should not carry any object from one domain into another domain on the Sabbath.

ii. According to Jewish Law, a Jew must not travel on foot more than two thousand cubits (one cubit is the equivalent of approximately a foot and a half) from any point of the city limits, unless for the purpose of saving a life.

iii. The concept of establishing an *eruv* was instituted only for the purpose of allowing a person to fulfill a commandment that required some traveling (e.g., attending a ceremony of circumcision). The word, *eruv,* literally means "blending" or "intermingling." It is a way of symbolically combining several domains for the purpose of making it lawful on the Sabbath to transport things from one to the other. There are various types of the *eruv.* The *eruv techumim* was prepared as follows: all the tenants joined in providing an article of food, which was deposited in an appropriate place on Friday, as if to say, "We are all associated together and possess one and the same food, and none of us holds a domain distinct from the domain of the other. Just as we have equal rights in the area which remains a common domain, so have we all equal rights in each of the places held by the various tenants respectively."

iv. The *eruv chatzerot* (blending of the courtyard): carrying in a public domain was forbidden on the Sabbath. One could not carry an object from one house to another's house. However, if, in a large courtyard, all the tenants would contribute food and place it at a central point before the Sabbath, the courtyard would be symbolically transformed from a series of individual private dwellings into one common group dwelling that belonged to the entire community.

v. The *eruv tavshilin* (blending of dishes): establishing this type of *eruv* rendered it permissible to prepare food on a holy day for the use on the Sabbath that immediately follows it. The permission to prepare food on holy days is restricted to food required for those days. However, if the preparation was begun before the holy day, it may be continued on the holy day itself. This is accomplished by symbolically singling out food for the Sabbath on the eve of the festival.

Commentators

Maimonides.

Quoting Menachem Habavli, Maimonides says that one's manner of walking on the Sabbath must not be like his manner of walking on a weekday. Since there is a so-called extra soul in a person on the Sabbath, he must devote his free time to the study of the Torah, and not waste the day walking by foot from place to place.

Ibn Ezra.

He states that the implication of this commandment is that a person should not go places on the Sabbath for any project that involves a type of work that is forbidden on the Sabbath.

Hinnuch.

He reminds us that God worked for six days to create the world and on the seventh day God rested. Thus, Jewish people should not use the Sabbath for going on a journey that is related to a weekday activity. Rather, they should use the Sabbath for strolling and for pleasure.

If You Want to Learn More

See Talmud *Sanhedrin* 66a; Talmud *Eruvin* 17b, 48a, 49a, 51a; *Sefer Mitzvot Gadol,* negative commandment 66; *Code of Jewish Law, Orach Chayyim,* 398; *Sefer HaHinnuch,* commandment 24.

5. Remembering and Observing the Holy Sabbath

"Remember the Sabbath day to keep it holy" (Exodus 20:8). "Observe the Sabbath day to keep it holy" (Deuteronomy 5:12).

i. The origin of the Sabbath dates back to the beginning of creation. The Bible relates that God made the world in six days. On the seventh day, God rested; He blessed the seventh day and made it holy.

ii. The commandment to remember the Sabbath is the fourth of the Ten Commandments. In the Exodus version of the Ten Commandments, the commandment is to remember (*zachor*) the Sabbath day. In the parallel commandment in Deuteronomy, the opening word is "observe" (*shamor*). According to the Midrash, the two words, "remember" and "observe," were, in a miraculous way, pronounced together by God.

iii. Not all Jews understand the commandment to observe the Sabbath in the same way, and thus, a great many observances have evolved. There are, however, many basic Sabbath customs and traditions that continue to be shared by many Jews today, including the lighting of Sabbath candles, the recitation of the blessing over the wine, and the blessing over the *challot* (Sabbath loaves), just to mention a few.

iv. The rabbis teach that the observance of the Sabbath involves, not only the fulfillment of certain commandments relating to the Sabbath, but also the refraining from work. *Melacha,* the term for "work" that is used in the Bible, generally applies to work that involves creation, production, or transformation of an object. There are thirty-nine categories of *melacha,* which the rabbis defined as based on the kinds of work that were involved in the building of the portable sanctuary in the wilderness. The source of the thirty-nine major categories lies in the biblical juxtaposition of the laws of the Sabbath with the description of the construction of the tabernacle (Exodus 31:12–17). The fact that the Sabbath laws immediately precede the account of the construction suggested to the rabbis that the term "work" covered all manner of work done in connection with the construction of the tabernacle. The categories of forbidden work included: sowing, plowing, reaping, binding, threshing, winnowing, selecting, grinding, sifting, kneading, baking, shearing, bleaching, carding, dyeing, spinning, making two loops, threading needles, weaving, separating, tying, untying, sewing, tearing, hunting, slaughtering, flaying, salting, treatment of skins, scraping, cutting, writing, erasing, building, demolishing, carrying, kindling or extinguishing fire, and putting the finishing touches on a manufactured object.

Commentators

Ibn Ezra.

"To remember" the Sabbath for Ibn Ezra means that one should always remember that God created the world.

Nachmonides.

His concern related to the word "remember" in the Exodus version of the Ten Commandments and the word "observe" in the Deuteronomy version. He states that the word "remember" was chosen for the first version over the word "observe" because it is more important for a person to remember the Sabbath in a spirit of loving reverence rather than to simply keep the Sabbath and follow the letter of the law out of the motive of fear.

Hinnuch.

Quoting the *Mechilta* (the oldest rabbinic commentary on the Book of Exodus), he states that to remember the Sabbath is to do so by drinking a cup of wine. Wine, he says, stimulates one's mind and allows for a more joyous appreciation of the Sabbath.

Philo.

He says that the commandment to observe the Sabbath really is in effect saying that we should always imitate God. This means that we should let that one period of seven days in which God created the world be for people a complete example of the way in which people are to obey the law. Also, since on the seventh day God beheld all of the works that He had made, this teaches that on the Sabbath people should contemplate the works of nature and all of the separate circumstances which contribute toward happiness.

Maimonides.

He states that remembering and observing the Sabbath means to recite certain words at the commencement and end of the Sabbath that mention the greatness, dignity, and holiness of the day, and its distinction from the other days of the week.

Abraham Joshua Heschel.

For Heschel, the meaning of the Sabbath is to celebrate time rather than space. Six days a week we live under the tyranny of things of space. The purpose of observing the Sabbath is to try to become attuned to holiness in time, to turn from the results of creation to the mystery of the creation of the world by God.

Leo Baeck.

He states that the Sabbath is not merely a day to celebrating one's stopping from work, but rather a day that allows one to renew oneself.

Samson Raphael Hirsch.

In arriving at his interpretation of work, he states that the Sabbath testifies to God as the Supreme Creator of heaven and earth. Man, however, is constantly engaged in a struggle to gain mastery over God's creation, to bring nature under his control. By the use of his God-given intelligence and skill, he has in large measure succeeded in this. Thus, man is constantly in danger of forgetting his own dependence on God for so many things. By refraining from work on the Sabbath, man renounces and ceases to use his own human power in order to proclaim God as the source of all power. In this way the observing of the Sabbath is a person's way of paying homage to God, creator of all.

If You Want to Learn More

See Talmud *Shabbat* 10b, 33b, 49b, 113b, 117b, 118b; Talmud *Berakhot* 20b; Talmud *Pesachim* 48a, 106a; Maimonides, *Mishneh Torah,* Laws of Shabbat; Maimonides, *Book of Commandments,* positive commandments 154, 155, negative commandment 320; *Code of Jewish Law, Orach Chayyim,* 242, 246, 260, 262, 289, 300, 305; *Sefer HaHinnuch,* commandments 31, 32, 85; Abraham Joshua Heschel, *The Sabbath;* Samson Raphael Hirsch, *Commentary on the Books of Exodus and Deuteronomy.*

6. The Prohibition of Lighting a Fire on the Sabbath

"You shall not kindle fire throughout your habitations on the Sabbath" (Exodus 35:3).

i. This commandment is one of the thirty-nine prohibitions of forbidden work on the Sabbath. This commandment affects any activity that involves the initiation, transferring, or prolongation of combustion.

ii. Rabbinic interpretation of this prohibition includes the striking of a match and the use of electricity on the Sabbath.

iii. Various forms of automation, such as an alarm clock or wine press whose operation proceeds automatically is permitted for use on the Sabbath, provided the machinery was set into motion beforehand.

Commentators

Hinnuch.

He states that the prohibition of kindling fire on the Sabbath is already implied in the fourth commandment ("Remember the Sabbath day to keep it holy"). The reason for stressing this commandment of prohibition is to teach us that courts of justice ought not to carry out work on the Sabbath. His reasoning goes as follows: if judges were to work on the Sabbath, it is entirely possible that a situation might arise where they would have to pass a death sentence on the Sabbath in a crime that called for death by fire. Since the law stated that a sentence ought to be carried out at the earliest possible time, a court of justice would be violating the Sabbath by requiring death by fire. Thus, this commandment is a reminder that judicial courts ought to be closed on the holy Sabbath.

Sforno.

Since most work that is forbidden on the Sabbath deals with work of creativity, one might think that the use of fire would be permitted since it is more often associated with destruction rather than creation. Nevertheless, the lighting of fire is strictly forbidden, since fire can also be used for works of creation (e.g., forging of metal).

Nachmonides.

He holds that since cooking and baking for that particular day is permitted on the three pilgrim holidays (Sukkot, Passover, and Shavuot), the prohibition of kindling fire on the Sabbath is intended to clearly show that the Sabbath is different from the other holidays. Baking and cooking are not permitted on the Sabbath.

Martin Noth.

He states that the prohibition of lighting fire on the Sabbath may relate to the connection that God was believed to have had with fire, and on Sabbaths and festive days God was honored with fire in the tabernacle and, later, in the Temple. Thus, this prohibition may have been an early attempt to centralize worship to some degree, meaning that the prohibition of fire applied only to one's private dwelling but not to the sanctuary proper.

Rabbi Menachem Habavli.

He states that the Sabbath may be profaned in order to save human life (even in cases of uncertainty). However, where the taking of a human life is concerned, observance of the Sabbath is of paramount importance. This is the meaning of the commandment of not kindling fire on the Sabbath (i.e., one may not punish another on the Sabbath by taking that person's life).

Kenite hypothesis.

This hypothesis suggests that Moses' religion had a special relationship to an itinerant tribe of smiths called the Kenites. They used fire prominently in their work, and thus a commandment to prohibit "work" on the Sabbath would have needed to have been highlighted by a special commandment not to kindle fire on that day.

If You Want to Learn More

See Talmud *Shabbat* 20, 70a; Talmud *Sanhedrin* 35b, 46a; Maimonides, *Book of Commandments* (Maimonides), negative commandment 322; *Sefer HaHinnuch,* commandment 114; Noth, *The Book of Exodus;* Eerdmans, *The Religion of Israel,* p. 29.

7. *Cessation of Work on Festivals*

"On the first day, you shall have a holy convocation . . . you shall do not type of servile work" (Leviticus 23:7). "On the seventh day is a holy convocation . . . you shall do no manner of servile work" (Leviticus 23:8).

i. These commandments, although pertaining in this specific instance to the festival of Passover, also apply to the major pilgrim festivals of Sukkot and Shavuot.

ii. These commandments are qualified by the biblical statement in Exodus 12:16: "On the first day you shall hold a sacred convocation, and on the seventh day, a sacred convocation. No work at all shall be done on them, except what every person is to eat, that alone may be prepared for you." This has been rabbinically interpreted to mean that unlike the Sabbath, when no work (including the cooking of food) is permitted, on festivals, work that is connected with the preparation of food is permitted. Transferring of fire and carrying things are also permitted on festivals.

iii. There are three divisions to the festivals of Sukkot and Passover: the first day (holy day with restrictions), the five intervening days (called intermediate days, or *chol hamo'ed,* with restrictions lifted), and the last day (holy day). In places outside of Israel (i.e., the Diaspora), the laws apply to the first two days, the four intermediate days, and the seventh and eight days. During the intermediate days of these festivals, the commandments are relaxed and the days appear to be more like regular weekdays.

Commentators

Nachmonides.

In his explanation of this commandment, he connects this commandment to a previous verse in Exodus 12:6, which forbids work on Passover but adds, "only what every person is to eat, that alone may be prepared for you." Thus, for Nachmonides, only work involved in preparing food for the festival is permitted, and all other kinds of work are forbidden as works of labor.

Hinnuch.

He states that the purpose of the commandment of refraining from work on a festival is to allow time to remember the miracles that occurred on those days, to take time to relate those to our children, as well as to visit synagogues and to participate in the study of the Torah. If working were allowed on festivals, their true significance would quickly be forgotten.

Maimonides.

He holds that festivals are appointed for happy, festive gatherings of people. If work were permitted on festivals, the opportunity to be together as a festive Jewish community would be eradicated.

If You Want to Learn More

See Talmud *Shabbat* 106b, 142b; Talmud *Makkot* 21b; Maimonides, *Book of Commandments,* positive commandments 159, 160, negative commandments 323, 324; *Code of Jewish Law, Orach Chayyim,* 495; *Sefer HaHinnuch,* commandments 297, 298, 300, 301.

8. *Counting the Omer*

"And from the day on which you bring the sheaf of wave offering, the day after the Sabbath, you shall count off seven weeks. They must be complete: you must count until the day after the seventh week—fifty days" (Leviticus 23:15–16).

   i. *Omer* (literally, "sheaf") refers to an offering from the new barley crop which was brought to the Jerusalem Temple on the sixteenth of Nisan, the eve of the second day of Passover. This was the beginning of the grain harvest in the land of Israel.

   ii. Today, *omer* has come to be the name of the period between the festivals of Passover and Shavuot. The counting of the days of the omer help to heighten one's anticipation of the celebration of the festival of Shavuot, which commemorates the revelation of the Torah to the Jewish people.

Commentators

Recanti.

The question that he attempts to answer concerns the period of seven weeks that elapsed before the Jewish people were given the Torah. He compares the Jewish people in Egypt to a menstruating woman. Both were unclean and must wait a period of days in order to become clean once again. God required the seven-week period of time as a period of cleansing and sanctification, after which He was prepared to reveal His Will on Mount Sinai.

Maimonides.

He states that the festival of Shavuot is the anniversary of the revelation on Mount Sinai. In order to emphasize the importance of this day, we count the days that pass from the preceding festival. This action is like that of the person who expects his most intimate friend on a certain day and begins to count the days and even the hours. Thus, this fulfillment of this commandment results in the counting of days from the anniversary of the Israelite departure from Egypt and the anniversary of the giving of the Torah on Mount Sinai.

Hinnuch.

He states the purpose of the counting of the omer is to give expression to one's deepest and innermost yearnings for the arrival of this day. The act of counting the days demonstrates that the totality of a person's desires and attentions are devoted to waiting for the time to draw nearer. The reason why the counting begins on the second day of Passover and not the first relates to the fact that on the first day, the whole being of the Israelites was concentrated on commemorating the miracle of the exodus from Egypt. In order not to divert the attention of the Israelites from this joyous day, the counting was commanded to commence from the second day of Passover.

Rabbi Cathy Felix.

She links the counting of the days between Passover and Shavuot to the theme of various transitions in our lives. As people grow, they grow through a variety of transitions: for example, changing jobs, getting married, moving to a new house. The omer teaches people how to manage these stressful times in their lives. It does this because the counting of the omer is a constant reminder that any transition is a slow process. It takes time to adjust to new situations. The Jewish people could not immediately move to Mount Sinai, for they needed time to make psychological adjustments. Rabbi Felix says that the omer is that period of limbo that people go through after they have said goodbye to the old but have not yet fully settled into the new.

Edward Greenstein.

He states that the omer ends after a count of seven weeks, seven times seven days from Passover to Shavuot. The symmetry of the period (7 × 7) symbolizes a special degree of holiness for Shavuot, the day of the great revelation on Mount Sinai. Similarly, the especially sacred parts of the tabernacle were square in shape and symmetrical: the altar and the holy of holies. What has symmetry to do with the holy? It is stable, even, balanced, and harmonious, and it shares the same measure.

Zalman Schachter Shalomi.

He says that while the giving of the Torah is what God does on Shavuot, the role of the Jewish people is to receive it. This is the purpose of the counting of the omer. During the so-called omer period, we form ourselves into vessels in order to receive the Torah. Each person creates a receptacle made of his needs and questions. This process precipitates the drawing down out of a universe saturated with blessings just those things that his vessel requires. This is each person's Torah.

If You Want to Learn More

See Talmud *Menachot* 45b, 65b, 66a; Talmud *Chagigah* 17b; Maimonides, *Book of Commandments* (Maimonides), positive commandment 161; *Code of Jewish Law, Orach Chayyim,* 489; *Sefer HaHinnuch,* commandment 306; Cathy Felix, "Finding the Significance of Counting the Omer," *Metro West Jewish News,* May 1993, p. 34; Michael Strassfeld, *The Jewish Holidays: A Guide and Commentary.*

9. Commemorating the Festival of Shavuot

"On that same day [Shavuot] you shall hold a celebration. . . . [Y]ou shall do no manner of work" (Leviticus 23:21).

    i. The festival in this commandment is that of Shavuot, sometimes called the festival of weeks. It always falls seven weeks after the festival of Passover.

    ii. The festival of Shavuot is the shortest of the three pilgrimage festivals. Although it lasts only two days, it continues to remain high in intensity of feeling since it reenacts the revelation of God at Mount Sinai and the giving of the Torah.

iii. Shavuot began as a spring harvest festival in Israel. The first wheat ripened approximately fifty days after the first barley. The first barley offering was brought to the Temple one day after Passover began. From that day on, the Jewish people were told to count seven complete weeks from one harvest to the other, and at the end of the counting, they were commanded to celebrate the festival of Shavuot, which literally means "weeks."

iv. The Torah also refers to Shavuot as *Hag HaBikkurim,* the festival of the firstfruits (Deuteronomy 26:1–11), during which Jews would make their pilgrimage to Jerusalem bearing gift offerings of firstfruits.

Commentators

Maimonides.

Maimonides is concerned with the reason why the festival of Shavuot is celebrated only for two days (in the Diaspora) and one day in Israel, while Passover is celebrated for many more days. He answers that the full influence of receiving the Torah took place in one day. When Shavuot is celebrated in one day, there can be no error as to its motive. The eating of unleavened bread on Passover is different, for one may eat matzah for several days without feeling anything unusual. When, however, a person eats matzah and no leaven for one whole week, it becomes self-evident that one is commemorating a very important event in Jewish history, namely, the freedom of the Jewish people from Egyptian slavery.

David Hoffman.

He asks why no symbolic ritual was instituted for Shavuot to mark the revelation at Mount Sinai. He answers that the revelation cannot be translated into the tangible language of symbol. The Israelites were simply commanded to commemorate this historical experience. In the words of the Bible, the Israelites were commanded to take heed that "you saw no likeness on the day that the Lord spoke to you at Horeb from the midst of the fire" (Deuteronomy 4:15).

Keli Yakar.

His concern related to the reason why the Torah did not specifically identify the festival of Shavuot as connected with the receiving of the

Torah. (This, incidentally, is a concern of a variety of biblical commentators.) He answers that the receiving of the Torah on Mount Sinai is an event that we ought to commemorate each and every day of our lives. Every time a Jew studies Torah, he ought to discover new things and new truths.

If You Want to Learn More

See Talmud *Chagigah* 17b; Talmud *Shabbat* 88a, 88b, 89a, 89b; Maimonides, *The Guide of the Perplexed,* pt. 3, sect. 43; Maimonides, *Book of Commandments,* positive commandment 162, negative commandment 325; *Code of Jewish Law, Orach Chayyim,* 495; *Sefer HaHinnuch,* commandments 308, 309; David Hoffman, *Commentary to Book of Leviticus.*

10, 11. Celebration of Rosh Hashanah and Sounding of the Ram's Horn

"In the seventh month, on the first day of the month, you shall observe complete rest, a sacred occasion with loud blasts. You shall not work at your occupations" (Leviticus 23:24–25).

i. This commandment refers to the commemoration of the festival of Rosh Hashanah.

ii. Rosh Hashanah, which means "head of the year," marks the beginning of the Jewish calendar. Interestingly, it falls on the first and second days of the month of *Tishri,* the seventh month of the Jewish calendar. Many years ago, the Jewish people had several dates in the calendar marking the beginning of important seasons of the year. The first month was *Nisan,* in the spring, when the Jewish people were freed from Egyptian slavery. The first of *Tishri* was the beginning of the economic year, the time when the old harvest ended and the new one began. In time, the first of *Tishri* became the beginning of the year.

iii. This commandment describes one of the oldest musical instruments, called a *shofar* (a ram's horn), which was sounded to announce the beginning of the new year. In modern times during the Rosh Hashanah service blasts of the *shofar* are sounded at various times during the morning service. It is a commandment to hear the sounding of the *shofar.*

iv. The *shofar* is a reminder for people to awaken and repent. It also is a reminder of the ram that Abraham sacrificed in the place of his own son Isaac. It is this story that is read on the festival of Rosh Hashanah.

Commentators

Hinnuch.

He states that at the root of this commandment lies the theme of God's kindnesses toward His people. The commandment is intended to help the people to recall them and regard their deeds one day in every single year, so that the transgressions should not become a great many, and there should be room for atonement. Thus we are to rejoice on Rosh Hashanah because God always tips the scales of justice toward loving-kindness and will pardon our sins.

Maimonides.

He states that the *shofar* is the way to awaken sleepers from their sleep, allowing them to search their deeds and ultimately repent for the sins that they committed.

Saadia Gaon.

He offers ten reasons for sounding the *shofar:*

   a. The *shofar* proclaims the sovereignty of God on Rosh Hashanah, the anniversary of creation.
   b. The *shofar* is used at wars and stirs the people to amend their life during the Ten Days of Repentance, beginning with the New Year.
   c. The *shofar* is a reminder of the revelation at Mount Sinai, when the Israelites said, "We will do and we will obey."
   d. The *shofar* brings to mind the prophetic warnings and exhortations.
   e. The *shofar* is reminiscent of the battle alarm in Judea.
   f. The *shofar* brings to mind the attempted sacrifice of Isaac by Abraham on Mount Moriah.
   g. The *shofar* inspires the heart with awe and reverence.
   h. The *shofar* reminds us of the Day of Judgment.
   i. The *shofar* inspires us with the hope for the final restoration of the people of Israel.
   j. The *shofar* is identified with the idea of the resurrection of the dead.

Saul Leiberman.

He has suggested that the sounds of the *shofar* are like prayers without words.

If You Want to Learn More

See Talmud *Rosh Hashanah* 16a, 32a, 32b, 34a; Talmud *Shabbat* 131b; Talmud *Megillah* 20b; Maimonides, *Book of Commandments,* positive commandments 163, 170, negative commandment 73; *Code of Jewish Law, Orach Chayyim,* 495, 585, 588; *Mishneh Torah, Mada, Laws of Repentance* 3:4; *Sefer HaHinnuch,* commandments 310, 311, 405.

12. Observance of Yom Kippur

"On the tenth of this seventh month is the day of atonement; there shall be a holy convocation for you, and you shall afflict your souls" (Leviticus 23:27).

i. This commandment relates to the commandment to observe the festival of Yom Kippur, the Day of Atonement.

ii. The Talmud rabbis interpreted the phrase "afflict your souls" to mean practicing various forms of self-denial. These included abstention from anointing oneself with oil, wearing shoes, washing, sexual intercourse, and food or drink.

iii. Fasting on Yom Kippur means complete abstinence from food and drink from sundown until the end of the next day. A fast, therefore, is approximately twenty-five hours in length.

Commentators

Philo.

He speaks of Yom Kippur as an occasion for self-restraint at a season when the fruits of the earth have just been gathered in and the temptation to indulge is even greater than usual. Abstinence at such a time is likely to raise a person's thoughts from the gifts to the giver who sustains all of life.

Hinnuch.

He states that at the root of this commandment is the kindness of God toward all His human beings. God set one day in the year to allow for atonement of one's sins with proper repentance. Therefore, fasting is a commandment on this day, because food and drink and the other pleasures of the sense of touch, arouse the physical self to be drawn after desire and sin.

Abrabanel.

He states four different reasons why it was the tenth of Tishri that was chosen by God for the Day of Atonement.

a. The creation of the world took place on the first of Tishri and there is a tradition that Adam repented on the tenth of that month. Thus we do the same.

b. Tradition relates the fact that Abraham performed his own circumcision on the tenth of Tishri, thus establishing his covenantal relationship with God.

c. Moses ascended Mount Sinai for the second time on the first of the month of Elul. Forty days later, on the tenth of Tishri, he descended with the second set of Ten Commandments. This symbolized the pardon of the Israelites for the sin of the golden calf, and is therefore an appropriate day each year for the Jewish people to ask God for His forgiveness.

d. There is a tradition that says that Moses crouched in a hole of the mountain and saw God's Presence pass by. At that very instant, God taught Moses how to gain forgiveness through His attribute of mercy and lovingkindness. Thus on Yom Kippur it is customary to recite aloud God's Thirteen Attributes of Mercy.

If You Want to Learn More

See Talmud *Yoma* 80a, 80b, 81a, 82b; Talmud *Rosh Hashanah* 20b, 30a, 30b; Talmud *Megillah* 7b; Maimonides, *The Guide of the Perplexed,* pt. 3, sect. 43; Maimonides, *Book of Commandments,* (*Maimonides*), positive commandments 48, 49, negative commandment 327; *Code of Jewish Law, Orach Chayyim,* 604–624; *Sefer HaHinnuch,* commandments 313, 315–317.

13, 14: Observance of the Festival of Sukkot

"On the fifteenth of this seventh month is the feast of tabernacles for seven days unto God" (Leviticus 23:34). "In booths you shall dwell seven days" (Leviticus 23:42).

i. This commandment refers to the celebration of the festival of booths, known as Sukkot. This holiday is a reminder that the Israelites many years ago lived in booths during their wanderings in the desert.

ii. The festival of Sukkot is the fall harvest festival. Thus it is sometimes called *Chag Ha'asif,* the festival of the ingathering.

iii. The *sukkah* had to be made of at least three walls, with a roof covering called *sechach,* consisting of anything that grew from the soil and had to be detached from the ground. The *sechach* had to be arranged so that there would be more shade than sunshine in the interior of the *sukkah*.

iv. The commandment of dwelling in the *sukkah* was rabbinically interpreted to mean that a person must eat, drink, and sleep in the *sukkah*. Nowadays most people do not sleep in the *sukkah* but many do eat their meals in it.

v. The blessing for dwelling in the *sukkah* is as follows:

בָּרוּךְ אַתָּה יהוה אֱלֹהֵינוּ מֶלֶךְ הָעוֹלָם, אֲשֶׁר קִדְּשָׁנוּ בְּמִצְוֹתָיו
וְצִוָּנוּ לֵישֵׁב בַּסֻּכָּה.

Praised are You, Adonai our God, who had made us holy by Your *mitzvot* and commanded us to dwell in the *sukkah*.

Commentators

Maimonides.

He states that the moral lesson derived from the festival is that a person ought to remember his bad times in days of prosperity, and thus will be induced to lead a modest life. This is the reason that God commands us to leave our elegant homes in order to dwell in booths that are reminiscent of desert life lacking in convenience and comfort.

Abrabanel.

He questions the length of the festival of Sukkot, and wonders how it was possible to observe an eight-day festival that would cause one to be absent from his fields for more than one week. He answers that the festival of Sukkot occurred during that time of year when the crops were already gathered and stored away for the winter. This would thus allow an observant person the opportunity to celebrate the joyous festival of Sukkot in a relaxed and peaceful manner.

Rashbam.

He states that the commandment requiring a person to dwell in a *sukkah* helps a person recall the Israelites who had no inheritance in the desert and no house in which to dwell. Celebrating the Sukkot festival reduces a person's possible pride in his well-stocked house, lest he say that "his own might has gotten him this wealth" (Deuteronomy 8:17). In fact, it is God to whom we must give thanks for our bountiful harvest.

Hinnuch.

He understands the festival of Sukkot and its ordinances as aimed at implanting within the Israelites a sense of thankfulness to God for His miracles in the wilderness.

Nachmonides.

He attempts to clarify two interpretations of the word *sukkah*. According to the first definition, the word *sukkah* means a tabernacle, and its purpose was to remind the Jew that although his life was altered because he had to live in a booth, nonetheless God denied him nothing and he always enjoyed God's bounty. In the second interpretation, the word *sukkah* means a "cloud of glory." Thus the Jewish people are commanded to always remember the protection that God gave the Israelite people when He caused His Cloud of Glory to shield them wherever they wandered.

Samson Raphael Hirsch.

He saw in the *sukkah* a symbol of universal peace and brotherhood.

Mordecai Kaplan.

He said that Jews relive their experience in the desert on Sukkot by living in booths. In this way, they are afforded each year an opportunity to place themselves in a frame of mind which enables them to detach themselves from the order of life which they had come to accept as normal and to view it critically.

Isaac Aboab.

He states that the *sukkah* is designed to warn us that a person ought never to put his strength in the size or beauty of his home, nor must he rely upon the help of any human being, however powerful. Only God can be trusted as always dependable.

If You Want to Learn More

See Talmud *Chagigah* 17a, 17b; Talmud *Sukkah* 2a, 6b, 27a, 27b, 55b; Talmud *Shabbat,* 133b; Maimonides, *Book of Commandments,* positive commandments 166, 167, 168, negative commandments 328, 329; *Code of Jewish Law, Orach Chayyim,* 495, 628, 630, 634; *Sefer HaHinnuch,* commandments 318, 319, 321, 322, 325; Isaac Aboab, *Menorat Hama'or III,* ed. Mosad Harav Kook, 4:6; Mordecai Kaplan, *The Meaning of God in Modern Jewish Religion.*

15. Four Species

"And you shall take for yourselves on the first day the fruit of goodly trees, branches of palm trees and boughs of thick trees, and willows of the brook, and you shall rejoice before your God seven days" (Leviticus 23:40).

   i. According to tradition, the four species specified in the above commandment refer to the *etrog* (citron), the *lulav* (palm tree), the *hadassim* (twigs of myrtle tree), and the *aravot* (twigs of the willow tree).

   ii. Rabbinic instruction states that the *lulav, hadassim,* and *aravot* are bound together and held by a person in his right hand, while the *etrog* is taken in the left. Holding both hands together, one says the blessings and waves the four species in all four directions, as well as upward and downward. The blessing is as follows:

בָּרוּךְ אַתָּה יְיָ אֱלֹהֵנוּ מֶלֶךְ הָעוֹלָם אֲשֶׁר קִדְּשָׁנוּ בְּמִצְוֹתָיו וְצִוָּנוּ
עַל נְטִילַת לוּלָב:

Praised are You, Adonai Our God, who made us holy by Your *mitzvot* and commanded us to wave the *lulav.*

Commentators

Hinnuch.

He explains the commandment of taking the four species as follows: God commanded the Israelites to celebrate the joyous festival of Sukkot, at which time they would thank God for their bountiful harvest and rejoice during these festival days. Since joy very often evokes the physical, material self and can make a person forget one's reverence for God, God commanded the Israelites to take in their hands objects that would remind them that all of their rejoicing should be for the sake of His glory. The Hinnuch also quotes another rabbinic interpretation when he says that the *etrog* resembles the heart (the seat of a person's intelligence); the *lulav* is like a person's spine, reminding us that we must always stand erect when praying to God; the myrtle resembles eyes, implying that one should never go straying about following his eyes on the day of his heart's rejoicing; and the willow is like one's lips, which a person ought to hold in restraint, focusing solely on being in awe of God.

Bachya ibn Asher.

In elaborating on several rabbinic traditions, he says that the *etrog* can be compared to Abraham because it is a beautiful fruit. Abraham's old age was beautiful. Isaac can be compared to the *lulav* by the wordplay on the word *kappot* ("branches"), as well as stemming from a root which means, "to bind." The *lulav* has branches, and Isaac was bound and ready to be offered as a sacrifice. Jacob is like the myrtle, which is thick with leaves, symbolizing Jacob's being blessed with many children. Finally, Joseph can be compared to the willow, which dries up quickly, since he died before all of his brothers.

Bachya also states that the four species reminds us of the four kingdoms that caused Jews to suffer—Babylonia, Persia, Greece, and Rome. Just as the Jewish people survived these political forces, so, too, with God's help, they shall survive others in the future.

Rabbi Yehuda Aryeh Leib of Ger.

He points out that in *gematria,* (a way of interpreting the Torah involving the explanation of a word of group of words through the assignment of a numerical value to the Hebrew letters), the Hebrew word *lulav* has the value of sixty-eight, which is the same as that of *chayyim* (life).

Edward Greenstein.

He states that the emphasis on the number four at Sukkot is most appropriate for a festival so rooted in the earth. The four winds, the four directions, and the four seasons are all reminders of how related to the growth cycle is the number four.

If You Want to Learn More

See Talmud *Sukkah* 29b, 32a, 32b, 33b, 43a, 43b; Talmud *Pesachim* 5a; Talmud *Rosh Hashanah* 16a; Maimonides, *Book of Commandments,* positive commandment 169; *Code of Jewish Law, Orach Chayyyim,* 651; *Sefer HaHinnuch,* commandment 324; Michael Strassfeld, *The Jewish Holidays: A Guide and Commentary.*

16. *Three Annual Pilgrimages to Jerusalem*

"Three times in a year shall all your males appear before God in the place which He shall choose: on the feast of unleavened bread, and on the feast of weeks and on the feast of tabernacles; and they shall not appear before God empty. Every man shall give as he is able, according to the blessing of the Lord your God which He has given you" (Deuteronomy 16:13–17).

i. These verses refer to the biblical commandment that requires every Jew to make a pilgrimage to the Temple in Jerusalem on three occasions during each year—the festivals of Passover, Shavuot, and Sukkot. Each person was to bring with him the necessary animals for the three different sacrifices.

ii. The three pilgrim festivals marked the spring (barley), summer (wheat), and autumn (fruit) harvests, respectively.

iii. Today, these same three festivals are celebrated with much joy and enthusiasm. However, since the Jerusalem Temple no longer exists, there is no longer a need to bring sacrifices. Praying in synagogues is the modern-day substitute for sacrifices.

Commentators

Sforno.

He states that the festive nature of these three pilgrimages to the Temple was intended to counterbalance the enthusiasm shown by the Israelites when they circled, danced, and prayed around the golden calf.

Ibn Ezra.

He states that the three pilgrim festivals were called *shalosh regalim* (literally, "three feet") because most of the people went to Jerusalem on foot. The traditional rule was that every person had to walk on foot at least the final stage of the journey up, from the city of Jerusalem to the Temple

Mount, since the expression, *shalosh regalim,* conveys the sense of "three times on foot."

Hinnuch.

He states that the purpose of the pilgrimages was so the Jew could say thank-you to God for the miracles that He had performed on each of the three festivals. Although one could feel grateful at home, the special aura of a sanctuary would add to the sanctity and specialness of the occasion.

Nachmonides.

He mentions the fact that each pilgrim festival coincides with a different season of the harvest. At each of these seasons—the seasons of rain, sun, and dew—God continues to provide us with much bounty. And this, therefore, is the root meaning for the commandment to visit the holy Temple of Jerusalem and offer thanks to God.

If You Want to Learn More

See Talmud *Kiddushin* 34a, 34b; Talmud *Sukkah* 49b; Talmud *Pesachim* 8b; Maimonides, *Book of Commandments,* positive commandments 52–54, negative commandments 156, 229; *Code of Jewish Law, Orach Chayyim,* 529; *Sefer HaHinnuch,* commandments 88, 450, 488–490.

Section V: Family

1. Procreation

"Be fruitful and multiply, and fill the earth and subdue it" (Genesis 1:28).

   i. To "be fruitful and multiply" is one of Judaism's most important commandments. It has been rabbinically interpreted to mean that a man must beget at least a son and a daughter in order to fulfill this commandment.

   ii. According to rabbinic tradition, when a man reaches the age of eighteen, he becomes subject to the commandment to marry and have children.

Commentators

Hinnuch.

According to the Hinnuch, the purpose of the commandment to bear children is in order that God's desire to have the world inhabited with people be fulfilled. For only with a world of people can God expect to have His commandments fulfilled.

Or HaChayyim.

The author states that unpopulated places in the world are likely to be areas in which phenomena harmful to humans may breed. Thus, it is the obligation to inhabit the world.

Nehama Leibowitz.

She states that the fish and the other animals do not qualify for a special address to them by God. They are simply granted the power to be fruitful and multiply which is their blessing. However, man, besides being given the power to be fruitful and multiply, is especially told by God to be fruitful and multiply and is conscious of his power to do so. Thus, what is an impersonal fact with regard to the rest of the animal kingdom is a conscious fact with regard to man.

Maimonides.

He takes a rationalist point of view and states that the purpose of begetting children is to perpetuate the species of humankind.

If You Want to Learn More

See Talmud *Yevamot* 61b, 62, 63, 65b; Maimonides, *Book of Commandments,* positive commandment 212; *Code of Jewish Law, Even HaEzer*, ch. 1; Talmud *Kiddushin* 29b; *Sefer HaHinnuch*, commandment 1; Nehama Leibowitz, *Studies in Genesis*.

2. Circumcision:

"Every male among you shall be circumcised" (Genesis 17:10).

i. The covenant of circumcision is first mentioned as a divine command to Abraham, who was told that every male eight days old shall be circumcised as a sign of the covenant.

ii. Circumcision must be performed on the eighth day after birth, even if the eighth day is on the Sabbath or Yom Kippur. If the child is physically unfit for circumcision, the ceremony may be postponed for these important reasons of health.

iii. The participants in a circumcision are the mother and father, the
mohel (person who performs circumcision), the *Kvater* (godfather) and
Kvaterin (godmother), the *sandek* (person who holds the baby while
circumcision is performed), the rabbi and or cantor, and the invited guests.
The Prophet Elijah is the invisible participant at circumcisions, being
referred to as the "angel of the covenant" (Malachi 3:1) and protector of
children.

iv. The blessing said by the *mohel* at the ceremony is as follows:

בָּרוּךְ אַתָּה יְיָ אֱלֹהֵינוּ מֶלֶךְ הָעוֹלָם, אֲשֶׁר קִדְּשָׁנוּ בְּמִצְוֹתָיו
וְצִוָּנוּ עַל הַמִּילָה.

Praised are You, Adonai our God, Ruler of the universe, who has made
us holy by Your *mitzvot* and commanded us concerning
circumcision.

After the circumcision the parents say:

בָּרוּךְ אַתָּה יְיָ אֱלֹהֵינוּ מֶלֶךְ הָעוֹלָם, אֲשֶׁר קִדְּשָׁנוּ בְּמִצְוֹתָיו
וְצִוָּנוּ לְהַכְנִיסוֹ בִּבְרִיתוֹ שֶׁל אַבְרָהָם אָבִינוּ.

Praised are You, Adonai our God, Ruler of the universe, who has
sanctified us by Your *mitzvot* and commanded us to bring our son in
the covenant of Abraham our father.

v. A male who converts to Judaism who was circumcised before his
conversion is required by traditional Jewish law to undergo a symbolic
circumcision. This is done by drawing one drop of blood from the place
where the circumcision is performed.

Commentators

Maimonides.

He speaks of circumcision in the following terms: it gives to all members of
the same faith a common bodily sign, so that it is virtually impossible for
any stranger to say that he belongs to them and then attack them. If the

circumcision surgery were postponed until the boy grew up, he might perhaps not submit to it.

Maimonides was a physician and also believed that one of the purposes of circumcision was to weaken the sex drive of a man, so that he would not be excessively stimulated.

Hinnuch.

He states that the purpose of circumcision is to physically distinguish the Jew from the non-Jew. The sex organ was chosen as the way to make this distinction because it was the organ of procreation.

Abrabanel.

He believed that circumcision's purpose was to atone for the original sin of Adam (when he ate of the forbidden fruit) and its sexual implications.

Nachmonides.

He saw a similarity between the procedure of circumcision and that of offering a sacrifice to God, when the blood of the animal was meant to atone for one's sins.

Herschel Matt.

He states that the circumcision of the foreskin was an outer sign of the circumcision of our inner hearts. The sign of circumcision was the genital organ in order to indicate that just as life is passed on from one generation to another, so too is the covenant passed on.

If You Want to Learn More

See Talmud *Shabbat* 132a, 135a, 137a; Talmud *Yevamot* 47b; Maimonides, *Book of Commandments*, positive commandment 215; *Sefer Mitzvot Gadol*, commandment 28; *Code of Jewish Law, Yoreh De'ah*, 260–266; *Sefer HaHinnuch,* commandment 2; Herschel Matt, "Circumcision," *Program Notes of the Rabbinical Assembly*, November 1963.

3. Honoring Parents:

"Honor your father and your mother, so that your days may be long upon the land which God gives you" (Exodus 20:12). "You shall fear, everyone, his mother and his father" (Leviticus 19:3).

i. This commandment is the fifth of the Ten Commandments. It is one of only two commandments for which a reward is offered (i.e., length of days) to the one who observes it. It is also one of a number of commandments for which a person is rewarded in both this world and in the World-to-Come.

ii. To fear one's parents has been rabbinically interpreted to mean not to sit in the seat reserved for them at the table, not to contradict them, and not to call them by their first names.

iii. To honor one's parents has been rabbinically interpreted to mean to provide them with food, clothing, and shelter.

iv. This commandment also applies to stepparents and anyone else with parenting responsibilities.

Commentators

Hinnuch.

He states that at the root of this commandment lies the thought that it is fitting for a person to treat with loving-kindness the person who treated him with goodness, and he should not be a scoundrel. Each person should always remember that his father and mother are the cause of his being in the world, and hence it is entirely proper for him to give them every honor and benefit that he can.

Ba'al Ha-Turim.

His concern with this commandment related to its placement in the Ten Commandments. He asks: "Why is this commandment to honor parents placed immediately before that of remembering the Sabbath to keep it holy?" He answers that it is to show that just as a person must honor the Sabbath as a way of praising God for His works of creation, so, too, a person must honor his parents because in doing so he will always remember God's partnership with the parents in the creation of each child.

Abrabanel.

He states that we must honor our parents in order to set an example for our own children to respect us.

Keli Yakar.

He explains that it is parents who provide their children with their physical bodies, but it is God who gives them their souls. Thus, because both God and the parents are in active partnership in the creation of one's whole self, they are both to be honored by virtue of this commandment.

Gunther Plaut.

He states that parents are God's representatives and partners in the rearing of their children, and children who fail to respect this position are offending God as well.

If You Want to Learn More

See Talmud *Kiddushin* 30b; Talmud *Sanhedrin* 50a; Jerusalem Talmud *Peah*, ch. 1; Maimonides, *Book of Commandments*, positive commandments 210, 211; *Code of Jewish Law, Yoreh De'ah*, 240; *Sefer HaHinnuch*, commandments 33, 212; W. Gunther Plaut, ed., *The Torah: A Modern Commentary*.

4. Rights of a Wife:

"If he takes for himself another wife, her food, clothing and her conjugal rights shall he not diminish" (Exodus 21:10).

  i. A husband's biblical obligations to his wife include supplying her with food and clothing and having sexual relations with her.

  ii. There are seven rabbinic obligations that relate to a husband's obligations toward his wife. They include the following:

  a. To fulfill the obligations of the *ketubah* (Jewish marriage contract), in which there is a monetary settlement in the event that a husband divorces his wife.
  b. To pay for her medical care.
  c. To ransom her if she is captured.
  d. To give her a dignified burial.
  e. To make provisions to support her with his assets should he die prior to her death.
  f. To provide for the support of their unmarried daughter after his death.
  g. To make provisions that if his wife should die before him, the sons that she bore him will inherit any property she brought with her as her marriage portion.

Commentators

Rashbam.

He explains that the Hebrew word *onah,* which is generally translated as "conjugal rights," ought to be interpreted to mean "a home" (from the word *ma'on,* meaning home). Thus, a husband must provide a suitable home for his wife.

Me'am Lo'ez.

Regarding the obligation of a husband to provide his wife with clothing, he elaborates by stating that the clothing must be in accordance with her social standing. Thus, she should have both summer clothes and winter clothing, since each season requires its own garments. Furthermore, he should not allow her to dress worse than any other women in their city. If the husband is wealthy, he must provide for her according to his wealth.

Maurice Lamm.

He states that although there is a commandment to procreate and have children, this commandment relates to marital sexuality (*onah* in Hebrew) that is beyond procreation. Healthy proper sexuality is an act of love in marriage that can bring it renewed freshness. Thus, the *mitzvah* of *onah,* quite distinct from that of procreation (mentioned in the Book of Genesis), serves the children already born by making the marriage a firmer and more loving partnership.

If You Want to Learn More

See Talmud *Ketubot* 47b, 48a, 61a, 66b; Talmud *Bava Metziah* 59a; Maimonides, *Book of Commandments,* negative commandment 262, *Code of Jewish Law, Even HaEzer,* 70, 73, 76; Yalkut Me'am Lo'ez, *Commentary to the Book of Exodus; Sefer HaHinnuch,* commandment 46.

5. Cursing or Striking One's Parents:

"One who curses his father or his mother shall be put to death" (Exodus 21:15). "One who curses his father or his mother shall be put to death" (Exodus 21:17). "Everyone that curses his father or his mother shall be put to death" (Leviticus 20:9).

i. A person who cursed his parents by using the name of God was subject to stoning to death. Striking one's parents was subject to the penalty of strangulation by death.

ii. According to rabbinic interpretation, striking a parent meant injuring a parent and blood was seen. In cases where there was no loss of blood, the punishment was flogging.

Commentators

Hinnuch.

He states that the penalty for cursing or striking one's parent was severe because it is one's parents that brings a person into the world by the will of God. Thus, cursing and striking are both an affront to one's parents and to God.

Maimonides.

He says that the person who strikes his father or his mother is put to death on account of his great audacity and because he undermines the constitution of the family, which is the foundation of the state.

Nachmonides.

His interest relates to why there were different punishments for cursing or striking a parent. He concludes that stoning (ordained for cursing) was a more severe punishment than strangulation (ordained for striking a parent). Since children are more likely to curse one's parent than to attack them physically, cursing one's parents was subject to the more severe punishment in order to deter others from sin.

If You Want To Learn More

See Talmud *Kiddushin* 30b, Talmud *Sanhedrin* 53a, 66a, 84b; Maimonides, *Book of Commandments*, negative commandments 318, 319; *Code of Jewish Law, Yoreh De'ah,* 241; *Sefer HaHinnuch*, commandments 48, 260; Maimonides, *The Guide of the Perplexed* 3:41.

6. Respect for the Elderly:

"You shall rise before the aged and show deference to the old" (Leviticus 19:32).

i. This commandment expresses the Jewish ideal regarding treatment of the elderly, who in biblical times were honored for their wisdom and life's experiences.

ii. The rabbinic attitude toward the elderly also reflects the importance of proper treatment toward the elderly. In *Ethics of Our Fathers* Antigonos of Socho says: "A person who learns from the young is compared to one who eats unripe grapes and drinks wine from a vat, whereas a person who learns from the old is compared to one who eats ripe grapes and drinks wine that is aged" (4:26).

iii. To meet the need for care for the elderly, the first Jewish home for the aged was established in Amsterdam in the mid-eighteenth century. Today, most Jewish communities have care facilities for the elderly.

Commentators

Hinnuch.

He states that the main point of a person's having been created in the world is for the sake of wisdom, so that he will become aware of his creator. It is therefore fitting, says the Hinnuch, for a person to honor one who has attained it. As a result, others will be bestirred.

Maimonides.

He states that this commandment is especially obligatory for a disciple who owes the greatest of respect to his teacher and has the duty of fearing him. (Note that the rabbinic sages have always regarded the learned as aged, irrespective of their actual age, thus teaching that the obligation to respect old age transcends the bounds of race or religion.)

Recanti.

He states that it is a positive injunction to revere a sage because world peace can only be sustained by the intelligence of wise human beings.

If You Want to Learn More

See Talmud *Kiddushin* 32b, 33a; Talmud *Berakhot* 28a; Talmud *Bava Metziah* 33a; Talmud *Sanhedrin* 5a; *Mishneh Torah, Laws of Talmud Torah*, ch. 6; Maimonides, *Book of Commandments*, positive commandment 209; *Sefer HaHinnuch*, commandment 257.

7. *The Adulterous Wife:*

"If a man's wife has gone astray and broken faith with him . . . then he shall bring her to the priest" (Numbers 5:11–31).

i. This commandment (described in Numbers 5:11–31) deals with the law of the suspicious husband who believes that his wife has been unfaithful
to him.

ii. The suspicions of a jealous husband are proved or disproved by giving his wife so-called "bitter water" and waiting to see the results of this ministration.

iii. Many ordeals of jealousy were known in the ancient Near East, including a parallel in the Babylonian Code of Hammurabi, where the river itself acts as the Divine judge.

iv. In this commandment, the Torah gives the male partner clear prerogatives by laying the burden of proof of innocence on the woman.

v. This commandment clearly implies that fidelity is an essential element in marriage and that jealousy is a legitimate sentiment, for trust is the foundation of the marital covenant.

Commentators

Maimonides.

He states that the procedure of this ordeal for the suspected adulterous wife was meant as a deterrent to all married women from engaging in extramarital sexual relations.

Nachmonides.

In his explanation, he notes the talmudic injunction that states that one should never rely on the occurrence of miracles. The exception, he states, involves the only biblical instance where a commandment is dependent upon a miracle for its effectiveness. This was purposely designed by God, so that a Jewish wife would never afford herself an opportunity to bear illegitimate children.

Abrabanel.

He states that the name of God was written on the scroll with the curses, and erased together with them by the water. The purpose of this was to show that through her dastardly deed, the suspected adulteress brought shame upon the people of Israel as well as disgrace to God himself.

Hinnuch.

He states that it is most noteworthy that the nation of Israel has a method for removing any suspicion from Jewish wives. He also mentions that whereas other nations would often terminate the life of a suspected adulteress without due investigation, the Jewish nation was different in that it required a thorough investigation.

If You Want to Learn More

See Talmud *Berakhot* 63a; Talmud *Ketubot* 51b; Talmud *Sotah* 2a, 2b, 3a, 4a, 6a, 7a, 24a, 26a, 47b; Maimonides, *Book of Commandments*, positive commandment 223, negative commandment 104; *Code of Jewish Law, Even HaEzer*, ch. 11, p. 178; *Sefer HaHinnuch*, commandments 365–367; Philo, *Of Special Laws*, X.

8. Prohibition against Intermarriage

"You shall not intermarry with them; do not give your daughters to their sons or take their daughter for their sons" (Deuteronomy 7:3).

   i. Marrying within Judaism has always been encouraged among the Israelites. In one of the earliest Bible stories, Abraham instructs his servant Eliezer to find a wife for his son Isaac from his own family.

   ii. By the time of Ezra (400 B.C.E.), intermarriages were deemed socially and politically so undesirable that they had to be dissolved.

Commentators

Hinnuch.

He states that the reason for this commandment is for the protection of the Israelite children. Children who are products of a so-called mixed marriage cannot be expected to have solid convictions in matters of religion.

Abrabanel.

He states that in the case of an intermarriage, the true attraction between the Jewish person and the Gentile can only be sexual. Such a marriage, Abrabanel says, can most easily lead to the abdication of the Torah.

Morris Joseph.

He states that every Jew who contemplates marriage outside of his or her religion must be regarded as paving the way to a disruption that would be the final disaster in the history of the Jewish people.

If You Want to Learn More

See Talmud *Kiddushin* 68b, Talmud *Sanhedrin* 82a; Talmud *Shabbat* 56b; Maimonides, *Book of Commandments*, negative commandment 52; *Code of Jewish Law, Even HaEzer*, 16; *Sefer HaHinnuch,* commandment 427; Morris Joseph, *Judaism as Life and Creed*.

9. Divorce

"When a man takes a wife and marries her, and it happens that she finds no favor in his eyes, because he has found some unseemly thing in her, then he writes her a bill of divorce" (Deuteronomy 24:1).

    i. In biblical times, if a man found fault with his wife he was instructed to issue her a bill of divorce.

    ii. An entire talmudic volume called *Gittin (Divorces)* elaborates on the rabbinic specific details related to the divorce procedure.

    iii. Jewish law has provided that a man can divorce his wife if:

    a. she refuses conjugal relations;
    b. she has no children after having been married ten years;
    c. she commits adultery;
    d. she is lax in religious observance.

    iv. In about the year 1000 C.E., Rabbi Gershom, an important European Jewish legal authority, issued his famous edict which stated that a man may not divorce his wife except with her consent.

    v. Today, according to traditional Jewish law, a *get* (written bill of divorce) is required for every Jewish divorce. The *get* is written by a trained scribe and contains these components:

    a. A statement that the husband divorces his wife without duress.
    b. A statement that after the *get* the husband and wife may have no further sexual relationship.
    c. The time and place of the writing of the *get*.
    d. Complete Hebrew names of husband and wife, including any nicknames or added names by which they may be known.

Commentators

Maimonides.

In presenting reasons for a wife to ask her husband for a divorce, he says that if the husband debars his wife from participating in certain joyous functions or prevents her from wearing costly dresses and jewelry that he can afford to buy, she may sue for and be granted a divorce.

Abrabanel.

He states that a husband's obligation is to provide for his family, which often necessitates his going out into the world of competitive business. Thus, when a man chooses a wife, he expects help and compatibility at home. If there is not love and compatibility, a husband may divorce his wife.

Hinnuch.

He makes a case for the superiority of Judaism when it comes to the laws of divorce. Citing the fact that some religions forbid divorce under any circumstances, the Hinnuch states that it is far more sensible to dissolve a marriage when there is incompatibility rather than to continue with constant stress and strain.

If You Want to Learn More

See Talmud *Sotah* 5b; 16a; Talmud *Ketubot* 46b, 47a, 74a; Talmud *Gittin* 10a, 20a, 20b, 21b, 85a, 87a, 90a, 90b; Maimonides, *Book of Commandments*, positive commandment 222, negative commandment 356; *Code of Jewish Law, Even HaEzer*, ch. 10, pp. 115, 178; *Sefer HaHinnuch*, commandments 579, 580.

Section VI: Diet

1. Prohibition of Eating the Thigh Muscle

"Therefore the children of Israel are not to eat the thigh vein which is on the hollow of the thigh, unto this day, because he touched the hollow of Jacob's thigh, even in the sinew of the thigh vein" (Genesis 32:33).

   i. In Genesis (chapter 32) we are told that Jacob wrestles with an angel, after which his name is changed to "Yisrael" (Israel). This struggle left its mark, for Jacob leaves while limping on his thigh. Because of this, rabbinic law has forbidden the eating of any part of the thigh muscle of a kosher animal, including the area known today as the "sirloin."

Commentators

Sforno.

He says that the significance of the prohibition of eating the thigh muscle is to symbolically demonstrate that a Jew must never allow a physical handicap to discourage him in his fight for survival.

Hinnuch.

He says that at the root of this commandment lies the purpose that Jewry should have a hint that even though they will endure great struggles in the exiles at the hands of the nations and the descendants of Esau, they should remain assured that they will never perish, but their children and their name will endure forever. Thus, for the Hinnuch, the commandment to prohibit eating of the thigh muscle is a symbol of Israel's eternal survival.

Maimonides.

He states that the prohibition of eating the sinew of the thigh vein, even though found in the Book of Genesis, was commanded at Mount Sinai. Therefore we are simply obliged to keep this commandment because God the Commander commanded it.

If You Want to Learn More

See Talmud *Chullin* 89b, 96b; Maimonides, *Book of Commandments,* negative commandment 183; *Code of Jewish Law, Yoreh De'ah,* 65; *Sefer HaHinnuch,* commandment 3.

2, 3. Prohibition of Eating the Flesh of a "Torn Animal" or an Animal That Dies Otherwise Than by Correct Ritual Slaughter

"You shall not eat any flesh that is torn by beasts in the field. You shall cast it to the dogs" (Exodus 22:30). "You shall not eat of an animal that dies of itself" (Deuteronomy 14:21).

i. The first dietary commandment forbids the eating of any animal or fowl that was killed by a predatory animal. Such an animal is called a *terefah*. Rabbinically interpreted, the *terefah* has also come to refer to an animal (or fowl) that had physical defects or injuries with which it could not have survived for a year. The flesh of such an animal is forbidden food, even if the animal were Jewishly ritually slaughtered in the proper way.

The second dietary commandment forbids the eating of an animal or fowl that dies by itself (i.e., by natural causes). Such an animal has been termed a *nevelah*.

ii. The defects that would render an animal unfit for consumption according to rabbinic interpretation include an animal or fowl in any of the following conditions.

    a. Torn by a bird of prey or wild animal.
    b. Perforated vital organ.
    c. Underdeveloped organ.
    d. No liver
    e. Cut windpipe
    f. Torn membrane.
    g. Loose limbs as a result of a fall.
    h. Fractured ribs.

Commentators

Hinnuch.

His reason for not eating animals that had been killed by a beast of prey relate to health. He states that such animals are unhealthy and are therefore not to be eaten.

Maimonides.

He states that the meat of an animal that has died a natural death is indigestible and harmful as food.

Ibn Ezra.

He was interested in why the torn animal was to be disposed of by being cast to the dogs. He answers that dogs were the guardians of the animals, and their occasional reward for protecting the animals when an animal strayed and was killed by another was being fed meat.

J. P. Hyatt.

In his anthropological answer, he states that the prohibition of not eating flesh torn by beasts is an old taboo, based on the belief that the wild animal transferred its evil power to the torn animal.

If You Want to Learn More

See Talmud *Chullin* 37a, 47b, 102b, 114b, 115a, 115b; Talmud *Avodah Zarah* 67b; Talmud *Zevachim* 69a, 69b; Maimonides, *Book of Commandments,* negative commandments 180, 181; *Code of Jewish Law, Yoreh De'ah,* 15, 16, 29; *Sefer HaHinnuch,* commandments 73, 472; J. P. Hyatt, "Exodus," in *New Century Bible Commentary* (Grand Rapids, MI: Eerdmans, 1980).

4. *Prohibition against Mixing Meat and Milk and Eating Them Together*

"You shall not cook a kid in its mother's milk" (Exodus 23:19; Exodus 34:26; Deuteronomy 14:21).

    i. The prohibition against mixing meat and milk is mentioned in three different places in the Torah.

    ii. Rabbinically speaking, this commandment has been interpreted to mean that milk and meat cannot be eaten together or cooked together, and it is forbidden to derive benefit from food containing a milk and meat mixture.

    iii. Rabbinic law designed a waiting period between the eating of milk and meat. This period of waiting ranges from one to six hours, depending on which branch of Judaism one belongs to.

Commentators

Ibn Ezra.

He explains that cooking a kid in its mother's milk was a form of extreme barbarism, and that is why it was forbidden to mix meat and milk together.

Rashbam.

Similar to the reasoning of Ibn Ezra, he, too, believes that the ancient practice of cooking a kid in its mother's milk was a form of barbarism and cruelty to animals.

Maimonides.

He states that there are idolaters who worship their idols by an act of mixing meat and milk. Therefore, the Torah outlawed this mixture so that the Israelites would refrain from imitating idolaters.

Nachmonides.

He states that it is a sadistic act to boil a kid in its mother's milk and a cruel thing for any member of a holy nation to do.

Hinnuch.

He does not believe that the mixing of meat and milk is injurious to one's health. Rather, he states that the mixing of meat and milk is an interference with the very laws of nature themselves.

Samson Raphael Hirsch.

He states that this prohibition is intended to maintain the natural order of God's world. He states that the Jewish people have their place in the universe, and that they are not to mix with others. The prohibition of mixing meat and milk is another way of separating the Jewish people from the other nations of the world.

Abraham Joshua Heschel.

He states that the reason for this prohibition may be that the goat provides humans with the single most perfect milk in the world. It is the only food that, by reason of its composition of fat, carbohydrate, and protein, can by itself sustain the human body. How ungrateful we would be to kill the child of an animal to whom we are so indebted and cook it in the very milk that nourishes us and is given to us freely by its mothers.

Othmer Keel.

He emphasizes the intimate relationship between the mother and the kid. Keel informs us that the artistic image of the mother animal suckling its young is frequently found in ancient Near Eastern art. Killing the young with its mother would be a denial of the life process that allows for a mother to give birth to and nurture its young. Life can not be sustained if we tarnish the relationship between mother and child.

If You Want to Learn More

See Talmud *Chullin* 105a, 113b, 114a, 115b; Talmud *Shabbat* 130a; Maimonides, *The Guide of the Perplexed,* pt. 3, sect. 48; Maimonides, *Book of Commandments,* negative commandments 186, 187; *Code of Jewish Law, Yoreh De'ah,* 87; *Sefer HaHinnuch,* commandments 92, 113; James Lebeau, *The Jewish Dietary Laws: Sanctify Life.*

5. Prohibition of Eating Blood

"You shall eat no manner of blood" (Leviticus 7:26). "Be sure that you do not partake of the blood; for the blood is life, and you must not consume the life with the flesh" (Deuteronomy 12:23).

    i. Rabbinically interpreted, this commandment requires that before meat can be eaten, all of its blood must be drained by soaking and salting using coarse salt or by broiling it.

    ii. According to traditional Jewish Law, liver, because it contains so much blood, must be broiled before it is eaten.

    iii. As soon as an animal is slaughtered according to prescribed Jewish Law, it is positioned to allow its blood to drain. Since some blood remains, the meat is purged to remove all residual blood. The butcher removes veins, sacs, and the various membranes that collect blood, and then either the butcher or the traditional homemaker soaks, salts, and rinses the meat to further extract the remaining blood.

Commentators

Nachmonides.

It was his opinion that the reason for this prohibition against eating the blood was to prevent our bodies from absorbing animalistic characteristic. If humans refrain from consuming blood, which is the source of life and the very soul of the animal, they will be less likely to take on the animal's vitality or instincts.

Maimonides.

He ascribed special powers to the blood and suggested that the Jews were forbidden to consume it in an attempt to wean them away from idolatry, which held that blood provided nourishment to the so-called spirits.

Joseph Hertz.

He states that the prohibition of the consumption of blood tamed man's violent instincts by weaning him from blood and implanting within him a horror of all bloodshed.

If You Want to Learn More

See Talmud *Chullin* 64b; Talmud *Kritot* 20b, 21a; Maimonides, *Book of Commandments,* negative commandment 184; *Code of Jewish Law, Yoreh De'ah,* commandment 65; *Sefer HaHinnuch,* commandment 148; Joseph Hertz, *Commentary on the Five Books of Moses.*

6. Permitted Foods

"These are the living things that you may eat among all the beasts that are on the earth. Whatsoever parts the hoof, and is wholly cloven-footed, and chews the cud, among the beasts, that you may eat" (Leviticus 11:2ff.). "You may eat whatever has fins and scales in the water" (Leviticus 11:9).

i. The term *kashrut* (literally, "fit to be eaten") refers to those animals that meet the requirements for traditional Jewish consumption. The Bible states that animals that have split hooves and chew their cuds may be eaten. All fish that have fins and scales are also permissible to be eaten.

ii. The rabbis said that the dietary laws belong to the class of commandments which must be obeyed, although the reasons for them transcend human understanding.

iii. The dietary laws have been tenaciously kept to this day by the traditional Jewish people in lands around the world.

Commentators

Philo.

He states that the dietary laws are intended to teach the Jewish people control of their bodily appetites. He further finds a symbolic meaning in the permission to eat of animals that chew their cud and have divided hoofs. He says that man grows in wisdom only if he repeats and chews over what he has studied and if he learns to divide and distinguish various concepts.

Maimonides.

Somewhat similar to the reasoning of Philo, he states that the purpose of keeping the Jewish dietary laws is to inculcate self-control, but to this he also added that these regulations are also health laws. Many of the forbidden animals are injurious to human health, and in addition are also aesthetically repulsive (e.g., eels and roaches).

Nachmonides.

Specifically regarding the prohibition of eating fish that do not have fins and scales, he says that fish with fins and scales swim close to the water's surface where they frequently come up for air. This warms their blood, and unlike fish that do not have fins and scales, allows them to rid themselves of various impurities.

Recanti.

He states that the purpose of the dietary laws was to purify one's soul as a person draws its sustenance from the food in accordance with its refinement and purity.

Samson Raphael Hirsch.

He suggests that a rejection of the dietary laws makes the Jewish people "impure" and denies them holiness.

Joseph Hertz.

He suggests that outward consecration was symbolically to express an inner sanctity. By keeping the Jewish dietary laws, the people of Israel would always remind themselves of their status as a holy people, separate from the other nations of the world.

Mary Douglas.

She suggests that holiness means keeping distinct the categories of creation. She believed, therefore, that the biblical categories would classify as unacceptable or unclean any foods from species which are imperfect members of their class, or whose class itself confounds the general scheme of the world. The dietary laws are, therefore, signs that inspire meditation on the oneness, purity, and completeness of God. By rules of avoidance, holiness is given a physical expression in every encounter with the animal kingdom and at every meal.

Isaac Klein.

He believes that the dietary laws are designed to add holiness to the lives of the Jewish people. When one invites a friend for dinner, a new dimension is added to eating, which becomes a social act. Similarly, when a meal takes place in connection with a Jewish life-cycle event (e.g., wedding or circumcision), it becomes a solemn act that helps add significance to the occasion.

Jacob Milgrom.

He says that keeping the Jewish dietary laws is an instrument to sustain and perpetuate life—to elevate, revere, and sanctify it.

If You Want to Learn More

See Talmud *Kiddushin* 57a; Talmud *Chullin* 42a, 59a, 66b, 140a; Maimonides, *Book of Commandments,* positive commandments 149–152; *Code of Jewish Law, Yoreh De'ah,* 80, sect. 1–3, 5; *Sefer HaHinnuch,* commandments 153, 155, 158, 470; Isaac Klein, *A Guide to Jewish Religious Practice* (on dietary laws); Samson Raphael Hirsch, *Commentary on the Book of Leviticus.*

7. *Forbidden Foods*

"You shall not eat of their flesh and their carcasses you shall not touch" (Leviticus 11:8). "Whatever has no fins or scales in the water is a detestable thing to you" (Leviticus 11:12). "And these shall be an abomination among the fowls, and they shall not be eaten" (Leviticus 11:13). "And all the winged swarming things are unclean to you, and you shall not eat them" (Deuteronomy 14:19).

    i. In these verses the Bible designates all of the so-called forbidden foods (i.e., unkosher). These include fish that have no fins and scales, certain kinds of insects, animals that do not chew their cuds and have divided hooves, and certain kinds of fowl.

    ii. Although enumerating various varieties of forbidden fowl, the Torah does not list the physical characteristics of forbidden fowl. The ancient rabbis listed the following criteria for the so-called forbidden fowl:

    a. Birds of prey.
    b. One toe must be larger than the others.
    c. Birds must have a crop.

d. Birds must have a gizzard of which the inner lining can be easily removed.

iii. According to the Torah, locusts were permitted if they had four
wings that covered most of the length and breadth of their bodies, four feet,
and jointed legs.
iv. The product of an insect that was not a part of its body is permissible
to be eaten (e.g., honey from bees).

Commentators

Nachmonides.

Regarding the prohibition of eating fish that do not have fins and scales, he
states that such fish are stationary and are more like earth-bound creatures.
Thus, they are out of their element in the water and therefore forbidden to be
eaten.

Maimonides.

He states that insects are repulsive and therefore ought not to be eaten.

Ibn Ezra.

He states that it is impossible for a person to have a pure, clean, and holy
conscience if he eats insects and snacks.

If You Want to Learn More

See Talmud *Chullin* 59a, 60b, 63b, 66b, 126b, 127a; Talmud *Bava Metziah*
61b; Talmud *Pesachim* 23a; Talmud *Shabbat* 33a, 90b, 145b; Maimonides,
Book of Commandments, negative commandments 172–179; *Code of
Jewish Law, Yoreh De'ah,* chs. 79, 80, 83, 84; *Sefer HaHinnuch,* commandments 154, 156, 157, 159, 162–165, 471.

SECTION VII: JUSTICE

1. Prohibition against Murder

"You shall not murder" (Exodus 20:13).
i. This is the sixth of the Ten Commandments.

ii. Murder is one of the cardinal sins in Judaism. The penalty for murder in the Bible was death. The rabbis emphasis on the value of human life is expressed in many passages. For example, "whoever saves a single life, Scripture regards the person as though he/she has saved the entire world, and whoever destroys a single life, scripture regards the person as though he/she destroys the entire world" (Talmud *Sanhedrin* 4:4).

iii. In the second century c.e., capital punishment was decried by most of the rabbinic scholars. In Israel, crimes of treason and genocide are punishable by death.

Commentators

Nachmonides.

He is interested in knowing the reason for the prohibition of murder following the commandment to honor one's parents. He sees the logic as follows: God is the partner of every mother and father, and it is surely a crime to destroy that which was created by such a holy partnership.

Keli Yakar.

He suggests that since man was made in the image of God, if one man took the life of another, it would be as if he denied the godliness of his fellowman.

Abrabanel.

Referring to various rabbinic explanations, he states that the prohibition of murder extends in its meaning to also refer to withholding deeds of kindness from the poor or public humiliation of another. These are also considered forms of murder and are thereby expressly prohibited.

Hinnuch.

He states that the root meaning of this precept ought to be plainly obvious to everyone. Since God structured the world and commanded people to be fruitful and multiply, it would be totally antithetical to this structure for a person to murder another person.

If You Want to Learn More

See Talmud *Makkot* 6b, 12a; Talmud *Bava Kamma* 83b; Talmud *Sanhedrin* 72b; Maimonides, *Book of Commandments,* negative command-

ments 289, 292, 295, 296; *Code of Jewish Law, Choshen Mishpat,* 425;
Sefer HaHinnuch, commandments 34, 409, 413.

2. Prohibition against Stealing

"You shall not steal" (Exodus 20:13). "If a person steals an ox or a sheep, he
shall pay five oxen for an ox and four sheep for a sheep" (Exodus 21:37).

i. The Torah relates the prohibition against stealing several times (Exodus
20:13, Exodus 21:37, Leviticus 19:11, and Deuteronomy 19:11). Rabbinic
interpretation has suggested that the prohibition in Exodus and Deuteronomy is directed against stealing a human being (kidnapping) while the
prohibition in Leviticus is against stealing property. With regard to restitution, the Torah states that "if a person steals an ox or sheep he shall pay five
oxen for the ox and four sheep for the sheep."

ii. Rabbinic tradition recognized various categories of theft. They included: deceit or fraud; using false weights and measures to steal; stealing
something forbidden to be used or that was useless, for which no restitution was required; stealing documents, for which simple restitution must
be made; stealing animals and garments, which required double restitution;
stealing and selling or slaughtering oxen or sheep, for which the restitution
was fivefold and fourfold, respectively; and kidnapping, which was punishable by death.

iii. Rabbinic interpretation extends the prohibition against stealing to
include the "stealing of a person's heart" (e.g., inviting a person to be a
guest when one does not really wish to host the person).

iv. In modern times, acts such as copyright infringement and plagiarism
are also considered forms of stealing.

Commentators

Maimonides.

His concern related to the assessment of restitution as stated in Exodus
21:37 (i.e., five oxen for an ox, but only four sheep for a sheep). He states
that restitution for stolen property relates to the risk that the thief runs in
committing the crime. The less the risk, the less the punishment. If a person
steals in a situation where there is a large crowd, the risk is higher and the
restitution need only be twice the value of the stolen property if apprehended. Stealing sheep in an open field involves even less risk, since it is
impossible for any shepherd to be watching his flock at all times. If the thief
is caught, the risk is fourfold restitution. If a person steals an ox which is in

the habit of fleeing from the herd the risk is even less because it is very difficult for a person to watch over all oxen with care. Thus if caught, the restitution is fivefold.

Akedat Yitchak.

He states that the thief is treated differently from the one who causes damage. The latter who caused damage through his ox or pit did not intend to deprive his fellow of anything. He is therefore required to make half or total restitution. The thief who deliberately sets out to inflict loss upon another deserves to have a taste of his own medicine—to lose the same amount that he stole from his fellow man. This can only be achieved through double restitution.

Ibn Ezra.

He states that the damage caused to the owner of the ox is more because he ploughs with it. He also suggests that the penalty for ox stealing is heavier because the thief cannot hide it as easily as sheep. Only an expert thief can execute such an operation.

If You Want to Learn More

See Talmud *Bava Metziah* 61b, 112a; Talmud *Bava Kamma* 57b, 62b, 67b, 79b; Talmud *Sanhedrin* 72b, 86a; Maimonides, *Book of Commandments,* positive commandment 239, negative commandments 243, 244; *Code of Jewish Law, Choshen Mishpat,* 348, 359; *Sefer HaHinnuch,* commandments 36, 54, 224.

3. Bearing False Witness

"You shall not bear false witness against your neighbor" (Exodus 20:13; Deuteronomy 5:17).
  i. This is the ninth of the Ten Commandments.
  ii. The reliability and dependability of witnesses was very important in a court of justice.
  iii. Rabbinic interpretation suggests that this prohibition covers not only the act of witnessing but addresses itself to the character of a person. A false testifier not only lies and infects himself and the social fabric, but when he practices his deceit in court, the damage is doubly destructive.

iv. The severity of breaking this commandments is reflected in this statement from a midrash that says that "one who bears false witness against one's neighbor commits as serious a sin as if one had borne false witness against God, saying that God did not create the world" (*Mechilita* to Exodus 20:13).

Commentators

Ibn Ezra.

He attempts to understand why the text did not say "false testimony" rather than "false witness." He concludes that it is actually addressed to a false witness, as if it read: "Do not testify, if you are a false witness."

Meshech Chochma.

He responds to the Ibn Ezra puzzlement as to why the text stated "false witness" instead of "false testimony". He states that the reason is obvious: Though the actual testimony is true but he was not a witness to it— knowledge without sight—though it is not false testimony, he is nevertheless a false witness. This is the force of the text, "you shall not bear false witness."

Maimonides.

Quoting the *Mechilta,* he states that the person who bears false witness against his fellowman commits as grave a sin as if he had borne false witness against God, saying that He did not create the world.

Hinnuch.

He says that who suppresses testimony is compared to a person who stands idly by the blood of one's neighbor

If You Want to Learn More

See Talmud *Makkot* 2b, 4b, 5a, 5b; Talmud *Ketubot* 20a, 33a; Talmud *Sanhedrin* 37a, 90a; Maimonides, *Book of Commandments,* positive commandment 110, negative commandment 216; *Code of Jewish Law, Choshen Mishpat,* 28, 38; *Sefer HaHinnuch,* commandments 37, 524.

4. Prohibition against Coveting

"You shall not covet your neighbor's house, nor his wife, nor his man-servant" (Exodus 20:14; Deuteronomy 5:18).

    i. This is the last of the Ten Commandments. This commandment is in that category of commandments that deal with a person's feelings, in this case, the feeling of jealousy.

    ii. Prophets such as Micah and Habakkuk considered envy to be at the root of social injustice.

    iii. Rabbinic interpretation has suggested that if being envious of another leads a person to steal the possessions of another, he has violated the commandments of envy in thought, deed, and in theft.

Commentators

Maimonides.

He derives two separate negative commandments from this tenth commandment, based upon the two different Hebrew words *tachmod* ("covet") and *titaveh* ("desire") appearing in the two slightly different versions. Maimonides says that *tachmod* connotes only an actual plan to acquire another's property, while the latter refers even to desiring something that belongs to someone else. To desire an object is forbidden because, according to Maimonides, one's love for the object will eventually become so strong that one will ultimately devise some scheme to obtain it.

Sforno.

He states that if a person begins to envy an object belonging to his neighbor that he must train himself to pretend that the object does not exist at all. Otherwise, coveting will lead to lust, theft, and eventually even to the possibility of murder.

Malbim.

He states that the word "envy" in the Exodus version of this commandment refers to a physical experience—the actual impact of something that is pleasant to the eye. On the other hand, "desire" in the Deuteronomy version refers to the person who expresses the desire even for something which is not present and which is not outwardly beautiful. The person himself experiences a longing for it.

Samson Raphael Hirsch.

He suggests that coveting one's neighbor's wife refers to the act of pressuring her husband to divorce her so that he can marry her.

If You Want to Learn More

See Talmud *Sotah* 9a, 9b; Talmud *Bava Batra* 21a; Talmud *Bava Metziah* 5b; Maimonides, *Book of Commandments,* negative commandments 265, 266; *Code of Jewish Law, Choshen Mishpat,* 359; *Sefer HaHinnuch,* commandment 38.

5. Capital Punishment

"He that strikes a person so that he dies shall surely be put to death" (Exodus 21:12).

i. Prescribing capital punishment for a variety of offenses is both believed to be a deterrent as well as the fact that the perpetrator was detrimental to the community because in a sense, he had offended God.

ii. In the Torah, the death penalty was prescribed for many different crimes, including murder, adultery, blasphemy, false evidence in capital cases, false prophecy, idolatry, incest, striking one's parents, profaning the Sabbath, and witchcraft.

iii. Under Jewish law, capital punishment was imposed only when the Jerusalem Temple was still in existence.

iv. Rabbinic authorities made every effort to have judges avoid imposing capital punishment. We are told in the talmudic tractate of *Sanhedrin* (63a) that the members of a court that pronounced a capital sentence were obliged to abstain from all food on the day of execution.

v. The four types of capital punishment known in bygone years were death by strangling, sword, fire, and stoning.

vi. In the case of only causing injury to another person (see Exodus 21:18), the injured was entitled to compensation based on loss of time from work and medical treatment. Rabbinic law expanded compensation to include compensation for physical disability, pain, and indignity.

vii. Modern Israel has no capital punishment except for participation in genocidal activities and under certain conditions of warfare.

Commentators

Hinnuch.

He states that the root reason for this precept is to instill fear in the heart of the potential killer. He states that if it were not for the fear of justice, people would kill one another. This is the reason why God charged that a killer be put to death. ·

Maimonides.

He states that it was of cardinal importance to know which penalty was relevant to which crime. Thus, in his view, each individual procedure in the capital punishment arena was a commandment by itself.

If You Want to Learn More

See Talmud *Sanhedrin* 43b, 44a, 45a, 46a; Talmud *Ketubot* 30a; Maimonides, *Book of Commandments,* positive commandments 226–229; *Sefer HaHinnuch,* commandments 47, 50, 555.

6. Prohibition against Witchcraft

"You shall not tolerate a sorceress" (Exodus 22:17).
    i. It was considered a grave sin to mislead people by using forms of sorcery.
    ii. The pretended holding of communication with evil spirits or sorcery was regarded as a form of idolatry and rebellion against God, punishable by death.
    iii. Since immorality was closely connected with witchcraft, the law of the sorceress is preceded in the Torah by the section against sexual license and is followed by the regulation against unnatural vice (see Exodus 22:15–18).

Commentators

Maimonides.

He says that sorcery was a cardinal crime punishable by death because it was a way of exploiting the illiterate and causing them confusion.

Hinnuch.

He states that a sorceress was able to cause persons many misfortunes and were extremely dangerous people. Furthermore, sorceresses could cause people to divert their minds from belief in God's perfect work. This is why they were condemned to death.

If You Want to Learn More

See Talmud *Sanhedrin* 56b, 67a, 67b; Maimonides, *The Guide of the Perplexed,* pt. 3, sect. 37; Maimonides, *Book of Commandments,* negative commandment 310; *Sefer HaHinnuch,* commandment 62.

7. Prohibition against Cursing

"You shall not curse a judge, and a ruler of your people you shall not revile" (Exodus 22:27). "You shall not curse a deaf person" (Leviticus 19:14).

    i. Among ancient and primitive peoples, a curse was more than an expressed wish for evil. It was considered a method of making the potential harm become a reality.

    ii. Curses were often pronounced in the name of a god or demon. Belief in the power of curses was most prevalent among the ancient Babylonians, who relied on professional sorcerers to curse their enemies before battle.

    iii. The Torah approaches the act of cursing with great seriousness. When Balaam, the Moabite prophet (Numbers 25) prepares to curse the Israelites, God makes sure that his curse will be deflected and turned into a blessing.

    iv. Under biblical law, one who used God's name for purposes of cursing was subject to execution by stoning.

Commentators

Hinnuch.

He states that when a person curses a judge he defies, not only the court, but also God Himself, since the court is acting in the name of God.

Recanti.

He states that although a curse cannot in reality cause a person bodily harm, it does have the potential of causing emotional harm and mental anguish.

Maimonides.

He states that although a curse cannot really harm one's victim, it is forbidden to curse because the desire to curse someone is usually a result of some pent-up feeling of anger or hurt. Thus, the prohibition against cursing is an attempt to wean a person from feelings of anger.

If You Want to Learn More

Talmud *Shavuot* 35b; Talmud *Sanhedrin* 56b, 85a; Midrash Rabbah, *Shemot, Mishpatim,* ch. 31, secs. 8, 17; Maimonides, *Book of Commandments,* negative commandment 315; *Sefer HaHinnuch,* commandments 69, 71, 231.

8. Pursuing Truth in Justice

"You shall not utter a false report" (Exodus 23:1).

i. Truth is given high priority in the Torah. One of the Ten Commandments states that one is forbidden to tell a lie.

ii. This commandment has been rabbinically interpreted to warn a person against slander. The rabbis included this prohibition in the laws concerning fairness in court, because slander is a form of unfair behavior toward an often defenseless victim.

iii. On the basis of this commandment, the rabbis ruled that a litigant must not state his case to the court in the absence of the other litigant.

Commentators

Hinnuch.

He states that falsehood is abominable and corrupt in the eyes of all. Since God is a God of Truth, it is of utmost importance to stay far away from falsehood, since falsehood distances a person from God's Presence.

Nachmonides.

He states that God's laws are the very embodiment of justice. A judge, therefore, is expected to dispense God's law, since in essence he is acting as God's emissary in making legal decisions.

If You Want to Learn More

Talmud *Pesachim* 118a; Talmud *Sanhedrin* 6b, 7a, 7b; Maimonides, *Book of Commandments,* negative commandments 276, 281; *Code of Jewish Law, Choshen Mishpat,* 12, 17; *Sefer HaHinnuch,* commandments 74, 415.

9, 10. *Prohibition of Partiality in a Lawsuit and Not Accepting a Bribe*

"You shall not favor a poor person in his cause" (Exodus 23:3). "You shall accept no bribes" (Exodus 23:8).

i. The biblical view of justice is most noted for its unbending insistence on the strictest impartiality. If the matter in dispute is a question of money between a rich and a poor man, the judge is not to give a wrongful verdict in favor of a poor man on the plea that the rich person would not miss the sum involved.

ii. Biblical law also demands (see Leviticus 19:13) that the court not favor so-called important people in a lawsuit.

iii. A judge must never accept a gift from a litigant.

Commentators

Hinnuch.

He states that the reason for this commandment is already known to all. It applies in every place and in every time, for impartiality, no matter who the litigants are, is a noble, proper, and worthy matter.

If You Want to Learn More

See Talmud *Chullin* 134a; Talmud *Sanhedrin* 36b; Talmud *Ketubot* 105a; Maimonides, *Book of Commandments,* negative commandments 274, 275, 277–279; *Code of Jewish Law, Choshen Mishpat,* 9, 17; *Sefer HaHinnuch,* commandments 79, 81, 83, 234, 521.

11. *Prohibition of Trapping the Uninformed*

"You shall not put a stumbling block before the blind" (Leviticus 19:14).

i. This verse is a general warning against leading the young and morally weak into sin. It is not, as it appears on the surface, directed against taking advantage of an individual's physical handicap.

ii. Most rabbinic authorities understand this commandment to mean that one ought not take advantage of one who is ignorant of a particular situation, for example, sending a person on a dangerous journey where the person thinks there is no danger or offering a drink to a Nazirite (one who has vowed to abstain).

Commentators

Rashi.

He states that this commandment is not referring to the literally blind person, but rather to a person who is ignorant or blind to a particular situation.

Maimonides.

He further elaborates on the implication of this commandment by stating that it is forbidden to sell a heathen weapons of war, nor can we sell them knives, iron chains, or anything else that is a public danger. However, we may sell them shields, which are only for defense purposes. Maimonides says that whatever is forbidden to sell to a heathen is likewise forbidden to sell to a Jew who is a robber, since in doing so we make ourselves an accessory to a criminal and tempt him to unlawful acts. Whoever, therefore, misleads an innocent person (literally, the blind in the matter) and gives him dishonest advice violates this negative commandment.

Hinnuch.

He states that this commandment is intended to serve to improve society and order its communal life in order to guide people and give them good advice in all their activities.

If You Want to Learn More

See Talmud *Pesachim* 22b; Talmud *Kiddushin* 32a, 32b; Talmud *Chullin* 7b; Talmud *Avodah Zarah* 14a; Maimonides, *Book of Commandments,* negative commandment 299; *Sefer HaHinnuch,* commandment 232.

12. Requirement of Two Witnesses

"Whoever kills a person, the murderer shall be slain at the mouth of two witnesses, but one witness shall not testify against any person that he die" (Number 35:30; also Deuteronomy 17:6).

　　i. This commandment refers to the requirement of two witnesses to testify in the case where a death sentence is involved.

　　ii. Qualifications of witnesses were of utmost importance, since most trials were based completely upon the testimony of eyewitnesses. Among those rabbinically excluded from giving testimony in capital cases were women, minors, professional gamblers, and all of those who knowingly transgressed the laws of the Torah or were ignorant of them.

Commentators

Abrabanel.

He suggests that since one man is on trial, it logically follows that more than one witness is needed to prove his guilt, as if there was need of only one witness, then the case would be one person's word against another.

Hinnuch.

He suggests that mankind has a natural proclivity toward evil. A person who has a negative feeling toward another will work diligently to bring his enemy down. He may even be likely to distort his testimony since he is filled with such ill-will. However, it is less likely that two trustworthy witnesses will conspire to distort the truth. For this reason, this commandment requires the testimony of two faithful witnesses.

If You Want to Learn More

See Talmud *Sanhedrin* 33b, 34a, 84b; Talmud *Ketubot* 21a; Talmud *Gittin* 71a; Talmud *Bava Kamma* 70b, 90b; Maimonides, *Book of Commandments,* negative commandments 288, 291; *Sefer HaHinnuch,* commandments 411, 523.

13. Appointing Judges

"Judges and officers shall you make in all of your gates . . . and they shall judge the people with righteous judgment" (Deuteronomy 16:18).

    i. This commandment suggests those provisions necessary for an ordered civil government.

    ii. The highest court was the Great Sanhedrin, which was composed of 71 judges. The head of the Sanhedrin was called the *nasi* ("president"), and to the right of the *nasi* sat the *av bet din,* the "father of the court." A smaller Sanhedrin was composed of 23 sages for communities where there were fewer than 120 people.

    iii. According to talmudic tradition (*Sanhedrin* 17a), only those were appointed to the Sanhedrin who had stature, wisdom, good appearance, maturity, and familiarity with languages.

iv. In 1806 Napoleon brought about a revival of a Sanhedrin when he convened an assembly of Jewish notables for purposes of Jewish legislation. It consisted of forty-five rabbis and twenty-six lay people.

Commentators

Or HaChayyim.

The author was interested in the reason why the judges were selected by the people, which might lead to judges who could easily be swayed by those electing them. *Or HaChayyim* answers that this was the true test of a strong society, one who could appoint judges and submit with humility to their authority.

Nachmonides.

He questioned why there was the necessity of a smaller Sanhedrin when the Great Sanhedrin met daily in Jerusalem. He answered that the smaller courts alleviated some of the potential judicial burden of the Great Sanhedrin, allowing cases to be tried quickly without delay.

Maimonides.

He states that the purpose of the judges was to enforce the observance of the Torah's commandments, to compel those who strayed from the truth to return to it, to command the performance of what is good and the avoidance of that which is evil and to inflict the penalties on the sinners, so that the commandments and prohibitions of the Torah shall not be dependent upon the will of the individual.

If You Want to Learn More

See Talmud *Sanhedrin* 2b, 3a, 7a, 7b, 16a, 17b; Talmud *Makkot* 7a; Talmud *Shabbat* 10a, 139a; Maimonides, *Book of Commandments,* positive commandment 176, negative commandment 284; *Code of Jewish Law, Choshen Mishpat,* chs. 1, 5; *Sefer HaHinnuch,* commandments 141, 491.

14. Making a Parapet for the Roof

"You shall make a parapet for your roof, so that you do not bring bloodguilt on your house if anyone should fall from it" (Deuteronomy 22:8).

i. This commandment deals with safeguarding one's roof by building a parapet around it. Modern building codes have similar regulations.

ii. It was customary in bygone years for people to go up to the roofs. Without a railing or a guard there was always the possibility of one falling off the roof. This commandment would prevent accidental falls.

iii. Rabbinic tradition added that any form of danger created by humans, such as digging a well and leaving it uncovered, was a violation of Jewish law.

Commentators

Hinnuch.

He states that even though God pays careful attention to the details of human beings and knows all their deeds, nevertheless, one always must guard oneself from chance occurrences. Similarly, a person must take safeguarding measures to help protect his fellowman as well.

Maimonides.

He says that an important feature of this commandment is that just as it makes it obligatory to remove all obstacles that might endanger other people's lives, it equally imposes upon everyone the obligation to safeguard his own life. In like manner it is also obligatory to remove and to guard against every obstacle that constitutes a threat to life.

Abrabanel.

He states that although it is true that any person who falls from a roof to his death was predestined to die (because of his own sins), why should that death occur in one's house, due in part to one's own negligence? This explains the commandment to surround your roof with a guardrail.

If You Want to Learn More

See Talmud *Shabbat* 32a; Talmud *Sukkah* 3b; Talmud *Chullin* 136a; Maimonides, *Mishneh Torah: Laws of the Murderer*, ch. 11; Maimonides, *Book of Commandments*, positive commandment 184, negative commandment 298; *Code of Jewish Law, Choshen Mishpat*, 427; *Sefer HaHinnuch*, commandments 546, 547.

Section VIII: Relationships

1. *Prohibition against Adultery*

"You shall not commit adultery" (Exodus 20:14).

i. This is the seventh of the Ten Commandments. Dealing with the sanctity of marriage, this command is directed to both the man and the woman, and both are to be executed if found guilty (Leviticus 20:10).

ii. The purity and honor of a family are important values in Judaism. Thus adultery is called "the great sin" in the Bible (Genesis 20:9) and "the sin" in the Talmud (*Sanhedrin* 74a). It is thus considered one of the three sins (along with idolatry and murder) that people should avoid, even on pain of death.

iii. Other ancient Near Eastern law collections also prescribe the death penalty for adulterers, but, by treating adultery as an offense against the husband alone, permit the aggrieved husband to mitigate the punishment.

iv. Because the marriage bond is divinely sanctioned and the prohibition of adultery is of divine origin, God as well as the husband are offended by adultery.

Commentators

Keli Yakar.

He uses the logic of the structure of the Ten Commandments in his reasoning. The right tablet of the Ten Commandments has five commandments, each of which deals with the relationship between God and man. The left tablet bears five commandments dealing with the relationship between man and his fellowman. The prohibition against adultery (the seventh commandment) appears directly opposite the prohibition of idolatry (second commandment). According to the Keli Yakar, this was to demonstrate that adultery was forbidden because it could lead to idol worship.

Hinnuch.

He presents several reasons why adultery was prohibited:

    a. No species ought to become intermingled with another. Children should always know their mother and father.

    b. Children born of an adulterous relationship will never be able to honor their parents.

    c. It will lead to murder because a jealous husband may kill his wife's lover.

Samson Raphael Hirsch.

He says that one might think that if the husband does not mind, it is permissible for the wife to commit adultery. That is why the Torah qualifies "another man"—even though he be "your neighbor," and if it is with his consent that you do it, your sin is not diminished, for you have offended God (see Leviticus 20:10).

If You Want to Learn More

See Talmud *Shevuot* 47b; Talmud *Pesachim* 113b; Talmud *Kiddushin* 21b; Maimonides, *Book of Commandments,* negative commandments 347; *Code of Jewish Law, Even HaEzer,* 17, 20, 26; *Sefer HaHinnuch,* commandment 35.

2. Forbidden Relationships

"None of you shall approach to any that is near of kin to him, to uncover their nakedness. . . . I am God" (Leviticus 18:6).

"The nakedness of your father and mother, you shall not uncover" (Leviticus 18:7).

"You shall not uncover the nakedness of your sister, the daughter of your father, or the daughter of your mother, whether born at home, or born abroad" (Leviticus 18:9).

"You shall not uncover the nakedness of the daughter of your son or of the daughter of your daughter" (Leviticus 18:10).

"You shall not uncover the nakedness of the daughter of your father's wife, begotten of your father: she is your sister, and you shall not uncover her nakedness" (Leviticus 18:11).

"You shall not uncover the nakedness of the sister of your father" (Leviticus 18:12).

"You shall not uncover the nakedness of the sister of your mother" (Leviticus 18:13).

i. Various kinds of sexual control are found in almost all human societies. Among the most widespread of these is the prohibition of marriage and sex relations between blood relatives. The extent of these prohibitions varies, but everywhere sexual contact between parent and child is forbidden.

ii. Biblical law forbids not only unions between close blood relatives but also, in certain instances, those between persons connected by marriage. Thus, one may not marry the widow of his father, uncle, or son.

iii. Surprisingly missing from the list of forbidden relationships is that of the father and daughter. The ancient rabbis had to infer it from the prohibition of a union between grandfather and granddaughter.

iv. The passage from chapter 18 is included as the Torah reading for the afternoon of the Day of Atonement. It was selected to impress upon people the need of maintaining Israel's high standard of chastity and family morality. Impurity in marriage, incestuous promiscuity among close relatives, and other abominations were condemned and regarded as unpardonable sins.

Commentators

Ibn Ezra.

He considered the act of sex to be distasteful in the eyes of God. It is for this reason that he believed that God asked the Israelites to sanctify themselves by separating themselves from their wives before receiving the Ten Commandments. Although clearly acknowledging that man was created with a sex drive, Ibn Ezra held that some restrictions ought to be placed on a him, including the prohibition of conjugal relations with close relatives, who were readily available to him.

Maimonides.

He argues that sexual relations ought to be kept in moderation. He also stated that it was scandalous for two blood relatives to have conjugal relations.

Nachmonides.

He could not understand why sexual relations between relatives would be forbidden, since the Torah permitted a man to marry literally hundreds of wives. He guesses that perhaps it was not medically advisable for close relatives to have relations.

Hinnuch.

He states that from uncovering the nakedness of one's close relative many misfortunes and harms would result. He calls such relations with one's own relative ugly and abominable.

If You Want to Learn More

See Talmud *Sanhedrin* 28b, 38a, 57b, 58b, 75a, 76a; Talmud *Yevamot* 3b, 8b, 13a, 13b, 21b, 23a, 54a, 55a; 57a; Talmud *Sotah* 44a; Maimonides,

Mishneh Torah: Laws of Forbidden Relationships, chs. 1, 2; Maimonides, *Book of Commandments,* negative commandments 331–345, 351, 352; *Code of Jewish Law, Even HaEzer,* chs. 15, 16, 21–33, 34; *Sefer HaHinnuch,* commandments 188–206.

3. Abstinence from Sex during the Woman's Menstrual Cycle

"You shall not approach a woman to uncover her nakedness as long as she is impure by her uncleanliness" (Leviticus 18:19).

i. The laws of menstruation fall under the rubric of family purity.

ii. Ten chapters of a talmudic tractate called *niddah* are devoted to so-called ritual uncleanliness caused by menstruation and childbirth.

iii. Jewish law forbids a husband to approach his wife during the time of her menses, generally from five to seven days, and extends the prohibition of any physical contact beyond this period for another seven days, known as the "seven clean days." At the end of the two weeks, the menstruant (known as a *niddah*) must immerse herself in a body of water (called a *mikveh*) and recite a special blessing in which she praises God for sanctifying us with His commandments and commanding us concerning immersion.

Commentators

Maimonides.

He suggested that the prohibition to have relations with one's wife during her menstrual cycle was meant to help to suppress a man's sexual lust and control him from spending whole days in the company of many women.

Nachmonides.

Taking a very practical viewpoint, he suggests that since the ultimate purpose of sex is to reproduce and have children, a man must abstain from sexual contact with his wife during her menstrual cycle, since she cannot possibly conceive at this time.

Hinnuch.

Quoting the Sages, he stated that one of the reasons to keep a husband away from his wife in her menstrual cycle was to make her more beloved to him after she becomes "clean."

Maurice Lamm.

He suggests that whereas unrestricted approachability leads to overindulgence and often boredom and marital disharmony, the separation of husband and wife can bring a refreshing zest to love.

Rachel Adler.

She articulates the symbolic meaning of the ritual bath by stating that a woman's monthly period is a nexus point between life and death. The flood of blood marks a brush with death, and a potential child will not be born. The *mikveh,* on the other hand, is a sign of life. Its waters are called living water, and immersion in the ritual bath signals that the potential begins anew for a child to be born.

Elyse M. Goldstein.

She suggests that to go back to the waters of the *mikveh* is a wholly female experience. Just as Miriam's well gave water to the Israelites, so, too, will the *mikveh* give strength back to Jewish women. Water is the symbol of both birth and rebirth.

If You Want to Learn More

See Talmud *Makkot* 14a; Talmud *Sanhedrin* 37a; Talmud *Niddah* 13b, 31b, 64b; Maimonides, *Book of Commandments,* negative commandment 346; *Code of Jewish Law, Yoreh De'ah,* 183; *Sefer HaHinnuch,* commandment 207; Maurice Lamm, *The Jewish Way in Love and Marriage;* Rachel Adler, Strassfeld et al., "Essay on the *Mikveh,*" in *First Jewish Catalogue,* ed. Elyse M. Goldstein: "Take Back the Waters: A Feminist Re-Appropriation of Mikvah," *Lilith,* no. 15 (Summer 1986), pp. 15–16.

4. Prohibition of Homosexuality and Bestiality

"Do not lie with a male as one lies with a woman; it is an abhorrence" (Leviticus 18:22). "Do not have carnal relations with any beast and defile yourself thereby, and let no woman lend herself to a beast to mate with it. It is perversion" (Leviticus 18:23).

   i. In this passage the Torah condemns homosexuality between males and sexual acts with animals. Although the death penalty was prescribed for such offenses, we have no record of a death sentence for these crimes being carried out under Jewish auspices.

ii. Female homosexuality is not prohibited in the Bible itself, and there are very few condemnatory references to the subject in the entire Talmud.

Commentators

Nachmonides.

He states that homosexuality is loathsome and is forbidden because it does not allow the sexual act to be fulfilled through the birth of children.

Ibn Ezra.

He states that homosexuality is contrary to the laws of nature and is a perversion.

Hinnuch.

Similar in viewpoint to Nachmonides, he states that since there can be no fruitful benefit of offspring in a homosexual relationship, it is therefore expressly forbidden.

Herschel Matt.

He states that although marriage in Judaism has always been heterosexual and its purpose for procreation, it is not the sole purpose of marriage. Sexual pleasure and release are also one of marriage's purposes, as well as trust, companionship, moral and spiritual support, and the overcoming of loneliness. He concludes by saying that unlike celibacy and masturbation, a homosexual relationship can bring into being a union of a caring and loving relationship. He further says that modern homosexuals have no choice in their orientation. As such, they ought to be considered exceptions to traditional Jewish Law, and we ought not be so presumptuous as to deny God's right to create or permit the "homosexual exceptions."

Janet Marder.

She believes that Jewish Law does, indeed, condemn the way of life of a homosexual, but in her opinion, Jewish Law is not binding since it was the work of human beings. The Judaism that she cherishes affirms love of humanity and respect for the spark of divinity in every person and the human right to live with dignity. Therefore, she states that God endorses loving, responsible, and committed human relationships, regardless of the sex of the persons involved in them.

Judith Plaskow.

She states that we ought to see all of sexuality as part of what enables people to reach their level of spirituality. Each person, she states, needs to find that place within himself or herself where spirituality and sexuality come together. Plaskow maintains that for any homosexual to be involved in a heterosexual relationship out of conformity to Jewish law would be a transgression. A gay person can often only find spirituality in a homosexual relationship, which then becomes a *mitzvah.*

If You Want to Learn More

See Talmud *Nedarim* 51a; Talmud *Sanhedrin* 54a, 54b, 55a, 60a; Talmud *Gitten* 85a; Maimonides, *Book of Commandments,* negative commandments 348–350; *Code of Jewish Law, Even HaEzer,* ch. 24; *Sefer HaHinnuch,* commandments 209–211; Hershel J. Matt, "Sin, Crime, Sickness or Alternative Life Style? A Jewish Approach to Homosexuality," *Judaism* 27:1 (Winter 1978): 3–7; Janet Marder, "Jewish and Gay," *Keeping Posted* 32:2 (November 1986): 7; Judith Plaskow, *Standing again at Sinai: Judaism from a Feminist Perspective* (San Francisco, CA: Harper and Row, 1990).

Section IX: Torts

1. Causing Injury to Another When in a Fight

"If men quarrel, and one smites the other with a stone or with his fist and he does not die, but keep his bed. . . . If he rises again, and walks abroad with his staff, then shall he that smote him go unpunished, except that he must pay for his idleness and his cure" (Exodus 21:18–19).

    i. A person is responsible for any damage that he or she inflicts upon another.

    ii. Today, the passage related to "an eye for an eye" (Exodus 21:24) has been reinterpreted rabbinically to mean monetary compensation for an eye.

    iii. An injured person, according to the *Code of Jewish Law,* is entitled to compensation for physical disability, pain, medical treatment, the loss of earning power resulting from the injury and compensation for the indignity and shame inflicted upon him. The Talmud also states that one is not forgiven until he asks for pardon (Talmud *Bava Kamma* 92a).

Commentators

Ibn Ezra.

He understood the phrase, "an eye for an eye," to mean that the person who caused another to lose an eye had to pay the injured monetary compensation.

Hinnuch.

He states that this law of compensation for causing injury is self-understood as a primary axiom of justice. Without such a law, injustice would run rampant in a community.

If You Want to Learn More

See Talmud *Bava Kamma* 83b, 84a, 85a, 91a, 92a; Talmud *Sanhedrin* 58b; *Mishneh Torah, Laws of Sanhedrin,* ch. 5, sect. 10; Maimonides, *Book of Commandments,* positive commandment 236; *Code of Jewish Law, Choshen Mishpat,* 1, 420; *Sefer HaHinnuch,* commandment 49.

2. Damage Caused by Animals: The Ox That Gores

"If an ox gores a man or woman so that they die, the ox must be stoned and its flesh must not be eaten" (Exodus 21:28).

    i. Jewish Law requires that people are responsible for the animals that they own. If one's animal causes injury to another, the owner is liable for the damage.

    ii. The law of the ox that gores is a case law that is also found in the famous Code of Hammurabi. The major difference is the disposition of the offending animal in the Bible. The ox becomes taboo following the incident and, after being destroyed, is not allowed for food.

    iii. Jewish Law differentiates between two kinds of destructive animals:

        a. *Tam* ("unconfirmed"): This is an animal that causes damage in a manner that is unexpected. For example, a young ox is likely to cause damage by eating someone's property, but would not be expected to gore a person using its horns. If it does gore, the owner is liable for only one half the damage.

b. *Mu'ad* ("confirmed killer"): An animal that causes damage in a manner that may usually be expected if it is not under control. Here the owner of the animal is liable for the total amount.

Commentators

Hinnuch.

He states that the root meaning of this precept is obvious and needs no explanation. If people were not held responsible for damage caused by their animals, there would be no true justice and owners would not be careful to control animals that potentially could cause another damage.

Bachya ibn Asher.

He compares the so-called animal that is a "confirmed killer" with the serpent in the Genesis story who also was instinctively conscious of the harm it inflicted. Similarly, the confirmed killer animal type is also somehow aware of the evil it is doing, and therefore one cannot have any benefit from it after its death.

If You Want to Learn More

See Talmud *Bava Kamma,* chs. 1–5; Talmud *Pesachim* 22b, 112b; Maimonides, *Book of Commandments,* positive commandment 237, negative commandment 188; *Code of Jewish Law, Choshen Mishpat,* 389–400; *Sefer HaHinnuch,* commandment 51.

3. Laws Pertaining to the Loan and Safekeeping of Property

"When a man gives money or goods to another for safekeeping, and they are stolen from the man's house, if the thief is caught, he shall pay double" (Exodus 22:6).

"When a man gives to another an ass, an ox, a sheep or any other animal to guard, and it dies or is injured or is carried off, with no witness about. An oath before God shall decide between the two of them to see that the one has not laid hands on the property of the other; the owner must acquiesce and no restitution shall be made" (Exodus 22:9–10).

"When a man borrows an animal from another and it dies or is injured, its owner not being with it, he must make restitution" (Exodus 22:13).

i. These laws deal with the responsibility that a person has who is entrusted with the property of another.

ii. The Talmud distinguishes different categories of persons who guard another's property. They include the *shomer chinam* (person who guards another's property without being paid for his services), the *shomer sachar* (person who guards another's property but is paid), the *socher* (person who hires the property of another person), and the *sho'el* (person who borrows another's property).

iii. In all of the above cases, the person who is guarding another person's property, hires the property, or borrows property is obligated to return the property in the same condition in which it was found.

Commentators

Hinnuch.

He states that these laws are reasonable, self-understood axioms of justice.

Maimonides.

He also writes that fairness of the law is evident. That is to say, if one guards the property of another without remuneration and without deriving any benefit from it for himself that such a person is free from all responsibility. However, if a person takes money for keeping the property or pays for using it and something happens to the property, the losses must be divided between the guardian of the property and the owner.

If You Want to Learn More

See Talmud *Bava Metziah* 41, 42a, 94a, 95a,b; Talmud *Bava Kamma* 63a, 93a; Maimonides, *Book of Commandments,* positive commandments 242–244, 246; *Code of Jewish Law, Choshen Mishpat,* 87, 293, 303, 306; Maimonides, *The Guide of the Perplexed,* pt. 3, sect. 42; *Sefer HaHinnuch,* commandments 57–60.

Section X: The Sabbatical Year

1. The Sabbatical Year

"During the seventh year you shall let your land rest and lie fallow" (Exodus 23:11). "The land shall be a sabbath for God" (Leviticus 2:2).

i. The sabbatical year occurs every seventh year, at which time the land was to lie fallow.

ii. Any fruit or vegetation that grew on their own in the seventh year was deemed public property and could be taken by anyone who wished it.

iii. During the sabbatical year it was forbidden to do any work that could be considered as preparation of the land for cultivation the following year.

Commentators

Ibn Ezra.

In his explanation he parallels the plan of God with that of humankind. Just as God rested on the seventh day from His creation, so too man is commanded to rest the soil. For Ibn Ezra, each year is the equivalent of one day of creation.

Maimonides.

He states in his scientific explanation that to allow the land to lie fallow in the seventh year gives it an opportunity to rejuvenate itself and yield more abundant crops in the years to come.

Keli Yakar.

He states that this law presents people with their opportunity to show faith in God. That is to say, one must certainly have faith that God will provide adequate crops in every sixth year if one is commanded to let his land lie fallow in the seventh.

Abrabanel.

In his spiritual explanation he states the purpose of the seventh year is to provide time for humankind to stop pursuing material gain and allow turn for more spiritual pursuits.

Hinnuch.

Similar in explanation to the Keli Yakar, he states that the law of letting the land lie fallow in the seventh year helps a person increase his trust in God. In addition, by allowing any produce that grows on its own in the seventh year to belong to all people, it helps to shape and increase one's desire to share with others perhaps less fortunate.

If You Want to Learn More

See Talmud *Rosh Hashanah* 8b; Talmud *Sanhedrin* 39a; Talmud *Sukkah* 40a; Maimonides, *Book of Commandments,* positive commandments 134, 135, negative commandments 220–223; *Sefer HaHinnuch,* commandments 84, 112, 326–329.

2. The Jubilee Year

"You shall count seven sabbaths of years" (Leviticus 25:8). "You shall hallow the fiftieth year and proclaim liberty throughout the land" (Leviticus 25:10).

i. The fiftieth year, known as the "jubilee year," rests on the same principle as the sabbatical year. The fiftieth year, occurring after seven times seven years had been counted from the last jubilee, the land was to lie fallow.

ii. Just like the sabbatical year, the year of the jubilee was designed to give the land a rest from agricultural work. Only the spontaneous produce of that year was to be enjoyed and shared with the poor and the strangers.

iii. In the year of the jubilee, all slaves were to be set free if they desired their freedom and debts were to be remitted to Israelites. All property was to revert to the original owner who, through poverty, may have been obliged to sell it at some time during the previous years.

iv. The fiftieth year was marked by the sounding of the ram's horn on the Day of Atonement, hence the Hebrew name *yovel,* which means a "ram's horn."

v. The words "you shall proclaim liberty throughout the land" are inscribed on the Liberty Bell, which announced the signing of the U.S. Declaration of Independence.

Commentators

Maimonides.

He states that the laws of the jubilee year were intended to train a Jewish person to be compassionate and merciful to his fellow man.

Hinnuch.

He states that the root meaning of this commandment of the jubilee is that God desired to convey to His people that everything belongs to Him, and ultimately everything will return to whomever He wished to give it originally. By counting the years to the jubilee each year, the Hinnuch believed that people will be reminded that the earth belongs to God and that they will be more likely to keep away from taking the land over their fellow brothers and sisters.

Ibn Ezra.

He comments upon the Hebrew word *dror,* which is usually translated as "liberty." He tells us that the word "dror" is derived from the Hebrew word for "swallow," a bird that, in captivity, bitterly cries. Man, too, would be a constant slave to his owner (and crying in pain like the swallow) if it were not for the sabbatical and jubilee years which were created to liberate a slave from his servitude.

Rashi.

Also commenting on the Hebrew word *dror,* he relates it to the Hebrew word *dror* ("generation"), because "a generation comes and a generation goes," signifying that liberty insures the survival of the entire human race.

If You Want to Learn More

See Talmud *Rosh Hashanah* 8b, 9a, 9b, 26a, 27b; Talmud *Moed Katan* 2b, 3a; Maimonides, *Book of Commandments,* positive commandments 136, 137, 140, and negative commandments 220–226; *Sefer HaHinnuch,* commandments 330–335, 339–341.

3. Remission of Debts in the Year of Release

"Every creditor shall remit that which he has lent to his neighbor. He shall not exact payment of his neighbor and his brother" (Deuteronomy 15:2).

i. The year of the jubilee included the cancellation of all debts that were outstanding at the end of the sixth year of the seven-year cycle.

ii. Under this biblical law the debtor was absolved of all obligation to repay the loan.

iii. During talmudic times, it was found that as the year of the jubilee approached, people became more reluctant to lend money to one another for fear of forfeiting their claim to it with the arrival of the sabbatical year of release. Rabbi Hillel introduced a method whereby the year of release did not affect the debts that had been turned over to the court. The creditor signed a document called a *prozbul,* formally transferring the debt to the *Bet Din* (Jewish Court), which could reclaim payment even during or after the jubilee year and hand over the sum to the original lender.

Commentators

Abrabanel.

He questions why the Torah emphasizes the canceling of debts over other cases of Jewish charitable giving. In his answer, which uses educational psychology, he states that the Torah intended that the repayment of the loan be annulled because all money in a sense belongs to God and therefore, God has the right to tell people what is best to do with His money.

Hinnuch.

He states that the purpose of the cancelling of the debt is to instill in the spirit of people the quality of generosity and continued and expanded trust in God.

Nachmonides.

He compares the annulment of the debt in the seventh year of release to the cessation of work on the holy Sabbath. It is important for one who observes the Sabbath, not only to stop work, but to have no thought of work in one's mind. Similarly, in the case of the canceling of the debt, the very thought of collecting must be prevented from entering one's mind.

Maimonides.

Quoting the Mishnah, he states that if a person should decide to repay a debt in the seventh year, the Sages will be pleased with him (Talmud *Shevi'it* 10:9). He however, does caution that the creditor may accept payment only if the debtor expressly insists on his doing so, and that the latter may offer such payment only on condition of it being regarded as an absolute gift.

If You Want to Learn More

See Talmud *Arakhin* 28b, 33a; Talmud *Gittin* 36a; Tosefta *Shevi'it,* ch. 8; Maimonides, *Book of Commandments,* positive commandment 41, negative commandments 230–231; *Code of Jewish Law, Choshen Mishpat,* 67; *Sefer HaHinnuch,* commandments 475, 477, 480.

Section XI: Social Obligations

1. Prohibition of Demanding Usurious Interest

"If you lend money to any of my people, you shall not be to him as a demanding creditor. Exact no interest from him." (Exodus 22:24).

   i. Throughout the ancient Near East taking interest on loans was permitted, with certain restrictions. For instance, in Old Babylonian law, the legal maximum was 20 percent for money and 33 percent for grain. Here in the Bible we see that the preference was for an interest-free loan.

   ii. According to Jewish Law, a lender must not cause the borrower embarrassment. If the lender knows that the borrower may be so poor that he or she cannot repay the loan, then the lender must not ask for repayment.

   iii. Rabbinic law has stated the importance of loans of money being carried out in the presence of two eye witnesses.

   iv. The Midrash (*Exodus Rabbah* 31:4) has stated that a rich person who gives to charity and lends money without interest is considered as a person who observes all of the commandments!

   v. Many Jewish communities today have set up free loan societies, fashioned using this biblical law of lending without interest as its model.

Commentators

Ibn Ezra.

He states that any person who is able to lend money to another is dependent upon God who helped him reach that position of creditor. Thus, according to Ibn Ezra, it would be inappropriate for a lender to humiliate the borrower or to be overcome with a feeling of haughtiness, since the lender owes his good fortune to the powers of God.

Hinnuch.

He reiterates the importance of lending to the poor over giving them outright charity. Perhaps, the Hinnuch states, such a loan will help the borrower with another relief so that he or she will not have to ask for outright charity again. The root reason for not demanding interest, according to the Hinnuch, is to instill in the lender the qualities of mercy, kindness, and compassion.

Recanti.

He draws the analogy between the galaxies in space and the interdependence of people. Just as the galaxies are dependent upon their interaction with each other for survival, so, too, do people need to interact with one another through the mechanism of lending and borrowing.

Keli Yakar.

He states that the lender receives greater benefit from giving away a loan than does the borrower who receives the loan. The borrower receives assistance in this world, whereas the lender, because he has assisted the poor, is rewarded in the World-to-Come!

If You Want to Learn More

See Talmud *Shabbat* 63a; Talmud *Bava Batra* 10a; *Ethics of Our Fathers,* ch. 2; Midrash *Rabbah Shemot* 31, sect. 3; Maimonides, *Book of the Commandments,* positive commandments 142, 197, negative commandment 234; *Code of Jewish Law, Choshen Mishpat,* 97; *Sefer HaHinnuch,* commandments 66, 67, 476.

2. Helping One's Fellowman and His Animal

"When you see the donkey of your enemy lying under its burden and would refrain from raising it, you must nevertheless raise it with him" (Exodus 23:5). "You shall not see your brother's donkey or his ox fallen down by the way and withdraw yourself from them. You shall surely help him to lift them up again" (Deuteronomy 22:4).

i. Judaism has always been concerned with welfare of animals. In this biblical law we see that whether it is owned by a friend or an enemy, a passerby must help an overburdened animal to rise and move along its way.

ii. Animals have always been the concern of God, and they were especially important in biblical times, where they were well used in an agricultural society.

iii. The commandment to care for animals in rabbinic literature has come to be known as *tzaar baalei chayim*—"compassion for the pain of animals." The rabbis included in this commandment that of feeding all of your animals before you yourself have been fed (Talmud *Berakhot* 40a).

Commentators

Hinnuch.

He states that the root meaning of this law is to instill compassion in people, whether they be our friend or our enemy.

Rashi.

He is especially intrigued with the Hebrew word *imo,* which means "with him." Rashi explains that this means that once a person (even our enemy) begins to make the effort to help lend a helping hand to the animal, the other person must also lend a hand. In this way, the two persons work together to lighten the animal's burden.

Maimonides.

He states that the object of this law is to enhance man's capability of showing mercy and compassion to all living creatures.

Benno Jacob.

He states that in the course of helping to release the animal, a minimal exchange of words becomes necessary, which might lead to reconciliation and the disappearance of animosity between the two persons.

Keli Yakar.

He states that only when one person is willing to share the work with the other is the other obliged to help. But not otherwise. This, he states, is a lesson to some of the poor people who often rely on the community to support them, refusing to work for their living even when they are fit and able. The poor person must, says the Keli Yakar, do all he can to help himself.

If You Want to Learn More

See Talmud *Bava Kamma* 54b; Talmud *Bava Metziah* 30b, 31a; Maimonides, *Book of Commandments,* positive commandments 202, 203, negative commandment 270; *Code of Jewish Law, Choshen Mishpat,* 272; *Sefer HaHinnuch,* commandments 80, 540, 541.

3. Prohibition against Stealing and Lying

"You shall not steal, neither shall you deal falsely, nor lie to one another" (Leviticus 19:11).

i. Telling the truth and being an honest person is one of Judaism's highest values and ideals. The Talmud (*Shabbat* 55a) states that "the seal of the Holy One, blessed be He, is truth."

ii. One of the seven characteristics of a wise person listed in the Ethics of the Fathers is that of acknowledging the truth and not telling lies (Talmud *Avot* 5:9).

iii. The talmudic rabbis (*Tevamot* 65b) believed that occasionally the telling of a "white lie" is permissible. It is allowed to tell a white lie where the intention is clearly to promote peace and harmony.

iv. Most of the commentators state that the practices referred to in this law refer to the forbidding of deceit in matters of property entrusted to one's keeping and concerning loans and the making of fraudulent claims.

Commentators

Hinnuch.

He states that the rationale behind this commandment of not telling lies is self-evident and that it requires no explanation. The same holds true for Abrabanel, who states that the law of telling the truth is a common-sense one.

Maimonides.

Quoting from the talmudic tractate of *Shavuot*, Maimonides states that the person who swears falsely in repudiation of a debt transgresses two negative commandments: "You shall not swear falsely by My name" and "You shall not lie one to another."

Ibn Ezra.

He states that to witness a theft and keep silent about it is also tantamount to actually having committed the theft.

If You Want to Learn More

See Talmud *Shavuot* 31b, 36b; Maimonides, *Book of Commandments,* negative commandments 248, 249; *Code of Jewish Law, Choshen Mishpat,* 294, 360, 366, 367; *Sefer HaHinnuch,* commandments 225, 226.

4. Prohibition against Taking Revenge or Bearing a Grudge

"You shall not take revenge, nor bear any grudge against the children of your people" (Leviticus 19:18).

i. This commandment is one of a series in the Torah that deals with a person's feelings. Here the Torah forbids a person to bear a grudge or seek revenge against another.

ii. The rabbis (Sifra) present this classic example of the attitude to which this prohibition applies. "A" refuses to lend his spade to "B"; "B" later refuses to lend "A" his ax—that is vengeance. But if "B" lends the ax to "A" and says, "See, I have let you have it even though you wouldn't lend me your spade"—that is bearing a grudge, and this is also forbidden.

Commentators

Rashi.

He states that taking vengeance implies that the person harbors the grudge inwardly though he does not actually take vengeance. Thus for Rashi, both vengeance and bearing a grudge are the product of hate, the former in deed and the latter in thought.

Nachmonides.

In wishing to rule out the taking of the law into one's own hands, he states that vengeance and bearing a grudge are condemned when they involve no definite obligation (i.e., such as "lend me your sickle"). However, no person is required to forgo a monetary debt such as damages, but he may claim it through the court. The guilty party is obliged to pay what he borrowed or stole. This applies with even greater force in capital offenses. Vengeance must be taken and a grudge harbored till the life of one's brother has been paid for, through due process of law as prescribed in the Torah.

Hinnuch.

He states that the reason for the prohibition of taking vengeance upon another is that vengeance is the domain of God. In a sense, the theology of the Hinnuch here is that since God wills everything, it is God, and only God, who has the right to take out vengeance upon another person. Therefore, when a person suffers insult or hurts he should realize that his own sins are responsible and that God decreed it this way. The Hinnuch concludes by stating that this commandment is very beneficial in removing hatred from a person's heart.

Alshech.

He states that one ought not to take out vengeance on another since it is entirely possible that the guilty party will eventually make amends on his or her own.

Biur.

He states that were vengeance and bearing a grudge to be approved of even in cases outside the discretion of the court, human society would be riddled with hate and dissension. The Torah thus forbade it and admonished people to rise above such pettiness.

Maimonides.

His basic premise for this commandment is that most things in life are quite trivial and not worthy of taking vengeance over. Grudges, he states, also make for uncivilized life and difficult social intercourse.

If You Want to Learn More

See Talmud *Yoma* 23a; Maimonides, *Book of Commandments,* negative commandments 304 and 305; *Sefer HaHinnuch,* commandments 241–242; *Sefer Mitzvot Gadol,* negative commandments 11, 12.

5. Loving Your Neighbor

"You shall love your neighbor as yourself" (Leviticus 19:18).

i. This is another in a series of biblical commandments that relate to a person's feelings. Here a person is told to love his neighbor as himself.

ii. The rabbis of old have stated that this commandment is one of the basic pillars upon which the entire Torah is erected.

iii. The fulfillment of this law of loving one's neighbor includes good deeds such as visitation of the sick, comforting the bereaved, and providing dowries for impoverished brides.

Commentators

Hillel.

He transposed this positive commandment into a negative one because he was convinced that it was easier to understand. Thus, he stated that "what is hateful to you, do not do to your neighbor'' (Talmud *Shabbat* 31a). In this way, a person is able to identify what hurts and harms him and, in doing so, then knows those things that must be avoided.

Ibn Ezra.

He explains that one is responsible to love other human beings because the One God has created all of them.

Maimonides.

He understands this command to mean that a person should love his neighbor with all of the qualities and modes of love with which a person loves himself. In other words, the quality and nature of a person's love must be of the highest category, parallel to that which we employ in promoting our own welfare.

Nachmonides.

Like Maimonides, he also senses that loving another person with the same intensity that one has for oneself may not always be possible. Thus, what the Torah really means by the command to "love your neighbor as your-self'' is that people should wish their neighbors well in all things, just as they wish success for themselves.

Malbim.

Disagreeing with Maimonides, he argues that the matter of loving one's neighbor is not an expression of feelings or wishing others success in things. Instead, the commandment relates to how one behaves toward another in action rather than in thought. Thus, Malbim understands this commandment to mean that a person should try to do everything that is to the advantage of his neighbor.

Pinchas Peli.

He states that the real challenge in performing this commandment is the loving of a person who is not particularly lovable in one's eyes. Thus, he understands the command to mean that a person should love one's fellow human being *as* himself, with all of one's own faults and shortcomings, and accept others in the very same way.

Biur.

He takes the view that the phrase "as yourself" is not as qualifying the degree of love, but as motivating the principle embodied in the text. Thus, "as yourself" is to be interpreted as "similar to you." Consequently, it means that a person must love his neighbor because he is similar to himself. (i.e., a human being).

Ramban.

He states that "love your neighbor as yourself" means to love your fellow human being with all the qualities of love with which you love yourself. Thus, according to him, the commandment is concerned with love in its *qualitative* and not its *quantitative* sense.

Sforno.

He states that to love your fellow human being means to put yourself in his position. That is to say, in thinking of a friend who is sick, one would ask, "If I myself were ill, what blessing would I seek from God?" Then he should pray that the other receive that very same blessing.

If You Want to Learn More

See Talmud *Shabbat* 31a; Talmud *Niddah* 17a; Talmud *Sanhedrin* 45a; Maimonides, *Book of Commandments,* positive commandment 206; *Sefer HaHinnuch,* commandment 243; Pinchus Peli, *Torah Today,* p.141; Moses Maimonides, *Mishneh Torah, Hilchot Evel* 14:1; *Ethics of Our Fathers* 1:14.

6. Prohibition against Falsifying Weights

"You shall not falsify measures of length, weight or capacity. You shall have an honest balance, honest weights" (Leviticus 19:35).
    i. This biblical commandment warns that people should be careful to have exact weights and measures.
    ii. The rabbis cautioned that weights should be kept clean from rust, since a coat of rust adds its own weight.
    iii. The rabbis of old insisted that the sin for falsifying weights was greater than that of incest!

Commentators

Recanti.

He draws an analogy between the parts of a scale and the balance of man. Just as both parts of a scale have to be parallel in order to be accurate, so too, he states, a person must be well balanced and try to stay far from extremes. Thus Recanti is in favor of a life of moderation, a value espoused by many rabbis in ancient times and even today.

Abrabanel.

His comments relate to the placement of the command to have just weights immediately before the next sentence in Leviticus which states ''I am God who freed you from Egypt. From the juxtaposition of these two verses, Abrabanel concludes that God reminded the Israelites about having just weights at the same time as He asked them to remember their slavery in Egypt. This was purposely done to remind them that the concept of freedom is forever to be equated with just laws, and that people must always set standards of justice when dealing with their fellow human beings.

Ba-al Ha-Turim.

He reminds us in his commentary that any person who violates the laws of just weights also rebels against God and all of God's commandments. No person should pretend to serve God and at the same time deceive other people.

Ibn Ezra.

He states that one can only have true civilization if justice prevails, and that if one perverts justice by falsification of weights, it will lead to the deterioration of the society.

If You Want to Learn More

See Talmud *Bava Batra* 88b, 89b; Talmud *Bava Metziah* 49b; Maimonides, *Book of Commandments,* positive commandment 108, negative commandments 271, 272; *Code of Jewish Law, Choshen Mishpat,* 231; *Sefer HaHinnuch,* commandments 258, 259, 602.

7. *Loving the Stranger*

"You shall love the stranger, for you were strangers in Egypt" (Leviticus 10:19).

i. There are more than thirty references in the Bible related to loving the stranger!

ii. The frequency of this command in the Bible suggests that strangers and foreigners had a difficult time finding acceptance in society.

iii. The Torah gives an explicitly stated reason for the commandment to love the stranger, calling on the Israelite's compassion: "You shall not oppress a stranger, for you know the feelings of the stranger, having yourselves been strangers in Egypt" (Exodus 23:9). In this way, the Israelites are told to be empathetic to all strangers, since they themselves were strangers in Egypt.

iv. Rabbinic interpretation has come to understand the word for "stranger" to mean a "proselyte" or "convert."

Commentators

Hinnuch.

He states that any person who leaves his or her religion in order to become Jewish is certainly deserving of our complete and whole-hearted love.

Rashi.

He states that when people know how painful it is for the stranger, they can better empathize with him. That is why, he states, it is important for the Jewish people to remember always what it felt like to be slaves in Egypt.

Samson Raphael Hirsch.

He states that the treatment of the stranger is a special test of ethical living. Because of their history of persecution, Jews should be more sensitive to the suffering of foreigners or strangers. Every stranger, he states, is a human, and Jews, in order to remain a holy people, are obliged to love the stranger.

Leo Baeck.

He states that this commandment is intended to teach us that no person is superior to any other person, and that all people in a sense are strangers and must care for one another.

Nachmonides.

He states that the recollection of what God did for the Israelites in Egypt is meant to encourage the Jewish people to help the oppressed. God, too, will stand by the persecuted.

Alshech.

He maintains that the Torah's linkage of the warning about "knowing the feelings of the stranger" with the reminder that "you were strangers in Egypt" is to teach us not to oppress the stranger by noting our own treatment by God. Clearly, Alshech states, those who recall their origins before being given the Torah will be more sensitive to the feelings of strangers and will treat them with more understanding.

If You Want to Learn More

See Talmud *Bava Metziah* 59b; Talmud *Gittin* 57a; Maimonides, *Book of Commandments,* positive commandment 207; *Sefer HaHinnuch,* commandment 431; Leo Baeck, *The Essence of Judaism* (New York: Schocken Books, 1936), pp. 197–198.

8. Being Charitable

"You must open your hand and lend him sufficient for whatever he needs" (Deuteronomy 15:8).

i. Charity is one of the most important pillars in all of Judaism.

ii. The word *tzedakah* in Hebrew literally means "righteousness," and is synonymous with the Hebrew word *mishpat* meaning "justice." Thus in Judaism, *tzedakah* is not a matter of philanthropic sentiment but an act of justice.

iii. In Judaism, the poor people are entitled to the help of other people.

iv. One tenth of one's annual income has come to be the official rabbinic reply to the question of "How much do I give?"

v. There have been many rabbinic statements written about righteous giving. Maimonides, who established his famous Eight Degrees of Charity, writes that the highest form of charity is when money is given to prevent another person from becoming poor, as by providing that person with a job or by lending him money to tide him over. There is no greater charity than this because it prevents poverty in the first instance!

Commentators

Ibn Ezra.

He comments upon the importance of one's attitude when doing righteous giving. He states that when one gives to the poor, one must give whole heartedly and never grudgingly.

Abrabanel.

He states that charity is an exercise in faith. Since one loses when one gives (at least arithmetically speaking), this commandment comes to teach us that God promises an increase when we give to others.

Hinnuch.

He states that this commandment is intended to teach us and educate us to become more compassionate and caring people. When we give to others, we become God's agents.

If You Want to Learn More

See Talmud *Bava Batra* 9b, 10a; Talmud *Ketubot* 67b; Talmud *Shabbat* 151b; Maimonides, *Mishneh Torah: Hilchot Gifts to the Poor*, chs. 7–10, Maimonides, *Book of Commandments*, positive commandment 195; negative commandment 232; *Code of Jewish Law, Yoreh De'ah*, 247; *Sefer HaHinnuch*, 478, 479.

9. Returning Lost Property

"You shall restore them to your brother" (Deuteronomy 22:1).

   i. It is a positive commandment to return lost property to its rightful owner.

   ii. According to rabbinic law, when a person who has lost a prized possession has abandoned all hope of finding the object and the object is found, the law permits the finder to keep the object.

   iii. The commandment of returning lost property has been rabbinically interpreted to also include the obligation of everyone to care for the possessions of others.

   iv. Early rabbinic commentators insist that even if the lost item belongs to one's enemy, it must still be returned.

Commentators

Nehama Leibowitz.

She states that the commandment of restoring lost property involves not only the passive taking charge of the lost article until the owner claims it, but also an active concern with safeguarding a neighbor's possessions so that they remain intact and would be able to be restored.

Bachya ibn Pakuda.

He comments that the instruction to return lost property is in essence the fulfillment of the Bible's instruction to "love your neighbor as yourself" (Leviticus 19:18). Property is an extension of the human being, and loving one's neighbor means taking care of all that is of importance to him.

Hinnuch.

He states that a society of human beings needs to trust in one another. Thus a society in which people watch over and return the lost property of others is one in which people have faith in each other. This is the sign of a society in a good state of health.

Nachmonides.

He comments that the commandment to return lost property supersedes any inconvenience that might be caused to the finder. The sooner the announcement goes out that an object has been found, the better the chance of the one who lost it finding it, thus reducing his or her anxiety.

Pinchas Peli.

He states that from the moment one notices a lost object, one must get involved and try to find it. That is to say, people must be proactive when it comes to lost property.

Recanti.

He reminds us that people very much value their possessions, and when they lose something they can be extremely distressed. Thus, finding another's lost object can help ease the mental burden of the one who has lost it.

If You Want to Learn More

See Talmud *Bava Metziah* 23b, 25a, 26a, 27a; Talmud *Sanhedrin* 73a; Maimonides, *Book of Commandments,* positive commandment 204, negative commandment 269; *Code of Jewish Law, Choshen Mishpat,* 259, 263; *Sefer HaHinnuch,* commandments 538, 539; Nehama Leibowitz, *Studies in Deuteronomy, "parshat ki tetze"*; Pinchas Peli, *Jerusalem Post,* Sept. 7, 1985.

Section XII: Community

1. Law of the Half-Shekel

"This is what everyone who is entered in the records shall pay: a half shekel by sanctuary weight—as an offering to the Lord. (Exodus 30:13).

i. Biblical law required that the Israelites pay a levy of one half shekel for maintenance of the sanctuary.

ii. During the time of the Second Temple, this was revived as an annual levy paid by the Jews. Every year, during the month of Adar, each Jew was required to donate half a shekel to pay for the daily sacrifices brought by the priests on behalf of all of the people.

iii. In modern times we read the portion of the Torah dealing with the theme of the half shekel on the Sabbath preceding the month of Adar. This Sabbath is called *Shabbat Shekalim*—the "Sabbath of the Shekel."

Commentators

Da'at Zekanim.

The author questions whether a rich person was permitted to donate more than one-half shekel. The answer was that all persons were required to donate only one-half shekel. In this way, rich and poor alike were equal when it came to giving donations to the Temple.

Abrabanel.

Commenting with similar theme to that of Da'at Zekanim, he states that the reason why everyone was commanded to give one-half shekel and not according to their true financial ability was so that the rich (who were capable of giving more) would not do so, thus embarrassing a poor person.

Keli Yakar.

He states that the half shekel donation was intended as an atonement offering for the worship of the golden calf. The half shekel amount was chosen to symbolize the Ten Commandments that were broken apart by Moses after he saw the Israelites dancing around the golden calf.

Benno Jacob.

He states that the half shekel donation was intended as a ransom for one's soul. Thus, the soldier who is ready to march into battle is, in the eyes of God, a potential taker of life, though not a deliberate murderer, and therefore requires a ransom for his life.

Hinnuch.

He states that the purpose of the commandment of the half shekel was so that all of Israel should have an equal share in the sacrifices, and that both rich and poor alike should be equal in the eyes of God.

If You Want to Learn More

See Talmud *Megillah* 13b, 29b; Jerusalem Talmud *Shekalim,* chs. 1, 2, 3, 6; Maimonides, *Book of Commandments,* positive commandment 171; *Sefer HaHinnuch,* commandment 105.

2. Getting Involved When You See a Crime

"Do not stand idly by the blood of your neighbor" (Leviticus 19:16).

i. This biblical commandment suggests that people need to be involved when they see a crime being perpetrated upon another.

ii. A famous rabbinic adage states that "one who saves one person in Israel, it is as if that person saved the entire world."

iii. This commandment has been rabbinically understood in the field of medical ethics as justifying the destruction of an embryo in a woman's womb in order to save her life. In such a case, the embryo is regarded as the "pursuer," the mother as the victim, and the doctor as the rescuer.

Commentators

Hinnuch.

He comments that the root purpose of this commandment is self-evident. Just as one person will save his fellow human being, so will the other save him when necessary. This makes for the kind of world in which people help one another, and in this kind of society does God truly delight.

Ehrlich.

He understands the commandment to mean that a person should not act in such a way that one profits by the death or injury of another person.

Ibn Ezra.

He understands the verse to mean that a person ought not to associate with bloodthirsty people.

Maimonides.

He questions why we are permitted to kill a pursuer intent on murder (even before he has actually committed the deed) and were not permitted to act in a similar fashion to one who desecrates the holy Sabbath and worships idols. The answer is that there is a difference between a potential murderer, who once having committed the crime, the crime cannot be undone, and the idol worshiper, who may desecrate the Sabbath but always is given a second chance to repent.

If You Want to Learn More

See Talmud *Bava Kamma* 26a, 28a; Talmud *Sanhedrin* 72b, 73a; Maimonides, *Book of Commandments,* positive commandment 247, negative commandment 297; *Code of Jewish Law, Choshen Mishpat,* 425, 426; *Sefer HaHinnuch,* 237, 600, 601.

3. Cities of Refuge

"The manslayer may return to the land of his possessions" (Numbers 35:28).

i. In biblical times, if a person killed someone unintentionally, he could find security by fleeing to one of the six levitical cities of refuge.

ii. By fleeing into one of the cities of refuge, persons pursued by avengers of blood were protected against the ancient law of life for life.

iii. The Bible provided that the principal roads leading to the cities of refuge should be kept open, so that every homicide would be able to find a refuge. Only upon the death of the high priest could the unintentional manslayer leave the city of refuge.

Commentators

Hinnuch.

He states that even though a person may have killed unintentionally, it nevertheless has resulted in the death of a person. The city of refuge is a suitable place for such an unintentional murderer, allowing him to be protected from capital punishment but resulting in a loneliness of life which a city of refuge imposes upon him.

Bachya ibn Pakuda.

He reasons that an unintentional murderer was not penalized with the death punishment because there was not unity of action between his heart and body. Although his hands killed, his heart did not tell him to kill. This teaches that every person should attempt to coordinate the dictates of the heart with the desire to do that which God wants of people.

Gunther Plaut.

He states that the cities of refuge probably arose out of the need to end family feuds by taking the law out of private hands and placing it in public enforcement. He sees several purposes for these cities of refuge: to protect unintentional murderers from avengers, to punish them, and to isolate the sin that they committed.

Samson Raphael Hirsch.

He sees the cities of refuge as places to give the unintentional murderer an opportunity for forgiveness and rebirth.

Me'am Loez.

The purpose for the cities of refuge is to display compassion for the unintentional murderer by giving him a home where his life would be protected.

If You Want to Learn More

Talmud *Rosh Hashanah* 26a; Talmud *Sanhedrin* 18b; Talmud *Makkot* 7a, 9b, 11a, 11b; Maimonides, *Book of Commmandments,* positive commandments 182, 225, negative commandment 295; *Sefer HaHinnuch,* commandments 408–410, 413, 520; Gunther Plaut, *The Torah, A Modern Commentary,* pp. 1249–1250.

4. A City's Responsibility for a Murder Committed in Its Vicinity

"The elders of that town shall bring the heifer which has never been worked, which never pulled a yoke. . . . And they shall break the heifer's neck" (Deuteronomy 21:4–7).

i. The expiatory ritual for unsolved manslaughter has said to have dated back to the laws of the Hittites. Underlying the ritual was the concept that murder stained the land and that without punishment of the guilty the entire community was tainted.

ii. The community nearest the place of the murder was considered responsible and a heifer was chosen to ward off the wrath of God.

iii. Eventually, in talmudic times, when the crimes of murder multiplied, the performance of the ritual was no longer feasible and it ceased to exist.

Commentators

David Hoffmann.

He reasoned that the breaking of the neck of a heifer would attract so much public attention and interest that the level of communal responsibility would be raised by this ritual as much as by the execution of the apprehended murderer.

Abrabanel.

He said that the shock value of the breaking of a heifer's neck would prevent the people from forgetting the act and would always serve to keep alive the search for the offender.

Nehama Leibowitz.

She states that the responsibility for wrongdoing does not only lie with the murderer but that lack of care is also criminal. Whoever lies back passively and refuses to have anything to do with the evil in the world can never say, "Our hands have not shed this blood."

Hinnuch.

In his psychological answer, he comments that the purpose of the slaying of the heifer is to arouse the community to relate whatever they might know in relationship to the murder to the town leaders. As a result, they will purge the evil ones and the murderers from their midst.

Sforno.

He states that every community needs to have the attitude that it must not tolerate criminals not only within its own immediate area, but that it will help to assist to root out crime all over the land. Any community, Sforno states, that does not take this attitude, bears the guilt for any murder committed in its vicinity.

If You Want to Learn More

See Talmud *Makkot* 10b, 22a; Talmud *Pesachim* 26a; Maimonides, *Book of Commandments,* positive commandment 78, negative commandment 309; *Sefer HaHinnuch,* commandments 530, 531; Nehama Leibowitz, *Studies in Devarim, "parshat shoftim"*; David Hoffmann in *The Torah, A Modern Commentary,* ed. Gunther Plaut (New York: Union of American Hebrew Congregations, 1981), p. 1479.

Section XIII: War

Prohibition of Destroying Fruits Trees during War

"When in your war against a city you have to besiege it a long time in order to capture it, you must not destroy trees. . . . Only trees which you know do not yield food may be destroyed" (Deuteronomy 20:19–20).

i. This commandment falls under the rabbinic rubric of commandments called *bal tashchit* ("you shall not destroy"). Rabbinic law extended the concept of not destroying fruit trees in time of war to include the reckless destruction of things beneficial to humankind.

ii. The Code of Jewish Law (*Hilchot Shemirat Guf VeNefesh* 14) declares that it is expressly forbidden to destroy or injure anything capable of being useful to human beings.

iii. Human beings in Jewish tradition are seen as God's copartners in safeguarding the earth, since creation is an ongoing process.

iv. A well-known rabbinic teaching states that if one is in the midst of planting a tree and is told that the Messiah has arrived to bring peace to the world, you must not stop planting, but must first finish planting your tree!

Commentators

Ibn Ezra.

He states that since fruit trees yield food for humans, cutting them down is injurious to human health. Therefore the law of not cutting down fruit trees (even in time of war) was instituted to preserve the human species.

Hinnuch.

He states that this law is intended to train the human spirit to love what is good and beneficial. People who save trees will likely be peace-loving people who will do everything in their power to save other things from destruction.

Maimonides.

He extends the prohibition of destroying fruit trees to include the prohibition of obstructing the flow of streams and rivers in order to cause distress to the inhabitants of a besieged city.

If You Want to Learn More

See Talmud *Taanit* 7a; Talmud *Bava Kamma* 91b; Talmud *Makkot* 22a; Maimonides, *Book of Commandments,* negative commandment 57; Maimonides, *Mishneh Torah, Shoftim, Hilchot Melachim* 6, 10; *Sefer HaHinnuch,* commandment 529.

2. Exemption of a Newlywed from Going to War

"When a man takes a new wife, he shall not go out to war, neither shall he be charged with any business. He shall be free for his house for one year" (Deuteronomy 24:5).

i. The Bible provided exemptions for persons who recently built a house and had just started to live in it, or had planted a vineyard and started eating its fruits, or for one who was in his first year of marriage.

ii. The exemption from military service for a first-year husband applied only in cases of so-called optional wars.

Commentators

Hinnuch.

He asks the question related to why marriage should be sufficient grounds for a year's exemption from military service. He comments that there is always the possibility that the life of a soldier during war becomes promiscuous. For this reason, the Bible offers a first-year married man a military exemption from battle, thus allowing him the needed time to bond with his new wife.

Nachmonides.

Using his psychological rationale, Nachmonides argues that a newly married man who serves in battle will have difficulty focusing on the task at hand, thus endangering his life. The Bible, therefore, decided to provide a military exemption for a first-year married man, unless the war were a nonoptional one, in which case the exemption would no longer apply.

Abrabanel.

In a most unusual commentary, Abrabanel argues that the reason for military exemption is that the newly married husband would suffer anguish in not being able to fulfill the religious obligations associated with building a new home and planting a vineyard. In his argument, he states that the husband would not be able to bring the fourth-year fruit to the Temple as prescribed by the Bible, nor would he be able to erect a protective parapet around his new home as prescribed by the Bible.

If You Want to Learn More

See Talmud *Sotah* 42a 42b, 43a, 44a, 44b; Talmud *Kiddushin* 13b; Maimonides, *Book of Commandments*, negative commandments 58, 311, positive commandments 191, 214; *Sefer HaHinnuch,* commandments 526, 581, 582.

Section XIV: Animals and Agriculture

1. Forbidden Mixtures

"You shall not let your cattle breed with a diverse kind. . . . [Y]ou shall not sow your field with two kinds of seed . . . neither shall there come upon you a garment of two kinds of material mixed together'' (Leviticus 19:19). "You shall not sow your vineyard with two kinds of seed lest the fullness of the seed which you have sown be forfeited together with the increase of the vineyard" (Deuteronomy 22:9). "You shall not plow an ox and a donkey together" (Deuteronomy 22:10). "You shall not wear mingled stuff, wool and linen together" (Deuteronomy 22:10).

i. The interbreeding of different species of animals and the planting of different kinds of seeds was regarded in the Bible as contrary to the divinely appointed order of nature. The penalty for being engaged in the crossing of fruit species was flogging.

ii. Deuteronomy 22:11 defines the mixture of two kinds of seeds (in Hebrew called *shaatnez*) as referring to wool and linen. Traditional Jewish Law today limits the prohibition to this one mixture. However, wool or linen may be mixed with cotton, silk, and other fibers.

iii. Jewish Law forbids the use of an ox and a donkey together as a "team" for plowing or other work. These animals were not allowed to be mated, and since they differ substantially in strength, the donkey (the weaker of the two animals) would be placed under undue stress.

iv. Even today there are Orthodox Jewish authorities who will not permit the eating of genetically engineered fruits and vegetables.

v. An entire treatise of the Mishnah, called *Kilayim* (*Forbidden Mixtures*) is devoted to the laws of prohibited combinations of plants and animals.

Commentators

Nachmonides.

He states that each plant and animal created by God has its own distinct features. The right to produce new creatures belongs only to God, the creator of all, and therefore man does not have a right to tamper with the natural order of God's divine plan. Such tampering is a defiance of God.

Ibn Ezra.

Commenting on the prohibition of having an ox and a donkey plow together, he states that the motivation is God's mercy and compassion on His creatures. Since an ox is much stronger than a donkey, putting the two together would cause undue pain to the donkey.

Recanti.

He associates the prohibition of wearing garments from wool and linen with the narrative of Cain and Abel. In the Bible, Cain's offering came from the "fruit of the ground" (Genesis 4:3), while that of Abel was from the "firstlings of the flock" (Genesis 4:4). God's acceptance of Abel's offering over that of Cain led to the first murder in recorded history. Thus, for Racanti, the problem of mixing linen and wool has come to symbolize the incompatibility of the two.

Maimonides.

In his comments, he states that the prohibition against wearing garments of linen and wool relates to the fact that such mixed garments were worn by pagan priests. Since God would not want the Jewish people to be connected in any way with the unchaste practices connected with idolatrous rites, He prohibited the wearing of such garments.

If You Want to Learn More

See Talmud *Niddah,* 61b; *Mishnayot of Kilayim;* Talmud *Bava Metziah* 91a; Talmud *Bava Kamma* 54b; Talmud *Berakhot* 22a; Maimonides, *The Guide of the Perplexed,* pt. 3, sects. 26, 27, 37, 49; Maimonides, *Book of Commandments,* negative commandments 42, 193, 215–218; *Code of Jewish Law, Yoreh Deah,* 296–298; *Sefer HaHinnuch,* 244, 245, 548–551.

2. Leaving Gleanings for the Poor

"You shall not wholly reap the corner of your field" (Leviticus 19:9). "Neither shall you gather the gleanings of your harvest" (Leviticus 19:9). "You shall leave them for the poor and the stranger, for I am the Lord" (Leviticus 19:10).

   i. For the benefit of the poor, the fatherless, the widow, and the stranger, the Bible instructs the owner of a field or a vineyard not to gather the grain that the reapers have failed to remove or the grapes that remain after the vintage.

   ii. The term *gleaning* refers to the ears of corn that fall from the hand of the reaper.

   iii. Poor people were also entitled to *leket* (ears of corn that fall to the ground during reaping).

iv. The subject of the rights of the poor to the produce of one's land is discussed in the talmudic tractate called *Pe'ah,* which is the technical term for the corner of the field that must be left for the poor.

v. According to rabbinic law, the minimum part of the crop that the owner was required to leave for the benefit of the poor was one-sixtieth of the harvest.

vi. A description of the gleaning by the poor is preserved in the Book of Ruth (2:3–7). There it is told how poor people in Bethlehem followed along in the rows of grain after the reapers.

Commentators

Hinnuch.

The Hinnuch presents as one of the reasons for this commandment the attempt to inculcate a spirit of generosity within people.

Alshech.

He states that the law of leaving crops for the poor helps to solidify the important point that one's entire harvest belongs to God, the rightful owner of everything, and the fact that people are merely God's tenants. In addition, since the poor are entitled to part of the harvest they need not be embarrassed by having to ask for a handout. Rather, part of every person's crop belongs to them, and they are entitled to it.

Maimonides.

He states that the owner of the crop was forbidden to discriminate against the poor, and was even considered a robber of the poor if he prevented them from entering his field. If, however, there were no poor in the area, the owner was not obliged to seek them elsewhere but could keep the gleanings for himself.

If You Want to Learn More

See Talmud *Chullin* 131a, 131b; Talmud *Bava Kamma* 94a; Maimonides, *Mishneh Torah: Laws of Gifts to the Poor,* ch. 1; Maimonides, *Book of Commandments,* positive commandments 120–124, negative commandments 284–287; *Code of Jewish Law, Yoreh De'ah,* 332; *Sefer HaHinnuch,* commandments 216–223.

3. Prohibition against Killing an Animal and Its Young on the Same Day.

"And a cow or a ewe, it and its young shall you not slaughter on one day" (Leviticus 22:28). "You shall not take the mother bird with the young" (Deuteronomy 22:6). "You shall let the mother bird go" (Deuteronomy 22:7).

i. It was forbidden to kill an animal together with its offspring within a period of twenty-four hours.

ii. Similarly, it was not permissible to take a mother bird and its offspring together. Interestingly, this is one of only a couple of biblical commandments that promises the reward of a long life for performing it.

iii. The commandment regarding the prohibition of killing an animal with its young on the same day and releasing a mother bird before taking its eggs falls under the rabbinic value of *tzaar baalay chayim*—"not causing pain to animals." These laws were intended to instill in people compassion for the pain of all living creatures.

Commentators

Keli Yakar.

He notes that both the rewards for removing the mother bird before taking its eggs and the reward for honoring parents in the Bible are the same— namely, length of days. His reasoning for this is that if a person is going to behave tenderly toward a bird, how much more so is that person likely to honor and respect his or her parents. Thus, God's reward is one of longevity of life.

Maimonides.

He suggests that since humans are the highest form of animal, they must not use their domineering powers for purposes of hurting other animals. Rather, they must always consider the feelings of the animals which do have emotions and be careful to respect these emotions.

Abrabanel.

He states that the prohibition of not slaughtering an animal with its offspring together is intended to teach humans that they must always be careful not to kill a family of animals which eventually could have the potential of obliterating (if done enough) an entire species.

Hinnuch.

He states that the purpose of the commandment is to demonstrate God's concern for the animal kingdom and God's desire to protect them so that they will continue to endure. It is also the intention of this commandment to instill in humans a quality of pity for animals and remove the quality of cruelty.

Luzzato.

He holds an educational rather than a humane motive for this commandment. He states that as a person approaches a bird's nest, the mother will naturally leave her young in order to escape. However, her maternal instincts prompt her to risk her life and try to save her fledglings. The commandment prohibits a person from touching the mother bird so that her maternal instincts should not lead her to suffer. Thus, the commandment is intended to teach us to respect moral qualities and inculcate the idea that a person never suffers a loss for doing justly.

If You Want to Learn More

See Talmud *Berakhot* 33b; Talmud *Chullin* 78a, 78b, 79b; Maimonides, *Book of Commandments,* negative commandment 101, positive commandment 148; *Sefer HaHinnuch,* commandments 294, 544, 545.

Section XV: Idolatry

1. Prohibition against Divination

"You shall not practice divination nor soothsaying" (Leviticus 19:26).

i. The pretended holding of communication with evil spirits, witches, and so forth was regarded in biblical times as a form of idolatry and a rebellion against God.

ii. The forms of communication that were expressly forbidden included the use of stars to guide one's plans in life, turning to ghosts and spirits, turning to persons who attempted to perform supernatural acts, and dealing with persons who attempted to contact the dead in cemeteries.

Commentators

Maimonides.

In his commentary he discusses the sheer nonsensical aspects of those who purport to be sorcerers.

Hinnuch.

He comments that persons who engage in so called black magic can lead others astray from true, authentic religion. He cautions people who seek out a sorcerer who may by accident make a single correct prediction.

Nachmonides.

He reminds everyone is his commentary that God is the all-knower of things, and it is God who guides everything in the universe, including the stars and the lives of all people. Therefore, it would make sense to trust in God rather than in soothsayers for guidance.

If You Want to Learn More

See Talmud *Chullin* 7b, 95b; Talmud *Shabbat* 75a, 152a; Talmud *Sanhedrin* 65a, 65b, 66a; Maimonides, *The Guide of the Perplexed,* pt. 3, sect. 37; Maimonides, *Book of Commandments,* negative commandments 8, 9, 31, 33–38; *Code of Jewish Law, Yoreh De'ah,* 179; *Sefer HaHinnuch,* commandments 249, 250, 255, 256, 511–515.

2. Prohibition against Shaving

"You shall not round the corners of your head, neither shall you mar the corners of your beard" (Leviticus 19:27).

    i. It was forbidden in biblical times for a person to shave the corners of his hair or mar the edges of his beard. This has been explained as opposing some of the mourning customs connected with the ancient heathen worship of the dead.

    ii. Today this law has given rise to the practice among some observant Jewish men not to shave their beards or sideburns (*peot* in Hebrew.)

    iii. Yemenite Jews often leave the sideburns intact, when, according to the custom among Oriental Jews, they perform the ceremony of giving the first haircut to a boy of four years.

Commentators

Maimonides.

He explains that shaving one's beard and corners of the head was prohibited because it was the pagan practice to do this, and the Jewish people ought not to emulate pagan idolaters.

Bachya ibn Asher.

He states that men were forbidden to shave the corners of their beard since facial hair was the natural way to distinguish men from women.

Hinnuch.

He explained, much like Maimonides, that to shave the corners of one's head was to mimic the idolaters. This was something that the Bible wished to prevent; hence this commandment not to cut the corners of one's hair.

If You Want to Learn More

See Talmud *Makkot* 20b; Talmud *Kiddushin* 35b; Talmud *Shabbat* 152a; Maimonides, *Book of Commandments,* negative commandments 43, 44; *Code of Jewish Law, Yoreh De'ah,* 181; *Sefer HaHinnuch,* commandments 251, 252.

3. Prohibition against Tattooing

"You shall not make any cuttings in your flesh for the dead . . . nor imprint any marks upon yourself" (Leviticus 19:28).

i. Inculcating reverence for the human body as the work of God, the Torah prohibits tattooing.

ii. Cutting the flesh and tattooing the skin were closely connected with idolatrous usages among the Canaanites. In their demonstration of bereavement, they gashed and mutilated themselves, offering their blood as a sacrifice to the dead.

Commentators

Hinnuch.

He stated that the Jewish people were not to emulate the pagans, and tattooing was therefore expressly prohibited because it was common practice among pagans.

Maimonides.

Similar in explanation to that of the Hinnuch, Maimonides writes that tattooing was a heathen custom, who used to so mark himself for idolatry, as much as to say that the tattooed person was a slave sold to the idol and marked for its service.

If You Want to Learn More

See Talmud *Makkot* 21a; Talmud *Kiddushin* 36a; Maimonides, *Mishneh Torah, Mada, Laws of Idolatry,* 12, 11; Maimonides, *Book of Commandments,* negative commandment 41; *Code of Jewish Law, Yoreh De'ah,* 180; *Sefer HaHinnuch,* commandment 253.

4. Dressing in Clothing of the Opposite Sex

"A woman shall not wear that which pertains to a man, neither shall a man wear that which pertains to a woman." (Deuteronomy 22:5).
    i. The Bible forbids the wearing of clothing customary for the opposite sex.
    ii. The Bible appears to wish to teach us that the sexes are sacred and ought to remain completely distinctive from each other. Any attempt to blend the sexes was considered contrary to God's plan for humans.

Comentators

Rashbam.

He attempts to present living examples of males and females dressing in each other's clothing. For example, he states that a woman who dresses in armor like a man going into battle will be led to a life of lewdness. Similarly, any man who chooses to dress and look like a woman could easily use this tact as a ploy to seduce her.

Abrabanel.

He states that homosexuality is an abomination, and that the interchanging of clothes by the sexes will surely lead to homosexuality.

Hinnuch.

He writes that men dressing like women and vice versa is sexually immoral. It leads to lewdness, and that is the reason why it is expressly forbidden in the Bible.

Maimonides.

He states that the interchange of clothing was connected with idol worship. In addition, he writes, the switching of clothing begets lust and leads to immorality.

If You Want to Learn More

See Talmud *Nazir* 59a; Talmud *Shabbat* 94b; Talmud *Avodah Zarah* 29a; Maimonides, *The Guide of the Perplexed,* pt. 3, sect. 37; Maimonides, *Book of Commandments,* negative commandments 39, 40; *Code of Jewish Law, Yoreh De'ah,* 156, 182; *Sefer HaHinnuch,* commandments 52, 543.

Section XVI: Ritual Purity

1. Uncleanliness of a Man and a Woman

"A woman who gives birth to a male child shall be unclean seven days" (Leviticus 12:2). "When a man has a discharge from his flesh, his discharge is unclean" (Leviticus 15:2).

i. According to biblical law, a discharge from the sex organs renders a person ritually unclean.

ii. The biblical laws of purity and impurity are not synonymous with the requirements of physical cleanliness, even though the two types sometimes coincide.

iii. A woman who has given birth becomes unclean and has to count fourteen clean days. She then immerses herself in a *mikveh*—a ritual bath— and is considered ritually clean again.

iv. Women also become ritually impure during their menstrual cycle.

v. A man with a discharge from his sex organs became unclean. Jewish Law divided the discharges into the categories of a discharge of semen and a person who suffered from a chronic discharge from the genitals. For both categories, immersion in a *mikveh* made the unclean man clean.

Commentators

Obadiah ben Jacob Sforno and Keli Yakar.

According to them, women were given their menstrual cycles as a punishment for the sin committed by Adam and Eve. Women were expected to atone for this sin. They did this by counting clean days and then immersing in a *mikveh,* a ritual bath.

Hinnuch.

He relates the connection between disabilities of the body and moral deficiencies. He thus says that a women's menstrual cycle is a sickness because of the overabundance of blood. Thus she needs to stay away from sexual relations with her husband until she immerses in a *mikveh* and again becomes ritually clean. This abstaining from sexual relations has the additional advantage of enhancing the desire for intercourse once the unclean period has ended.

If You Want to Learn More

See Talmud *Niddah* 21b, 24b, 36b, 37b; Talmud *Shabbat* 44b; Maimonides, *Book of Commandments,* positive commandments 99, 100, 104, 106; *Code of Jewish Law, Yoreh De'ah,* 183, 194, 196; *Sefer HaHinnuch,* commandments 166, 178, 181, 182.

2. Laws of the Red Heifer

"Speak to the children of Israel, that they may bring you a red heifer, faultless, wherein is no blemish, and upon which never came yoke" (Numbers 19:2).

i. The need to be cleansed after touching a corpse reflects an ancient fear of the dead.

ii. According to biblical law, the ashes of the red heifer purify a person who has become impure by contact with a corpse. This type of commandment was called a *chok* by the ancient rabbis, and was defined as an irrational law whose rationale is extremely difficult to determine.

iii. The red heifer's ashes mysteriously defiled the person who prepared the ashes for use in the first place.

iv. On one of the Sabbaths before the festival of Passover the chapter on the red heifer is read in traditional synagogues in addition to the weekly portion, and the sabbath is officially called *Shabbat Parah*—the "Sabbath of the Cow." The special reading is to commemorate the purification of the unclean so that they may be able to bring the Passover sacrifice in a state of ritual cleanliness.

Commentators

Nehama Leibowitz.

She writes that a sprinkling of water mixed with ashes from the red heifer possesses both educational and purifying powers. It not only purifies sin but is also a reminder that Jewish people are strictly forbidden from touching the bodies of the dead.

Sforno.

In his symbolic explanation, he states the priest takes cedar wood (identified with pride) because the cedar stands tall, and hyssop (identified with humility) because it is a low-growing plant, along with red-scarlet thread (symbolizing sin), and throws all three into the fire consuming the red heifer. For Sforno, the power associated with the red cow brings the sinner back from the evil of pride to the high ideal of humility.

Joseph Bechor Shor.

He adopts a rational approach, stating that the rites of the red heifer were designed to discourage association with the dead, which was prompted by the bereaved's love for the departed and excessive grief. In addition, he notes that people should not make it their practice of consulting the dead, and to that end the rite of the red heifer and the high degree of defilement resulting from contact from the dead was meant to discourage this practice.

Rabbi Yochanan ben Zakkai.

He comments that the ashes of the red heifer and the waters of the sin offering have no intrinsic properties that are able to purify. The law of the red heifer is simply a Divine commandment which by itself determines the defilement of the corpse and the purification properties of the red heifer ashes. It is the commandment that helps to refine the human soul.

Samson Raphael Hirsch.

He maintains that the ritual of the red heifer helps to enable people to overcome ritual contamination and go beyond the boundaries of life and death. The mixing of the red heifer's ashes (symbolizing the triumph over the animal within people) with the "living water" demonstrates that every person is given an immortal spiritual being that allows that person to shape all of the moral decisions that affect life.

Rashi.

Quoting the commentary of Rabbi Moshe Hadarshan, he states that the red heifer was analogous to the golden calf. The red heifer and its rite was created to atone for the sin of the Israelites at Mount Sinai.

Robert Kunin.

This research chemist comments that the Bible was aware of water pollution and how to treat water pollution. Looking at the red heifer ashes chemically, one sees a mixture of granular and powdered activated carbon and bone char, capable of removing various viruses and pollutants. Kunin goes on to note that the components of the ash and the basic method of treating water as described in the Book of Numbers is essentially the only method currently approved by the U.S. government.

Morris Adler.

He comments that the red heifer rite sheds light on how Judaism looks upon human beings. The rite of the red heifer is proof that no person has fallen to such a low level that he is incapable of being purified. The ritual of the red heifer is God's opportunity for humans to start anew and have a second chance.

Jacob Milgrom.

He comments that the rite of the red heifer was intended to purge the individual and the sanctuary from wrongdoing. As such, it is in a sense a ceremony of ethical cleansing.

Hinnuch.

He states that the laws of the red heifer totally defy all human logic, and thus he makes no comment. Indeed, there are other commentators who follow his lead and also are unable to offer a rationale for the commandment of the red heifer.

If You Want to Learn More

See Talmud *Yoma* 2a, 14a, 42b, 43a; Talmud *Niddah* 9a; Talmud *Megillah* 20a; Maimonides, *Mishneh Torah: Laws of Red Heifer,* chs. 1–5; Maimonides, *Book of Commandments,* positive commandments 108, 113; *Sefer HaHinnuch,* commandments 397, 399; Robert Kunin, "Mystery of the Red Heifer," *Dor le Dor,* Spring 1985, pp. 267–269; Morris Adler, *The Voice Still Speaks,* p. 333; Jacob Milgrom, *Jewish Publication Society Torah Commentary: Numbers* (Philadelphia: Jewish Publication Society, 1989), pp. 438–447.

LIST OF COMMENTATORS

Early Commentators

Abrabanel, Don Isaac. Fifteenth-century Spanish exegete and statesman.

Alshech, Moshe ben Chayim. Sixteenth-century commentator who lived in Safed, Israel. His commentary to the Torah contains his Sabbath sermons.

Ba'al Ha-Turim. Thirteenth-century German scholar whose name was Jacob ben Asher. He wrote an important collection of Jewish Law called *Arba'ah Turim,* "Four Rows." He often interpreted using the mathematical meaning of Hebrew words.

Bachya ibn Asher. In his commentaries, this fourteenth-century Spanish biblical commentator seldom wandered from the literal meaning of the text or from the logical implications of the commandments.

Bachya ibn Pakuda. Eleventh-century Spanish poet and author of the study of Jewish ethics called *Duties of the Heart.*

Bechor Shor, Joseph. French exegete of the twelfth century. His commentary on the Five Books of Moses is marked by originality and a critical, rationalizing tendency.

Biur. A commentary by the Russian-German eighteenth-century exegete Solomon of Dubno on the German translation of the Bible by Moses Mendelssohn.

Chizkuni (Chezekiah ben Manoach). Thirteenth-century French commentator. Tradition relates that it was in memory of his father that he wrote a commentary on the Five Books of Moses, which he called *Chizkuni* (Strengthen me), and which was printed in 1524.

241

Da'at Zekenim **(Ba'alei Tosafot).** This collection of commentaries on the Bible portions of the week contain both literal and homiletical explanations.

HaLevi, Judah. Eleventh-century Spanish philosopher.

Hillel. First-century scholar and ancestor of a dynasty of patriarchs that held office until the fifth century.

***Hinnuch, Sefer Ha-* (Aaron Ha-Levi).** Ha-Levi, a fourteenth-century Spanish exegete, wrote a monumental work called *Sefer HaHinnuch* (the *Book of Education*), in which are listed all 613 commandments as they occur in the weekly Bible portion. A rationale is provided for each one, and thus this book has become a classic in the field of *mitzvah* studies.

Hirsch, Samson Raphael. Eighteenth-century German religious commentator.

Ibn Ezra, Abraham. Eleventh-century Spanish exegete. His Bible commentaries were based on linguistic and factual examinations of the text, and occasionally even included hints that foreshadow modern biblical criticism.

Karo, Joseph. This sixteenth-century scholar compiled the most authoritative rabbinic code of Jewish Law, called the *Shulchan Aruch.*

Keli Yakar (Ephraim Solomon of Luntshitz). Known chiefly by his commentary on the Torah, the Keli Yakar also produced a commentary on Rashi.

Kimchi, David ben Joseph. Known as "Radak," this Franco-Spanish exegete and grammarian wrote a biblical commentary that influenced the Authorized Version of 1611. He also provided Bible students with logical, grammatical explanations of difficult words and passages.

Loez, Me'am. Eighteenth-century Bible commentary, conceived by Jacob Culi. His aim was to popularize Jewish lore by means of extracts from the Talmud, Midrash, and *Zohar.*

Luzzatto, Chayim. Eighteenth-century Italian mystic whose commentaries were popular among *chasidim.*

Maimonides, Moses. Eleventh-century medieval Jewish philosopher, whose *Guide for the Perplexed* deals with difficult Bible terms and conceptions. He was also known as "the Rambam," an acronym for Rabbi Moses ben Maimon.

Malbim. Known as Meir Lev ben Yechiel Michael, this nineteenth-century Bible commentator based his explanation on the *Midrash* of the early rabbis.

Mendelssohn, Moses. This eighteenth-century philosopher was the first to translate the Bible into German.

Nachmonides. A thirteenth-century Spanish biblical commentator and mystic, his real name was Moses ben Nachman (also known as "the

Ramban''). Unlike some commentators (Rashi, for instance), who simply bring the views of tradition to bear on the text under discussion, Nachmonides (like Abraham ibn Ezra), expressed his own view, which reflected the Torah as the word of God and the source of all knowledge.

Or HaChayim (**Chayim ben Moses Attar**). This Moroccan, seventeenth-century exegete was both a talmudist and mystic. His commentary on the Five Books of Moses was known as *Or HaChayim*.

Philo, Judaeus. First-century philosopher whose Greek writings focused primarily on the Torah.

Radbaz. Refers to David ben Zimra, a fifteenth-century Spanish exegete known for his mystical composition called *Magen David*.

Ralbag (Levi ben Gershom, Gersonides). This thirteenth-century commentator wrote commentaries in which he discusses philosophical and theological questions. In his commentary on the Five Books of Moses, he attempted to reconstitute Jewish law rationally.

Rashbam (Samuel ben Meir). This French, eleventh-century exegete wrote many commentaries on the Bible, usually stressing the literal meaning of the text rather than the homiletics.

Rashi (Solomon ben Isaac). This French, eleventh-century, leading commentator on the Bible and Talmud is most noted for commentaries that are a compromise between the literal and homiletical interpretations. Many of his comments are based on rabbinic sources.

Recanti, Menachem ben Benjamin. This thirteenth-century Italian commentator made many comments tinged with mystical ideas.

Saadia ben Joseph (Saadia Gaon). This ninth-century scholar combined Jewish and Arabic scholarship.

Sefer Mitzvot Gadol (**Semag; Moses ben Jacob of Coucy**). This thirteenth-century scholar arranged talmudic law in order of the biblical commandments and called the work, *Sefer Mitzvot Gadol (Semag)*. The book deals with each of the 613 commandments and is written with great clarity.

Sforno, Obadiah ben Jacob. This sixteenth-century Italian scholar is known for his literal commentaries on the Bible. His work reflects a fine knowledge of grammar and philology.

Targum, Jonathan. Early Aramaic translator of the Bible, his real name was Jonathan ben Uzziel, a student of Hillel.

Modern Commentators

Adler, Morris. This twentieth-century, Conservative rabbinic thinker and outstanding orator was known for his sermonic books and homiletical skills.

Baeck, Leo. This twentieth-century theologian won recognition after the publication of the *Essence of Judaism* (1936). He believed that ethics without religious certainty are reduced to mere moralism.

Cassuto, Umberto. Twentieth-century Italian exegete.

Chayim, Chafetz. Refers to Israel Meir haKohen, a nineteenth-century talmudist known for his book called *Chafetz Chayim,* which dealt exclusively with gossip and slander.

Douglas, Mary. Anthropologist and humanities educator, she authored *Purity and Danger* (1966). She served as visiting Professor in Anthropology and Religion at Princeton University in the 1980s.

Ehrlich, Arnold B. Russian-Polish commentator who published a commentary at the end of the nineteenth-century called *Mikra Kifeshuto.*

Felix, Cathy. A congregational rabbi (member of the Central Conference of American Rabbis) residing in New Jersey.

Gillman, Neil. Twentieth-century Conservative theologian.

Glustrom, Simon. Twentieth-century Conservative rabbi from the United States.

Greenstein, Edward. Twentieth-century biblical scholar and professor at the Jewish Theological Seminary of America.

Greenberg, Sidney. Twentieth-century rabbi known for his skills as an orator and writer of many books and articles.

Hertz, Joseph. Former Chief Rabbi of Great Britain, this twentieth-century Conservative rabbi was known for his eclectic biblical commentary on the Five Books of Moses, called the *Hertz Chumash.*

Heschel, Abraham Joshua. Twentieth-century philosopher who attempted to illumine the relationship between God and people.

Hoffmann, David. Leading German rabbi of the mid-nineteenth and early twentieth-century.

Kaplan, Mordecai. Twentieth-century philosopher and founder of the Reconstructionist movement.

Keel, Othmer. Swiss scholar who has written extensively on the rationale of the Jewish dietary laws.

Klein, Isaac. Conservative rabbi and scholar, and a contributor to leading scholarly journals.

Kunin, Robert. Twentieth-century research chemist from the United States.

Leibowitz, Nehama. Twentieth-century professor of Bible at Hebrew University in Jerusalem. Her commentaries were noteworthy for their psychological insights.

Lieberman, Saul. Twentieth-century talmudic scholar who served as rector of the Jewish Theological Seminary of America.

Matt, Herschel. Twentieth-century Conservative rabbi.

Mendenhall, George. Biblical commentator and author of *The Tenth Generation* (1973).

Milgrom, Jacob. Professor, University of California, Berkeley, Department of Near Eastern Studies.

Noth, Martin. Twentieth-century biblical commentator whose English-edition biblical commentary, *The Laws in the Pentateuch and Other Studies,* was published in 1962 by the Westminster Press.

Peli, Pinchas. Twentieth-century scholar and rabbi, whose "Torah" Today" column in the *Jerusalem Post* won him critical acclaim.

Plaut, Gunther. Twentieth-century liberal rabbi known for his editing of the commentary called *The Torah,* which is used in most Reform congregations today.

Plaskow, Judith. Feminist theologian.

Riskin, Shlomo. Orthodox rabbi currently living in Israel. His Torah commentaries appear each week in the international edition of the *Jerusalem Post.*

Sarna, Nahum. Professor emeritus of biblical studies at Brandeis University and an editor and translator for the Jewish Publication Society's new translation of the Bible.

Shalomi, Zalman Schachter. Ordained by the Lubavitcher Yeshiva in Brooklyn, he has served as professor of Jewish mysticism at Temple University.

Silverman, Morris. Twentieth-century Conservative rabbi.

BIBLIOGRAPHY

Adler, Morris. *The Voice Still Speaks.* New York: Bloch Publishing, 1969.

Alshekh, Moshe ben Chaim. *Torat Moshe.* Vols. 1, 2. Trans. Eliyahu Munk. Jerusalem: Rubin Mass, Publishers, 1988.

Appel, Gershon. *A Philosophy of Mitzvot.* New York: Ktav Publishers, 1975.

Bachya ben Asher. *Kad haKemach.* Trans. Charles B. Chavel. New York: Shilo Publishing House, 1980.

Birnbaum, Philip. *Maimonides' Mishneh Torah (Yad Hazakah).* New York: Hebrew Publishing Company, 1944.

Buber, Solomon, ed. *Midrash Tanhuma.* Vilna, 1885.

Cassuto, Umberto. *A Commentary on the Book of Exodus.* Jerusalem: Magnes Press, 1951.

Cohen, Philip. *Rambam on the Torah.* Jerusalem: Rubin Mass, Publishers, 1985.

"Commandments, Reasons for." In *Encyclopaedia Judaica,* vol. 5, cols. 783–791. Jerusalem: Keter Publishing House Ltd., 1972.

"Commandments, The 613." In *Enclyclopaedia Judaica,* vol. 5, cols. 763–782. Jerusalem: Keter Publishing House Ltd., 1972.

Douglas, Mary. *Purity and Danger: An Analysis of Concepts of Pollution and Taboo.* New York: Praeger Publishing, 1966.

Ganzfried, Solomon. *Code of Jewish Law: Kitzur Shulchan Aruch.* New York: Hebrew Publishing Company, 1961.

Glustrom, Simon. *The Language of Judaism.* Northvale, NJ: Jason Aronson, 1988.

Greenberg, Moshe. *Understanding Exodus.* New York: Behrman House, 1969.

HaLevi, Rabbi Aaron. *Sefer HaHinnuch: The Book of Mitzvah Education.*
New York: Feldheim Publishers, 1978.

Hertz, Joseph. *The Pentateuch and Haftorahs.* London: Soncino Press, 1988.

Herschel, Abraham Joshua. *The Earth is the Lord's and the Sabbath.* New
York: Harper and Row, in association with the Jewish Publication Society,
1962.

Hirsch, Samson Raphael, trans. *The Pentateuch.* London: L. Honig and
Sons, 1959.

_____. *Horeb: A Philosophy of Jewish Laws and Observances.* Trans. I.
Grunfeld. 4th ed. New York: Soncino Press, 1981.

Hyatt, J. P. "Exodus." *New Century Bible Commentary.* Grand Rapids,
Michigan: Eerdmans, 1980.

Isaacs, Ronald H., and Olitzky, Kerry M. *Doing Mitzvot: Mitzvah Projects
for Bar/Bat Mitzvah.* Hoboken, NJ: Ktav Publishers, 1994.

Kaddushin, Max. *Worship and Ethics: A Study in Rabbinic Judaism.* New
York: Bloch Publishing Company, 1963.

Kaplan, Mordecai. *The Meaning of God in Modern Jewish Religion.* De-
troit: Wayne State University Press, 1994.

Klein, Isaac. *A Guide to Jewish Religious Practice.* New York: Jewish
Theological Seminary, 1979.

Lamm, Maurice. *The Jewish Way in Love and Marriage.* San Francisco:
Harper and Row, 1980.

Lebeau, James. *The Jewish Dietary Laws: Sanctify Life.* New York: United
Synagogue of America Department of Youth Activities, 1983.

Leibowitz, Nehama. *Studies in the Bible.* 5 vols. Jerusalem: World Zionist
Organization, 1980.

Maimonides, Moses. *The Guide of the Perplexed.* Trans. Shlomo Pines.
Chicago: University of Chicago Press, 1963.

_____. *The Commandments.* Trans. Charles B. Chavel. New York: Son-
cino Press, 1967.

Mechilta de-R. Yishmael. Ed. Jacob Z. Lauterbach. Philadelphia: Jewish
Publication Society, 1933.

Mendenhall, George E. *The Tenth Generation.* Baltimore and London:
Johns Hopkins Press, 1973.

Neusner, Jacob. *Mitzvah.* Chappaqua, NY: Rossel Books, 1981.

Noth, M. *The Laws in the Pentuteuch and Other Studies.* Trans. D. R. Ap-
Thomas. Edinburgh and London: Oliver and Boyd, 1966.

Pakuda, Bahya ibn. *Duties of the Heart.* Trans. M. Hymanson. Philadelphia,
1925.

Peli, Pinchas H. *Torah Today.* Washington, DC: B'nai Brith Books, 1987.

Plaut, Gunther, ed. *The Torah: A Modern Commentary.* New York: Union of American Hebrew Congregations, 1981.

Schechter, Solomon. *Aspects of Rabbinic Theology.* New York: Schocken Books, 1961.

Strassfeld, Michael. *The Jewish Holidays: A Guide and Commentary.* New York: Harper and Row, 1985.

INDEX

About the Author

Rabbi Ronald Isaacs is the spiritual leader of Temple Sholom in Bridgewater, New Jersey. He received his doctorate in instructional technology from Columbia University's Teacher's College. He is the author of numerous books, including *Loving Companions: Our Jewish Wedding Album,* coauthored with Leora Isaacs; *The Jewish Information Source Book: A Dictionary and Almanac; Words for the Soul: Jewish Wisdom for Life's Journey; Close Encounters: Jewish Views about God;* and *The Jewish Book of Numbers.* Rabbi Isaacs is currently on the editorial board of *Shofar* magazine and serves as vice president of the New Jersey Rabbinical Assembly. He resides in New Jersey with his wife, Leora, and their children, Keren and Zachary.